EUROPE

THE IRISH EXPERIENCE

Edited by

Rory O'Donnell

INSTITUTE OF EUROPEAN AFFAIRS

Published by
The Institute of European Affairs
Europe House
8 North Great Georges Street
Dublin 1
Ireland
Tel: (01) 874 6756
Fax: (01) 878 6880
e-mail: info@iea.iol.ie

ISBN 1-874109-48-6

Cover Design by Victor McBrien
Origination by Alan Hodgson
Printed by
ColourBooks Limited
Dublin, Ireland

Contents

CONTRIBUTORS

Rory O'Donnell is Jean Monnet Professor of European Business Studies at the National University of Ireland, University College Dublin.

Peter Cassells is Secretary-General of the Irish Congress of Trade Unions (ICTU).

Sean Cromien is a former Secretary-General of the Department of Finance.

Martin Cullen, TD, is Minister of State at the Department of Finance with special responsibility for the Office of Public Works.

Garret FitzGerald is a former Taoiseach and Leader of the Fine Gael Party.

Tom Garvin lectures in Politics at the National University of Ireland, University College Dublin.

Brendan Halligan is the Chairman of the Institute of European Affairs, Dublin.

Brigid Laffan is Jean Monnet Professor of European Politics at the National University of Ireland, University College Dublin.

Dermot McAleese is Whately Professor of Political Economy at the University of Dublin (Trinity College).

Miriam Hederman O'Brien is Chancellor of the University of Limerick.

Liam Ryan lectures in Psychology at the National University of Ireland, Maynooth College.

The Taoiseach, Jack Lynch, TD (right), and the Minister for External Affairs, Dr P. J. Hillery, TD, signing the Treaty of Accession to the European Communities in the Palais d'Egremont, Brussels, 22 January 1972

Foreword

Terry Stewart

In the course of his contribution to this volume, Professor Liam Ryan offers the opinion that "Irish society has changed more over the past 25 years than at any time in its history". There may be some who would identify other quarter-centuries as being equally important but it would be difficult to find them.

It was in the spirit of Liam Ryan that the Institute of European Affairs (IEA) decided to mark Ireland's attainment of 25 years membership of the European Communities and Union by organising a series of lectures in the late autumn of 1998. Their collection as chapters in this volume is intended to form a permanent record of Ireland's experience in Europe. An Irish Rip Van Winkle who had gone to sleep in 1973 and had awakened at the end of 1998 would have found a country transformed – politically, economically, socially and administratively. What were the reasons for such an all-embracing transformation? For some, it was very simple: "money from Brussels". This thesis has been voiced around our fellow Member States, particularly in recent years. To the generation attaining political consciousness now (1999), without the experience of what has happened over the past 25 years, it might appear that this was true. And, in addition, that the path from 1973 up to today had been one of smooth and steady progress. In fact, it was anything but!

What emerges from the chapters in this collection is that the policies adopted in the 1960s are the key to explaining today's success. It was during this time that so much of the basis for this success was laid. Fundamental reforms were made in Irish education, vocational training, industrial development policy and tourism, and Irish industry began to prepare itself for the increased competition and – perhaps more importantly – for the opportunities created by free trade that would come from the opening up of markets. There was also the beginning of the debate which led to the restructuring of agriculture.

After the end of World War II, Ireland went through a period of virtual stagnation and by the mid-1950s the attempt to build a self-sufficient society and economy was seen to have failed. Although the general public was not aware of the changes taking place on mainland

Europe, some key members of the Irish policy community were, and their thinking brought about a total change in the country's economic strategy. The change of position was forced somewhat by the British government's decision to apply for membership of the (then) European Economic Communities and Ireland decided to apply at the same time, mainly as a result of the predominant role that Britain played in Irish external trade, a point made in Brendan Halligan's contribution to this volume.

It is interesting to speculate on what might have happened had the Irish application been accepted at that time. While Irish agriculture would undoubtedly have benefited, it is hard to see how the industrial and services sectors could have survived, even if granted a generous transition period. In a sense, the rejection of the British application gave Ireland a preparation period of eleven years which, in retrospect, was vital in getting the country ready for membership. This is a point which the present wave of applicants to the Union should bear in mind, although it is difficult for them to show patience. Given the circumstances from whence they come, their impatience to secure membership is understandable.

The economic benefits to Ireland of EU membership are there for all to see, and the financial transfers from Europe played a vital part in the changes, particularly in the field of infrastructure. But perhaps it was the change in attitudes which was most significant. No one foresaw the massive growth in confidence which was to take place amongst young Irish people as they became part of that wider community, and how this confidence would grow as a result of the direct and indirect interaction with their counterparts from around an expanding Union. These contacts brought a new awareness at all levels, as Brigid Laffan points out in her contribution. In addition, Irish society has changed out of all recognition. According to Liam Ryan, in the early days of independence the State was inward looking and the only window on the outside world for young people at that time was the Catholic Church, which explained the large numbers entering the priesthood to serve in the missions. Ryan argues in his paper that over the course of the past 25 years these roles have been reversed, with the EU now forming an important window on the wider world, while the Church has become inward looking and introspective.

The path of progress over the past 25 years has not been smooth, as nearly all of the contributors to this volume point out. There has been a learning process. There were many hard lessons to be learnt from the European experience; especially that what we signed up for in the Treaties would affect us directly and fundamentally. The first lesson, on the question of equal pay, occurred not long after Ireland's accession. This presaged the steady progress made in Ireland on the whole question of equality, and our membership of the EU contributed in a substantial way to progress in that field. Equally, in the economic field, membership of the ERM eventually brought about a realisation that Ireland was not an entity apart from the rest of the Union. The grave economic difficulties of the early 1980s forced the redressing of the state of the public finances in the mid-1980s while the Social Partnership agreements beginning in 1987 (including the adoption of the Maastricht Criteria before they were introduced at EU level) pointed to a maturing attitude on the part of Irish society at all levels.

In spite of the ups and downs of the past 25 years, the Irish policy of remaining close to the core countries (the original Six) of the Union has been a constant and was a strategy shared across the Irish political spectrum.

Although not treated as a separate subject in this book, membership of the Union has transformed our relations with the United Kingdom. Tom Garvin remarks that, sometime between 1973 and 1998, the 800-year war with England ended. A truly remarkable transformation. There are still differences between Ireland and the UK but the days of "megaphone diplomacy" across the Irish Sea are over. Ministerial contacts with the UK, and indeed the other Member States, are so normal and frequent that no one passes any remark about them: yet in the previous 25 years they were few and far between. This growing together between two old adversaries is particularly apparent in relation to Northern Ireland, where there is a shared determination on the part of the British and Irish governments to do everything possible to facilitate a solution. This is one of the most important effects of membership of the Union.

In 1972 there were numerous groups in Ireland opposed to entry to Europe, many of them afraid of the unknown. For most, the Referendum of 1972 answered their doubts and they fell in behind the process of European integration. We now have a growing population, a rapidly increasing standard of living and a standing in Europe and throughout the world which Ireland has never known. Irish people play a major role in key decision-making in the Union and it can be argued that sharing our sovereignty within the Union has given the country an enhanced standing in the worlds of business, the arts and academia which reflect this new confidence. One wonders what the alternative to membership of the EU would have been. But much remains to be done and the result of the recent referendum on the Amsterdam Treaty reinforces this point. For the most part, the pieces of the European economic jigsaw have been put into place, but the completion of this phase has emphasised the gaps, especially in legitimacy and accountability. The spotlight will now shine on these and other areas, such as in security and justice and asylum.

In a lecture in Bologna in November 1998, the distinguished Italian economist, and now member of the Executive Board of the European Central Bank, Professor Tommaso Padoa-Schioppa, referred to the EU as a "limited democracy". He referred to the fact that, in 1914, Europe had had 100 years of almost uninterrupted peace; people travelled without passports and the gold standard gave monetary union. In that year people thought that the age of war was over, as do many young people today. He warned that: "the European Union is unfinished work and the greatest risk that it runs is that the younger generations do not realise it".

The IEA hopes that this volume, which describes the sometimes "tortuous path" of Ireland's journey to EU membership, will give our young people an insight into this past and encourage them to continue with the completion of that "unfinished work".

On behalf of the IEA I would like to thank all of the contributors to this work. Their names are listed in the contents page and on its verso. As always, they gave of their time freely and willingly. A special word of thanks is due to Rory O'Donnell, Jean Monnet Professor of European Business Studies, who acted as editor and contributed the introduction and final chapter overviewing the period and the major impacts on Ireland. The project would not have come to fruition without the help of Iain MacAulay, who gave of his time and experience to oversee the publication of this volume, as he has for many other publications of the IEA.

To all my colleagues, in particular PG and CQ, I give grateful thanks for their various contributions and constant support in the publication of this book.

TERRY STEWART
Director General

INTRODUCTION
AND
BACKGROUND

CHAPTER 1

Introduction

Rory O'Donnell

It is now 25 years since Ireland's accession to the European Community. In late 1998, the Institute of European Affairs (IEA) organised a series of lectures to review the Irish experience of Europe. It was decided that in order to make a coherent contribution, the lectures, and subsequent papers, should address a common question: what difference has participation in European integration made to Ireland?

The papers which form Chapters 2-11 of this volume explore the impact of European Union (EU) membership on four spheres of Irish life: politics, society and culture, the economy and public administration. To facilitate this, two introductory chapters describe the political, economic, social and administrative system prior to Ireland's membership. The impact of EU membership on each area is considered by two authors, one analyst and one activist. For example, the economic impact is considered by Dermot McAleese of Trinity College Dublin, and Garret FitzGerald, former Minister of Foreign Affairs and Taoiseach. The impact on society and culture is considered by Liam Ryan of St Patrick's College, Maynooth, and by Peter Cassells, General Secretary of the Irish Congress of Trade Unions.

Each chapter provides a reflective appraisal, rather than an historical account, of the years since 1973. In many instances, the reflections are supported by reference to particular issues or episodes. Overall, the book seeks to provide an objective and balanced assessment of how the 25 years of membership have affected Irish politics, administration, economy and society. However, objectivity cannot be achieved through a series of dry papers. The period of membership has been one of dramatic change, in which actors and observers have inevitably been passionately engaged. The book aims to elicit, rather than exclude, the vigorous testimony of the authors.

The Community Ireland joined in 1973 has changed dramatically since the mid-1980s. The Single Act, the internal market, the Structural Funds and the transition to EMU have greatly increased the salience of Europe. The process of embedding the national in the

European, and the European in the national, accelerated in the mid-1980s. A series of enlargements have altered the Union. The authors take account of this deepening of European integration in their reflections on the effects and meaning of membership.
Many of the effects and the meaning of membership are unique to each Member State, and are shaped by indigenous social, economic and political factors. Likewise, the nature of the EU – and, indeed, of the modernism and globalism unleashed in this century – is partly shaped by the features of particular countries, including peripheral ones like Ireland. What features of Ireland have shaped the particular effects and significance of EU membership for us? How has EU membership affected the content and process of Ireland's long-standing contribution to international society? The authors address these questions, adopting an interactive outlook, hence our title – *Europe The Irish Experience*.
There is evidence of a deterioration in the quality of media and other discussion of the European Union in Ireland. Witness RTE's recent "Late Late Show" discussion of the Celtic Tiger, and whether "we did it ourselves" or "can they take that away from us too?" Without glossing over real conflicts of interest, this book seeks to convey a more accurate picture of the relation between the various European institutions and the Member States.
The opposite of the new hostility to "Brussels", is an old strand of Irish self-criticism for not being "good" or "real" Europeans. Together, these approaches create a dialogue of the deaf. In their irrelevance, they leave the field to a third view: that membership is mainly about manipulating diplomacy to achieve financial transfers. The chapters in this volume get beyond these stereotypical views, presenting a richer perspective.
Although state policy and inter-governmental negotiation are central to the European Union, the authors do not confine themselves to the action of states. Neither the Union nor its Member States retain control of what happens – in business, society, culture and personal life – in the European space which they jointly create. Even the creation and shaping of the European area are not confined to the EU institutions and the member states. Numerous other public agencies, firms, political actors, interest associations, social movements and individual citizens have an active role. It is largely their activity that makes the economy, society and culture of Europe, and Ireland. The national government is not their sole conduit to the formal European system. The authors reflect on Ireland's place in this wider process of Europeanisation.
While European integration is a major project in its own right, it is

never entirely separate from other substantive projects of a political, economic, social or cultural kind. The authors relate Ireland's participation in European integration to the major concerns of Irish life in the 20th century. While the EU has been preoccupied with finding and working a European-level system of collective policy, it can never ignore more general issues of governance: effectiveness, legitimacy, implementation, enforcement and monitoring. Indeed, it can be argued that substantive challenges and problems of economic and social governance are now at least as important as integration itself. Some see the EU as particularly handicapped in addressing current substantive challenges and problems of governance; others consider that promising new approaches to public policy are reflected more quickly in the EU because it is new, part-formed and unburdened by the large-scale apparatus of the post-war nation state. While the authors necessarily assess the implications of Irish membership for the *amount* of national autonomy, they also consider the impact on the substance of Irish policy and on the *patterns* of policy-making, implementation and organisation.

CHAPTER 2

The Way We Were

Miriam Hederman O'Brien

RETROSPECTION

The Israelites recorded their flight from Egypt (and, indeed, the manner of their arrival in that country) in a work which remains vivid and forceful, to believer and unbeliever alike, centuries after it was written. Surviving records of the Egyptians appear to ignore the presence of their restive immigrants and say nothing of the dramatic interventions recounted in the Bible. Was this because such events never happened? Or was it that they happened but were of much greater importance to one party than to the other, so that one race commemorated them from generation to generation and the other forgot? Or did they happen in a different way and were transmuted by one side into a code of conduct and a legacy of history, and by the other into a footnote to more important events? Or are there records which have completely disappeared which would tell yet another version of the story?

While no comparison can be made between the significance of the events described in the Book of Exodus and the accession of Ireland to the Treaty of Rome, the example of the subjective power of the historian and commentator needs to be acknowledged, even in such a modest exercise as these reflections.

Modern access to documentation of every kind carries with it a dangerous form of wish-fulfilment. If one wants to prove that there was significant support for a particular view at a certain time one can quote the number of articles written to that end and even the number of letters to the daily press. One can argue which were the more influential. Does a letter to the *Irish Independent* for example, score more highly than one to the *Irish Press*, because of the larger circulation of the former, or should it be the contrary because *Irish Press* readers were said to be more homogenous in their political views? Or does an article in *The Irish Times* carry more weight than one in *The Farmers Journal* or vice versa?

A long and scholarly work can set out the basis and logic for a particular thesis. This essay in retrospection is essentially impressionist and personal, coloured by a slight feeling that the past tends to be painted in deeper black or more radiant gold than was apparent at the time.

A STATE OF PREPARATION

Apart from some periods of apparent stagnation (providing conditions in which change can gestate and ferment), Ireland has been in a virtually perpetual state of transition since the foundation of the State in 1922. And so it continues.

During 1972-73 Ireland was offered membership of the European Communities, the electorate passed a referendum enabling the Government to accept and full accession followed. This was a period of obvious transition.

Changes, which had occurred since 1945, had transformed the prevailing cultural climate, the education system, the economy and the political contours. And it had been apparent since 1961, when Ireland's application for membership of the European Communities was first made, that Europe would feature significantly in Ireland's future. When and how membership could be achieved and what effect it would have, were the questions. Much of the complexity of a retrospective study of Irish affairs arises from the difficulty of accurately ascribing causes and effects.

To what extent, for example, did the arrival of an Irish television station affect the way in which TV influenced public opinion? Or did RTE merely reflect and promote a fairly profound change, which was taking place in Irish society? Did the publication of the OECD report "Investment in Education" in 1966 provide the economic priority for extending access to second-level education to a majority of children, or was there a political decision, on grounds of social justice, for which the report provided an economic argument? Was the idea of the Anglo-Irish "Free-Trade" agreement with the United Kingdom in 1965 a preparation for a wider economic market or a preliminary to a resumption of a single UK/Irish economy if the European option disappeared? Was Sean Lemass personally committed to membership of the European Communities because of the principles involved or was the prospect of such membership an opportunity to put pressure on Irish business, labour, agriculture and the public service to improve their performance so that the Irish government could meet its social and political objectives? The answer, on the evidence of his speeches and actions would appear to be "both".

As with any community in the throes of transition, the process of change which took place in Ireland generated a dynamic element which threw many of the forecasts off course and provided an impetus to some of the developments far greater than even their most optimistic proponents envisaged.

One of the most distinctive features of the period from 1961, when the first application for membership was made, is the active support given for accession by some sectors, in particular the farmers and certain sections of business and political life, and the lack of interest in many others. There was a considerable body of opinion which felt that enlargement would never happen.

Not surprisingly, members of the Oireachtas who had attended the Council of Europe as delegates tended to be more eloquent on European issues in general and the implications of accession to the European Communities than their colleagues who had not. The Fine Gael party was popularly perceived as being knowledgeable about Ireland and Europe, mainly as a result of the early involvement of Declan Costello, TD (until he became a judge) and that of Professor James Dooge and Dr Garrett FitzGerald (even before he became active in national politics). The latter, in particular, was a regular columnist and economic commentator and used this access to the public very effectively. Fianna Fáil, despite the backing of Lemass, was most consistently represented in discussions on Europe in the preparatory years by members of the Seanad, notably Ruairi Brugha, Eoin Ryan and Michael Yeats. Ministers such as George Colley, Charles Haughey, Dr Patrick Hillery and Jack Lynch naturally promoted government policy for full membership of the EEC. Of the Labour Party members of the Oireachtas, Barry Desmond, TD, and David Thornley, TD made a considerable contribution; other standard bearers were Brendan Halligan, (as a senator and member of the Party) and Tony Brown, who represented the younger generation of Labour trade union leadership.

THE FIRST TASTE OF MEMBERSHIP

Ireland had the benefit of twelve years in which to prepare for accession to the European Communities. The level of activity during that period was not uniform. The acceptance, both by the Six founding members and Ireland itself, that the applications of Ireland and the United Kingdom were inextricably linked led to periods when accession seemed unlikely as Britain and Europe (France in particular) blew hot and cold in turn. It was difficult to keep pushing for change when the goal of membership seemed to drift further and further over the horizon. Then Edward Heath would rally his troops or de Gaulle would lose power and interest would resume.

The issues which were of most concern to Ireland in 1973 were not greatly different from those which were at the top of the political agenda in 1961 – or, indeed, in 1945. Employment and emigration were twin evils in which cause and effect were clearly evident. The creation of sustainable jobs, however, required access to markets beyond those traditionally available in the UK and such markets were generally more competitive and demanding than those which most Irish business had previously experienced.

Agriculture had done badly out of the Anglo-Irish Free Trade Agreement in 1965.[1] Its leaders were clear that it also required access to new and more lucrative markets than that of Britain. The servicing of these would require radical restructuring of agriculture and the food industry.

Both industry and agriculture needed massive investments of capital and "know-how" in order to modernise and compete on international markets.

The Second Economic Programme was initiated to bring about the desired transformation in the period 1963-70. The Third Economic Programme (1969), designed to complete the process, immediately followed it.

The policy of actively wooing, through a policy of tax concessions and grants, foreign companies to set up in Ireland was designed to gain investment, expertise, employment and access to markets already served by the new-comers. Transnational companies which set up in Ireland between 1962 and 1973, with the assistance of the Industrial Development Authority, employed 25 per cent of the total manufacturing workforce by the mid-seventies and accounted for two-thirds of Irish goods exported outside the UK in 1973.

The Irish economy grew at about four per cent per annum, the highest national rate in Western Europe, during the period. Emigration declined and the population actually increased. Tourism was identified as an important source of jobs and revenue, and Bord Fáilte stepped up the drive towards the creation of an important service industry by improving standards and targeting international markets. Training for manufacturing and service industries was expanded.

The "sustainable" aspect of job creation, however, was less easily achieved. Irish business was not transformed. Indeed many native companies died and comparatively few sprang up to take their place. Agricultural employment fell at a sharper rate than had been anticipated. Unemployment remained stubbornly high and foreign borrowing increased.

Whatever the shortcomings of some of the preparation, it is clear with hindsight that Ireland needed the intervening years to equip itself socially, economically, politically and psychologically for membership of the European Communities and that, on the whole, it used that time well.

THE LINK WITH BRITAIN

Four aspects of the relationship between Ireland and UK profoundly affected the Irish approach to the European Communities.

The first, and one which has received relatively little attention, was the manner in which some Irish people accepted British political and media assumptions about the scope and remit of the European Communities, even though the majority of Irish people took a more positive view regarding membership. There was no great appetite in either country for exploring fully the political implications. Indeed, the Irish Council of the European Movement, with the assistance of some of the anti-membership group, was almost alone in pointing out that this Community was a unique, political structure, designed to achieve peace and social and economic security in Europe, which carried political obligations. It was not, and never could be, purely a "Common Market". The British flirtation with the European Free Trade Area, of which Ireland was never a member, blurred the issue for the electorate in the UK but there was no such excuse in Ireland. It was the inclusion of agriculture in the remit of the European Economic Community which created most favourable reaction to the EEC in Ireland, even from those who were not directly engaged in farming.

The second aspect, more dramatic than any development on the European stage, was the change which took place in Northern Ireland between the time of the Lemass/O'Neill meetings and the conflagration which followed the Civil Rights Movement. The manner in which this was handled produced new tensions in Anglo-Irish relations. (A senior German member of the Commission told me in 1977 that the EEC should have required Ireland and the UK to resolve the problem of Northern Ireland before admitting either to membership. He had the grace to admit that it had not occurred to him at the time.) It is interesting to note that Ireland, which had beaten the Partition drum so loudly in the early years of the Council of Europe, did not appear to raise issues relating to the existence of the two jurisdictions on the island in the course of negotiations, other than those relating to fishing. John Hume was the first Northern Irish politician to grasp the potential of membership of the EEC as a lever for change in Northern Ireland and the first to consistently promote the idea.

The third aspect related to the position of the Irish Labour Party and the trade union movement. The Irish Labour Party adopted the position of many of the British trade unions and the majority of the British Labour Party. The Irish trade union movement was in the process of healing its internal divisions. Some of the trade union leaders (notably those representing the public service workers and those whose headquarters were not in the UK) supported moves to prepare for accession to the Communities but the majority followed the anti-membership lead of the mainstream British Labour movement. Once the electorate had passed the referendum for accession, the members of the Labour movement in Ireland were free to support, oppose or ignore increased integration of Ireland into Europe. The general approach of the Irish Labour Party and trade union movement is more fully dealt with by Brendan Halligan in his response to this chapter.

The fourth aspect of the Irish-British relationship, which changed during the period, was that of trade between the two countries. Ireland and Britain represented a common labour market (as they still do) and they were also virtually a common trade and agriculture market, with Ireland producing the raw material in the form of "cattle on the hoof" and Britain adding value through processing. The conscious effort to attract non-British investment and expertise was designed to bring access to new markets and it was quite successful. Even as the Anglo-Irish Free Trade Agreement opened up an increased share of the Irish market to British exporters, exporters from Ireland were finding new outlets which provided more profitable returns than those available from the UK.

THE POLITICAL AND SOCIAL CLIMATE

Ireland's accession to the European Communities was signed by Jack Lynch, who had succeeded Sean Lemass as leader of the Fianna Fáil Party and subsequently as Taoiseach. Lynch was not of the generation which fought in the Civil War. He was fortunate in being able to build on the blessing which Sean Lemass had given to the European adventure, plus the solid support of the agricultural sector, so as to bring with him some of the more potentially isolationist elements of the electorate. "Europe" was perceived as being good for Ireland in social and political as well as in economic terms.

The international isolation which had been a feature of Ireland's position in the forties and fifties had declined as a result of membership of the Council of Europe, and the OEEC (subsequently

OECD). Accession to the United Nations in 1955 had been followed by active participation of Irish troops in the Congo during 1961-64, as a result of legislation enabling the Government to commit armed forces to peace-keeping operations abroad. This experience had a significantly positive effect on public opinion as far as Irish involvement in international affairs was concerned.

The growth of national self-confidence is a complex process and the interaction of cause and effect particularly difficult to disentangle. The positive mood of 1961 had been strengthened in the years up to 1973 by a combination of improved economic performance, better access to further education, and the greater international exposure (most of it positive) experienced by Irish politicians, civil servants and the electorate generally. Membership of the Community arrived just as Irish society was in a position to take advantage of the opportunities it offered for further educational and social achievement.

One of the areas in which membership of the European Communities had an immediate effect was that of the political alliances operated by the national political parties of the Member States for their mutual advantage. The Irish Labour Party, which was a very special bloom in the Socialist garden, joined its varied sister parties in the European Parliament. Fine Gael made common cause with the Christian Democrats. Fianna Fáil, which might have been happy enough in the same grouping, found an alternative with the French Gaullists. It is necessary to read the newspapers of the period in order to realise how little, in comparison to their current preoccupations, European or international dimensions concerned the majority of the members of the Oireachtas. Suddenly, the Irish members of the European Parliament were expected to study and make decisions on policies relating to the over-production of olive oil or the regulation of international rivers such as the Rhine and the Danube. Their status as "defenders" of Irish interests would come to depend to a considerable extent on the quality of their contributions to issues which were of immediate concern to their colleagues from France, Germany, Italy and elsewhere.

Some of the "social" regulation of the European Communities, such as equal pay for work of equal value, had been long resisted by those who argued that Ireland could not afford such a luxury. The prospect of a European imposition of such regulation was, therefore, welcomed by a considerable sector of the population. There were many aspects of life, not all of them so obvious, where the demands, regulatory and practical, of membership of the EEC were used to bring about reforms which would have been desirable in themselves.

Other movements, such as the freeing of frontier controls, are still constrained by the need to keep the Irish/UK frontier freely open – particularly with respect to Northern Ireland.

Fear of cultural subjugation was directed less towards Europe than to the growth in Ireland of US and British entertainment and media. If anything, Europe was perceived as being a cultural counter-weight to the US and England.

The limitations of national sovereignty in matters of trade, commerce and the financial markets were well known to the Irish sectors which were thus involved. This understanding was also found throughout the general population, particularly among those whose children had been forced to emigrate through lack of opportunities in Ireland. Neither political independence nor cultural distinction had been found to be sufficient to guarantee the quality of life which was sought by many.

The Irish Sovereignty Movement and "anti-Common Market" groups foretold dire consequences for national independence, severe job losses and an end to the traditional role of farming during the campaign in advance of the first referendum. The majority of the electorate decided that such threats, real as they were, emanated from elsewhere and that Europe offered an antidote.

Alongside the mood of improved confidence there was a very modest expectation of the political progress which might be expected from the new Communities. There is no evidence that the economic shocks of the oil-crisis were foreseen, nor were the steps which would be needed to counteract them. Neither was there much discussion on the likely development of the European Parliament or the role of the Commission. The evolution of a European stage for lobby groups was more quickly realised, with the agricultural bodies, yet again, leading the way. The role of the European Court attracted notice in legal and in some political circles (it had been one of the reasons why Ireland had to hold a referendum) and the appointment of the Chief Justice, Cearbhaill Ó Dálaigh, as the first Irish judge of the European Court was a recognition that the Court's role was being regarded seriously.

THE IMPACT OF IRELAND ON THE EUROPEAN COMMUNITIES

The impact of membership of the European Communities has been unique to each Member State. Other contributors to this volume deal with the effects on Ireland.

The contribution of the individual members to the development of the Communities, however, has also been various and has differed from time to time. Some have contributed significantly to the creation of the European "vision" and others to the practicalities of making the organisation work. Some have managed to do both.

An analysis of the level of a specific Irish contribution would probably show a fairly cautious start, given that the world economic crisis, which occurred in 1973, slowed down the development of Europe. There was also a natural settling down period for a new, small Member State.

A non-scientific assessment would indicate that, while most Irish efforts in the 25 years seem to have been directed towards maximising the benefits flowing into the Irish economy from Europe, the Irish approach towards the Communities was generally constructive. Successive Irish members of the European Commission took their portfolios seriously and Irish members of the Commission staff played a significant role in many of the improvements in European policies. The Irish members of the European Parliament have tended, particularly since the introduction of direct elections, to try to keep in touch with their electorate. The system of the rotating Presidency of the Community (subsequently the European Union) has given an opportunity for Ireland to maximise its influence, while bringing European issues closer to the citizens. Indeed, the 1996 Irish Presidency was particularly fruitful and the Irish approach to the Intergovernmental Conference and the preparation for the Treaty of Amsterdam were widely acclaimed.

If there is disappointment with the impact of Ireland's membership on the European Community it probably arises on two fronts. The first is that of security and foreign policy, where Ireland's much publicised dedication to international peace was not, until very recently, matched with policy initiatives on a European scale. The second is that of finding new methods of dealing with a range of issues which have arisen from changes brought about by enlargement, environmental protection, fisheries and agricultural policies. A blueprint on one or more of these currently intractable problems would be very welcome.

A small but positive contribution by Ireland has been its intermediary approach between the United Kingdom and the core mainland Member States of the Union. It is not in the interest of Europe or Britain that there should be a gulf between them. Neither is it to Ireland's advantage that the United Kingdom should operate as a semi-detached member of the European family. From the outset, when Ireland and the UK joined the Communities, Ireland has supported or opposed British proposals, depending on how advantageous or otherwise they appear but it has often appeared to act as an "interpreter" and rarely as a vehement opponent.

THE FUTURE – AS IT APPEARED IN THE PAST

Despite the success of the European Coal and Steel Community and of the early measures of the European Economic Community, it was not anticipated that the pace of political integration would quicken once Denmark, Ireland and the UK joined. Indeed, it could be said that it slowed appreciably and the prognosis was correct. Nonetheless, measures such as direct elections to the European Parliament, the growth and development of the European Presidency and the inexorable extension of European regulation in general (and social legislation in particular) have changed the political face of the European Union and its Member States far more quickly than was envisaged – even by enthusiastic pro-Europeans - in 1973.

The fears of those who opposed entry on the grounds that Irish national identity would be reduced to a homogenised European blancmange were not realised. On the contrary, Irish culture, albeit of a new type, became fashionable in Europe and flourished at home and abroad as a result.

The "Cold War" was built into the European view of the world in the seventies but the collapse of the Soviet bloc changed that view forever. Germany seized the opportunity to reunite and Europe played a minor role in the process. The fate of the countries in Central and Eastern Europe and in the Baltic region now impinge on their neighbours in a way which was not foreseen 25 years ago. The "Balkan Question" was considered to be ancient history and irrelevant to European development.

Globalisation of markets and the power of multinational corporations developed even more rapidly than had been foreseen. Awareness of the importance of the physical environment became more widespread, even as public confidence in the capacity of nation states to act together to safeguard it waned.

In general terms, Irish protagonists of European integration, would have outlined a gradual but smooth path towards what is now called "subsidiarity", (such a term would have been considered arcane in the seventies). Local and regional government would have been expected to develop as appropriate powers were exercised at European level. The road towards greater integration, however, has been much more rugged while local government, designed to exercise power at the most effective democratic level, remains largely ineffective in Ireland. The exercise of European control over some of the most powerful interests has been uneven. When the graph of progress at European level over the past 25 years is examined it shows at least two steps forward for every one backward. Despite the setbacks therefore, the progress has been significant.

HERE AND NOW

The condition of the European Union has waxed and waned over the past quarter-century. The issues of internal reorganisation and enlargement have come to dominate discussions on its future. As powers are allocated to European, national, regional or local jurisdictions, each Member State has to examine the effectiveness of its policies at every level. A "democratic deficit" at EU level may mask a more fundamental democratic failure at national or local government levels. A transfer of some areas of policy to the European stage should focus attention on the Member State's contribution to that policy and on the quality of its policy in the areas which remain within its competence. The accession of further members makes essential organisational reforms more urgent and political and economic development more pressing.

Monetary union is a matter of political decision, which will succeed or fail according to the economic performance of the states in the union. Ireland will have been a member from the outset. The political and economic implications of this union will be profound both for Ireland and the other members. It is to a great extent an act of faith, an act of hope, and an application of reason. It is an act of faith insofar as no group of states has ever combined its monetary systems by choice without creating, at the same time, a single government. Such a system can work only if the rules are obeyed and enforced, which is more difficult without a federal structure. It is an act of hope that the union will not be blown off-course by economic storms from without or within during the first few years. It is an application of reason because, without such a monetary union, the "Single Market" would remain incomplete and the European Union would be handicapped by its monetary diversity vis-à-vis the global market forces. Irish commentators have pointed out the implications, positive and negative, of the momentous decision. The acts of faith and hope have been made and the decision has been taken.

The social and political concerns inspired by unemployment, crime, international unrest and the destruction of the environment are felt from Ireland to the Urals and must be addressed by the politicians and policy-makers of Europe. It is on the quality of their solutions that they will be judged by the next generation.

What kind of European Union do we want? What kind of Europe did the protagonists of entry in 1972 want? The difficulty of answering the latter question with any certainty makes me wonder whether the relevant evidence exists. Perhaps we could interpret the arguments put forward by people as different as General M.J. Costello of the Sugar Company, Michael Killeen of the Industrial Development Authority, Juan Greene and Sean Healy of the National Farmers Association, Michael Sweetman of the Irish Council of the European Movement, academics such as Professors Louis Smith and Patrick Lynch, and the many others who laboured in the field to explain to the Irish people what was happening in Europe as requiring acts of faith, hope and rationality. I would not dare, however, to produce a blueprint and ascribe it to them. They sought a peaceful, fair and just Europe in which Ireland would realise an enlightened self-interest. They wanted Irish people to play an active role in developing the European community. A very few (notably General M.J.Costello) appeared to argue for an eventual federal solution. Most were not prepared to go so far. Nor did they rule it out.

Many of the "indifferent" in the sixties and early seventies became active partners in the European Community mechanism as soon as Ireland became a member.

The antagonists remain antagonistic, if on different grounds, to remind us that there is always another side to any proposal.

The electorate has become less enchanted as "Brussels" is made into a whipping boy as warts, in the form of scandals and inefficiencies, appear. But a member of 25 years standing should be in a position to take a mature stance. The scandals and inefficiencies of the EU lie within our power to rectify almost as much (if not quite) as the problems in our own state. There is no shortage of information about what is happening.

Twenty-five years hence our successors will ask about Ireland's contribution to the development and to the next enlargement of the EU. Having benefited so much itself, what did it do for the rest of Europe? How well did it manage prosperity? I hope that we will have measured up to the standards set by those who set off so bravely in 1973 to bring Ireland into full membership of the European Community.

1. A good account of the background to the agricultural sector is contained in *Farm Organisations in Ireland – A Century of Progress* by Louis P.F. Smith and Sean Healy (Dublin: Four Courts Press, 1996).

CHAPTER 3

What Difference Did It Make? – Setting the Scene

Brendan Halligan

INTRODUCTION

Ireland in 1972 was still part of the United Kingdom. I had first heard this proposition advanced by Professor Patrick Lynch when a student in UCD a decade earlier. After the initial shock had subsided I had to conclude he was right, at least in economic terms.

Two-thirds of our trade was with the UK; we shared a common labour market (even if the traffic was only one way); our currency was simply a derivative of sterling, consequently we had no need for separate monetary or exchange rate policies; interest rates were determined in London; agriculture was almost totally dependent on the British market; manufacturing exports (such as they were) went predominantly into the UK; and our external commercial policy was designed to accommodate to that of the British.

In now familiar terminology, Ireland was part of an economic and monetary union, with some minor modifications because of political independence. That independence had been dramatically expressed in 1939 when Ireland decided not to go to war on behalf of Britain, as the rest of the Commonwealth did; but in the prosaic world of peace, Ireland's political independence was heavily circumscribed in those mundane tasks which collectively are described as the national interest.

This period has been described in an IEA publication[1] as one of dependence on Britain and, if I may add my own colouring to that state of being, the freedom to win freedom, which Collins had identified in the Treaty, had not yet been realised. Dependence on Britain dominated official thinking on Ireland's approach to membership of the European Economic Community from the outset. The Taoiseach, Sean Lemass, had been blunt on the matter in two speeches in Dáil Eireann in 1960 and 1961. If Britain joined what he described as the Common Market then it was the government's view that "we should endeavour to secure terms of membership or association which would satisfactorily take account of our economic circumstances".[2] If Britain did not join then we should stay out.

18

ISOLATION FROM EUROPE

Moreover, it had already been decided not to join the European Free Trade Area because it did not encompass agricultural products and so would confer no economic advantages on Ireland given our trading pattern with Britain and our access to her agricultural market.[3] The upshot was that of the seventeen countries then part of what was called Western Europe, Ireland was one of a quartet not belonging to any international trade organisation; the other three being Finland (precluded by the Russian bear-hug), Spain (in diplomatic purdah because of Franco) and Greece (which at least enjoyed an association agreement with the EEC). This confirmed Ireland's isolation from the rest of Europe despite brave talk to the contrary because of our membership of the OEEC or the Council of Europe. Civilisation ended at the cliffs of Dover in a more meaningful way for us than for the country which had coined the phrase.

It has to be admitted that a sense of isolation from Europe did not greatly disturb the tranquillity of the Irish soul. When I became General Secretary of the Labour Party in 1967 it had no links whatever with any other social democratic party, not even in Northern Ireland or Britain, and when I proceeded to secure our membership of the Socialist International a year later[4] (and worse still to attend its meetings) the reaction of the party was that of an understanding and forgiving father towards an adolescent son who had temporarily gone off the rails. It simply was not serious politics to be consorting with continentals; for better to be in Bruree than in Brussels (even in Bruree there were more votes for Labour).

The same attitude prevailed in Fianna Fáil and Fine Gael, although in the latter case, Garret FitzGerald and Declan Costello were busy establishing contacts with the Christian Democratic parties. They too had indulgent and patient fathers who overlooked their transgressions. In a nutshell, Europe was a foreign place (except for Lourdes and Rome) and the psychological attitude or world view of most Irish people was best summed up as late as 1984 when a Cork law student on a trip to Strasbourg organised by Mary Robinson could tell me as an MEP that he felt more at home in Boston that he did in Brussels.

Indeed he did. The welcome given to President Kennedy on his visit here in 1963 was proof enough of this. So, it is not true to say that Ireland felt isolated from the world. On the contrary, it felt part of an international community composed of those countries where the emigrants had settled (and still does for understandable reasons) but it had no affinity with the community of European peoples and suffered no sense of loss as a result.

Irish politics had become truly insular by the end of the sixties, as the election campaigns of 1965 and 1969 testify. The only issue which mattered was whether Fianna Fáil could stay in office or be turfed out. Anglo-Irish relations no longer figured, as matters had been settled by the 1948 declaration of a Republic and partition had come to be accepted as a fact of life. A Gallup poll which the Labour Party commissioned early in 1969 could find no evidence of electoral interest in either issue; indeed, only one per cent of voters put Northern Ireland at the top of a list of national priorities, and none referred to the UK as an issue of national concern.

The political vocabulary of the period was so stunted that the word "socialist" could not be used in polite company (especially not in the presence of nuns) and the Labour Party's flirtation with socialism in 1969 was the very cause of its crushing defeat that year, or so it was said at the time. International politics did not feature much in political debate[5] and when in 1970 Dr Hillery, as Foreign Minister, was sent on an international mission in the wake of the Bogside violence that year, it was quickly apparent that we had no diplomatic superstructure in place to advance what had then become a burning national issue. A well-merited reputation at the UN for peace-keeping, and on disarmament and decolonisation, was no substitute for a real and continuous presence in international affairs.

None of this is intended to detract from the work of high officials in various government departments who had by 1972 developed a sophisticated understanding of the EEC, created a network of contacts with the institutions and Member States, and arrived at detailed conclusions about the national interest. It is simply to say that these officials, and some of their ministers, were unrepresentative of the body politic and were left free from vulgar interference in the conduct of affairs regarded by the great mass of politicians (and political journalists) as either arcane or simply irrelevant. That was the ethos of the Leinster House I haunted prior to 1973.

A POOR ECONOMY

If Ireland was isolated from Europe, and only externally associated with the English-speaking world, then what precisely were we on the advent of EEC membership? On the basis of this analysis, it can be said that we were a politically independent region of the British economy. But what sort of region economically? The answer is clear enough from the literature but, more importantly, from the personal life experiences on which the literature is based. Ireland was a poor region, euphemistically described as an economy in the course of development.

It was predominantly an agricultural economy depending in the main on one export market, which offered low prices.[6] It had few value-added agricultural products for export. Industry was generally small scale, inefficient, with poor management and few marketing skills, all of which can be read in the reports of the Committee on Industrial Organisation.[7] In short, Ireland was one of those regions of the UK which had not gone through the industrial revolution in the 18th and 19th centuries and had failed to do so in the 20th, despite achieving independence.

The social consequences of that sad history were only too familiar to those who lived with them; low incomes, continuous emigration, high unemployment and a quality of life limited by the poverty on which it was based. The dereliction of central Dublin[8] and other cities, or the standard of housing and living conditions in rural Ireland, can be recalled as tangible proofs of what the statistics indicate. On the eve of EEC membership Irish living standards were 62 per cent of the European average or, more graphically, about a third of what they are today.

Being a poor region of a mature metropolitan economy meant that economic development policies had long been imperative but, because of a self-imposed membership of monetary union with Britain, neither exchange nor interest rates could be employed to stimulate growth.[9] This restriction on the exercise of economic independence excited little political comment, and none at all from that class of academic economists which has been so critical of EMU in recent years on precisely these grounds. Those of us who did eventually raise the matter[10] were dismissed as eccentrics, despite the fact that the old Irish Parliament had the good sense to run its own exchange rate policy up to 1800.[11]

Deprived of the two policy instruments of exchange and interest rates the authorities could only resort to industrial development either behind a tariff wall or else go for free trade and encourage investment by a combination of state aids and tax incentives.

PREPARATION FOR THE EEC

Protectionism had been tried and had failed. By the mid-fifties emigration was so high that an American sociologist could write credibly of *The Vanishing Irish*. But crisis, as Monnet often observed, is the opportune moment for creativity and Whitaker's Grey Book on

"Economic Development" in 1958[12] revolutionised the way in which policy-makers viewed the Irish economy. His enduring insight was to the effect that a small regional economy could only prosper if it were fully open to the larger economy of which it was part and accepted all the policy consequences, in particular that exports were the key to survival and competitiveness the engine for growth. Ireland was a small economy. More particularly, it was a regional economy. Hence, it should be open.

It is to the undying credit of Sean Lemass that he immediately accepted the logic of this analysis, which is now a conventional feature of economic literature under the rubric of "a small open economy", although in our case with the added qualification of "with a fixed exchange rate with its largest trading partner". Having accepted the analysis, he implemented it with the Programme for Economic Expansion laid before the Oireachtas in November 1958.

The one set of weapons left in the government's hands in terms of development policy was thus used intelligently over the fourteen years that lay ahead before EEC membership. Industry was to be developed by state aids and tax incentives (there was a tacit understanding that agriculture offered little hope because of the UK cheap food policy). The IDA was established and a new tax regime fashioned, the essential features of the strategy remain intact to this day. By 1972, the effect was such that it had begun to transform the economy. Industrial output had more than doubled, exports quintupled and employment had risen by nearly a half.

More importantly for the voyage on which the economy was about to embark, diversification of exports had begun and a new managerial class was being fashioned under the tutelage of multinationals and the influence of the Irish Management Institute. An entrepreneurial class had not yet appeared, and there was no guarantee it would, but the sense that something significant had at last been done was palpable and explains the air of confidence with which the government asserted on the eve of EEC membership that industry could survive in a common market composed of nine economies. It also justified why the economy could by this stage be described as one in the course of development without provoking derision. Furthermore, it explains why the self-image of the Irish economy had changed from the predominantly rural economy, portrayed by Sean Lemass to the Council in 1962, to that of the industrialising economy presented by Jack Lynch as a fit candidate for EEC membership ten years later.

The transition from protectionism to free trade had been accelerated by the conclusion of the Anglo-Irish Free Trade Area Agreement in 1965, which would have led to full free trade for industrial products with Britain by 1975. The Agreement was not just the ante-room to the EEC, as was properly intended. To all intents and purposes, it was entry into Ireland's own common market.

It is intriguing to speculate that if De Gaulle had not departed the scene, or if his policies had been continued by Pompidou, Britain might have been kept waiting much longer for membership, and Ireland with it. From 1975 onwards we would by virtue of the Agreement have been a region of the British economy in a fuller sense than that described by Paddy Lynch in 1960. Doubtless, Lemass gambled that Britain would be admitted earlier and that the prospect of Home Rule under the guise of a Republic would be avoided. It was worth the try and he could at least claim that the results were worth it. Nevertheless, the actual situation in 1972 was that Ireland was locked into a bilateral common market with its largest trading partner. Its isolation from Europe was formally never more complete but, paradoxically, it was precisely at this moment Ireland was about to break out of a historical stranglehold and enter a new world.

At the risk of contradicting myself let me also add that the Ireland of 1972 had, in some respects, already begun its entry into the new world which awaited. After all, in that year the plane crash at Staines had deprived Irish business of some of its best minds, who had been on their way to Brussels to prepare for Ireland's EEC membership. The Confederation of Irish Industry had already produced its comprehensive report "Into Europe" on preparing Irish business for EEC membership. Around that time, Irish students unleashed their version of the French "events", a gentle revolution that produced a breed of young professionals open to new influences, such as Ruairi Quinn and Una Claffey. The civil service had completed its own preparations for membership and some politicians had even dipped their toes in the refreshing waters of European politics. All this is true, but does not detract from the general propositions that I have advanced.

Let me summarise at this point. I have painted a picture of Ireland in 1972 as a poor, underdeveloped region of the British economy, isolated from Europe and disengaged from international politics, save for the UN and connections with its diaspora, insular in its domestic politics but having had the courage to embark on a challenging path to economic development and with the first signs of success evident. I have used broad brush-strokes to portray Irish economics and politics, and the result may not be to everybody's liking but this is the landscape I saw or, more accurately, as I think I saw it then, as someone involved in left-wing politics. But there was more to be seen; economics and politics are but part of a greater picture, that of society itself and the state which tries to shape it. These are colours on the palette which must be daubed on the canvas if the portrait is to be realistic.

But before I do, two other colours must be used; orange and green. The cosy insular world I have described up to 1969 was, in that year, invaded by the North. The Civil Rights Movement appeared and the official response rapidly led to violence, precipitated a political crisis in the Republic, transformed the national agenda and made good working relations with the British government indispensable. Within three years, the Northern issue was to move from indifference to engagement, sometimes passionate. The British embassy in Dublin was burnt down after Bloody Sunday.

Thus, the negotiations for EEC accession were conducted in circumstances no one had foreseen. There were now three major preoccupations for government: a successful entry into Europe, maintaining the pace of economic development and managing the Northern crisis. It appeared that the government was handling all three with aplomb and it was rewarded by an increase in its vote in the 1973 general election (only losing power because of an effective electoral pact between its opponents).

This suggests that the capacity of the Irish political system to respond to new challenges was greater than had been believed. At the time, a clinical assessment along those lines would have been impossible due to the pressure of events, and would have been largely disbelieved. But the potential to adapt rapidly to a novel and complex agenda surely explains why Ireland slid so effortlessly into the new role that awaited it in the EEC, a thesis that will be explored by other contributors to this volume. I cannot say that from the vantage point of the Labour Party's head office I had detected this potential, for the good reason that there were many features of Irish society and public administration which suggested otherwise.

SOCIETAL VALUES

Labour Party members were by nature the outsiders in Irish society and, perhaps, best equipped to describe what a latter-day De Tocqueville might have found. Two features stand out; a rural ethos and a monolithic culture based on Catholicism. Reference to a rural ethos may be surprising. It is hard to pin down, but in 1972 there was still a feeling that the real Ireland lay outside towns, often diminished by the adjective "garrison", and that the values of this real Ireland should predominate. An antipathy to urban living partially (or wholly perhaps) explains the failure to engage in town and city planning or to develop the physical infrastructure. Ireland was badly in need of both in 1972.

Rural values were a sort of civil culture which reinforced the moral values of Catholicism and made it possible to claim the state was separate from religion, as in any good republic, but yet also made it possible for church and state to operate as if joined in some mystical union. The evidence of the church's civil role and political influence was clear enough. The church basically owned primary and secondary education and heavily influenced the universities, other than Trinity College Dublin. It owned and managed the hospital system and determined medical ethics. Its dominance in education, health and voluntary social services was the result of history, since the church had filled a vacuum within the British state structure in Ireland. It became, as it were, a state within a state. Having created this inner state, at great cost and effort, the church would not easily assign its role, rights and property to an independent Irish state and, by 1972, had not done so.

Although the 1937 Constitution could be offered to students of constitutional law as a model of church/state separation in a non-denominational republic this was not the case in practice, and everybody knew it. For example, the Constitution enshrined Catholic moral teaching on divorce and the law of the land prohibited the importation or sale of contraceptives. Those who contested this moral order immediately received a belt of the crozier (and some still bear the scars).

The position of women in Irish society directly reflected the unique and unified culture of rural Ireland and Catholicism. Even though a debate had begun on women's equality, society had not yet accepted that a woman was truly equal to a man, could work outside as well as inside the home, and was entitled to the same pay and career opportunities if she choose to do so. Women had to resign from the civil service on getting married.

The home in which the family lived was by law that of the husband, marital rape was not a crime, domestic violence seldom the subject of prosecution, and still less just cause for the husband being debarred from the home. Single mothers were denied social welfare assistance, as were spinsters, prisoners' wives and divorcees. In many pubs a women would not be served a pint and, in some, not admitted to male sanctuaries (a practice, too, of golf clubs).

At the risk of appearing too simplistic, Irish society could be characterised as male dominated, authoritarian, unequal and much given to the public expression of piety not always reflected in private life (the taboo on incest springs to mind). Perhaps this state of affairs arose from the peculiarities of Irish history, and its social effects, not least the low level of education. It had only been in 1968 that secondary education became free for all children and it was still too early in 1972 to see its effects on authority, male dominance and social inequality.

THE PUBLIC SERVICE

It is hardly surprising that, in these circumstances, the upper echelons of the public service (as well as business, commerce and education) were predominantly male. It is no less surprising that the public service was as insular as the political culture with which it related, the Department of External Affairs being a notable exception.

Yet, the civil service had great strengths. It inherited from the British a value system centered on earnest and patient pursuit of the common good and had internalised many of the better ideals of the independence movement. Generally speaking, it respected the principle that it was the apolitical servant of the government. It was better educated than society at large and was managed competently, if too cautiously at times. Taken in conjunction with the legal system, local government and a range of semi-state bodies, the civil service was an indispensable asset in the twin tasks of establishing and developing the state, the value of which has largely gone unrecognised.

Notwithstanding the conservative cultural norms which the civil service had inherited from the British, it had developed into a curious mix of planner and entrepreneur by 1972. Up to the forties a plethora of semi-state bodies had been the pragmatic response to the lack of entrepreneurship in developing natural resources and to the need to provide essential public services. But the creation of state development agencies in the fifties and sixties, particularly the IDA, was an imaginative step beyond those early initiatives and evidence of a determination to make things happen economically. Laissez-faire was not quite the dominant philosophy it appeared to be, and the hidden land sometimes had to be made visible.

The Programmes for Economic Development consistently defended themselves against charges that they were exercises in planning and insisted that market forces were the only engine of growth. Still, the Irish state by 1972 was closer to French *dirigisme* than it would have been prepared to admit, and it was already experimenting with a consensual macro-economic model which it would later perfect in the latter part of the eighties.

At the same time, the civil service remained largely faithful to the classical administrative culture which relies heavily on precedent, eschews risk-taking and distrusts change. This was the darker side. With others, I complained that the civil service seemed to expend as much energy preventing things from happening as it did in making them happen. If this seemed like institutional schizophrenia, it is easy in hindsight to diagnose the cause. Irish society was then in the midst of a re-awakening; while half-awake, it was still half-asleep. The civil service was no exception and was caught in the same process of change that was affecting the rest of society.

APPROACH AND EXPECTATIONS

Ireland was in mid-stream where one generation was yielding to another. The contrast between the two men who served as President and Taoiseach on the eve of EEC membership best exemplifies this argument. Mr de Valera had been the first President of the Irish Republic and personified the generation which had built an independent Ireland. Mr Lynch was the first Taoiseach not to belong to that generation and represented an Ireland willing, and indeed eager, to share its independence with other European states. That they both held office when the Treaty of Accession was signed in 1972 symbolised the break which was taking place and, with it, an irreversible change in values, self-image and world view.

The change in perception can be best seen in the different ways Mr Lemass and Mr Lynch presented the Irish case for EEC membership to the Member States and to the Irish people. Whereas for Mr Lemass the context was that of an agricultural economy whose interests had to be protected by following Britain (I intend nothing but respect for his pragmatism), for Mr Lynch it was that of a developing economy which wished to make a contribution to the task of uniting Europe.

Mr Lynch's statement in the Dáil in July 1967[13] on the reactivation of Ireland's application for EEC membership is remarkable not only for this change in tone but also for the confidence with which he contemplated Irish membership of the world's largest trading bloc and for the clarity with which he spelled out the political implications of membership. I remember it well because it was my first involvement as Labour's General Secretary in a major Dáil debate, and because it set the parameters for our negotiations and the subsequent referendum debate.

Rereading that statement and those which followed, such as the White Paper of January 1972,[14] it is clear that the Irish model of EEC membership corresponded with the political objectives of integration as expressed by the then Member States and differed markedly from the British or Danish. For those who wanted to hear (I have said earlier that they weren't too many) the message could not have been clearer. In his introduction Mr Lynch said:

> We do not look upon the EEC as merely an economic institution. The Treaty of Rome is the foundation stone of a much greater concept than the exchange of trading opportunities. This Treaty can rightly be regarded as the first decisive act in building up a new Europe.

He went on to say that Ireland looked forward with confidence to a united Europe and he recognised it would inevitably have political implications and would entail certain limitations on our national sovereignty. But, as far as we in Ireland were concerned, we remained determined to play our full part in the new and greater Europe, which we hoped would one day emerge. The statement is replete with such sentiments, which were reiterated in the 1972 White Paper and repeated in my hearing, in various pro-membership speeches throughout the referendum campaign.

In fact, by 1972, the government's internalisation of the European project was such that the White Paper summarised the two fundamental considerations underlying its policy in seeking EEC membership, as firstly, European unity and, secondly, the national interest. The ordering of objectives is interesting, and no doubt intentional. Membership would enable us to participate freely in the movement towards European unity and would simultaneously provide the conditions in which we could best pursue our economic and social development.

This was the battleground on which the referendum was then fought and if the goal of European unity did not figure prominently it was, at least, debated and inherent in the arguments on both sides. It explains, in great part, Labour Party opposition to membership. The Labour leader, Brendan Corish, and his Deputy Leader, Jimmy Tully, had no empathy with Europe and, paradoxically, had become the last defenders of the Sinn Féin philosophy, "ourselves alone". Labour opposition was also understandably founded on the fear that jobs would be lost. But the positions taken by the Irish Council of the European Movement and the Anti-Common Market Defence Campaign best dramatised the difference between those who were excited by a new European mission for Ireland and those who were more comfortable with old certainties; it was a contest between anticipation of the new and nostalgia for the old.

More importantly for the EEC membership which lay ahead, the government had positioned Ireland as a Member State which would contribute positively towards the creation of a united Europe. In short, it would be a psychological insider within the integration process. This was not a Pauline conversion for the sake of appearances.

Its origins lay as far back as the Whitaker Grey Book, which accepted trade integration as central to a new economic order; this insight had been advanced under Sean Lemass to become an embrace of the inevitable; and then refined by Mr Lynch to become a vision of a united Europe in which Ireland genuinely wished to play its part, however insignificant.

The analysis of what lay ahead had been developed consistently over two decades and reflects particular credit on those who fashioned it with sophistication and panache. Indeed, the 1972 White Paper is a model of its kind and could be studied with profit by the current applicant states. It served as the intellectual platform for what was to be Ireland's strategic orientation within the process of integration for the following quarter-century.

Of equal importance is that by 1972 the government, and Fine Gael as the main opposition party, had long arrived at definite conclusions as to where the national interest lay. Each Member State must necessarily see EU membership in terms of its own self-interests and seek to gain some unique benefit from the pooling of sovereignty. In Ireland's case, Mr Lynch had expressed the national interest in his 1967 statement with simplicity and force when he said:

> Our future lies in participation in a wider economic grouping. Failure to achieve this objective would result in economic and political stagnation.

The conjunction of political and economic stagnation is the best insight into the motivation within political and official circles for membership of the EEC. It explains, too, the robust dismissal of any alternative to full membership. Indeed, the 1972 White Paper was almost abusive in the manner it disposed of the Labour Party's preferred option of associate membership:

> There is no realistic alternative to membership of an enlarged Community which is compatible with the national objectives of increasing employment and improving the standard of living.

It is intriguing to recall that this "there is no alternative" line of reasoning was based on a modest enough expectation of Community transfers; that is to say, modest by the standards of today. There was no anticipation of a regional fund, still less of Structural Funds on today's scale, simply because they didn't exist (although a regional policy was in the offing). Indeed, Mr Lemass had said in 1962 that we did not anticipate it would be necessary to seek any special financial assistance from the Community but, by 1972, that had been moderated by an expectation of significant transfers via the CAP and the Social Fund. The farmers, as usual, had a simple and accurate view of what was economically best for them and led the stampede into the EEC (with 83 per cent of the electorate voting in favour of membership, no other description applies). Other economic benefits were primarily foreseen as bigger markets, more inward investment and an opportunity for growth. The balance of economic advantage in favour of membership was less clear cut than, say, at the time of the Maastricht referendum.

If it is surprising in retrospect that there was no grand expectation of massive transfers to oil our passage into the EEC, it may be equally surprising that there was an expectation that membership would result in an end to neutrality. Mr Lemass had been unequivocal on this point, as was Mr Lynch. The factual situation was spelled out that the EEC, as such, did not involve security obligations but there was an open acceptance of the likelihood that further integration could result in agreement on common security and Ireland would be willing to play its part on the principle that what was worth joining was worth defending. This was commendable in its honesty. It is intriguing that such admissions did not deter the electorate from voting "yes". Perhaps they didn't want to hear it or, if they did, were more concerned with the economic consequences of isolation.

The central thesis of this analysis has been the phenomenon of isolation; that in 1972 Ireland was a region of the UK economy and part of the Anglophone world, and was isolated from the rest of Europe and from world affairs (save for the UN). A complementary thesis would be that the economy had been launched on a development path, with no guarantee it would succeed. Politics were insular, even if recently exposed to the realities of the North, the demands of EEC membership and political developments in Europe and the US. Society was inherently conservative and bounded by a monolithic value system. The public administration was then a mixture of the planner/entrepreneur and cautious administrator. And yet, things were in a state of flux. The sixties had been a good time to be young and the seventies looked full of hope.

It is a truism to say that Ireland would have developed anyway over the following 25 years; the key question is, in what direction? Ireland was no Norway or Switzerland and the alternative to full EEC membership was foreseen as economic and political stagnation, the penalties of isolation, as Mr Lynch described them. Continued and even deeper isolation was the fear which haunted policy-makers should we exclude ourselves from Europe. It was the fundamental theme running through the government's analysis of the national interest.

Garret FitzGerald put the prospects of membership more positively and more prophetically when he wrote that EEC membership would be a psychological liberation. The electorate agreed overwhelmingly. Above all other considerations, the Irish psyche (more accurately, the psyche of those of us who chose or could afford to live and work at home) needed to be liberated from the chains of the past and to be given its first opportunity since independence to express itself as it wished, develop the economy and take its place among the nations.

The extent to which 25 years of EU membership made a difference in that search for a new Ireland is the subject of the chapters that follow.

1. *Britain's European Question*, IEA (1996).
2. "European Economic Community", Pr 6101 (1961) page 8.
3. ibid. page 7.
4. On foot of a resolution passed by the 1966 Annual Conference.
5. Except, perhaps, for the Vietnam War and apartheid in South Africa, which were mainly of concern to the Labour movement.
6. Because of a long established UK cheap food policy.
7. "Membership of the European Communities; Implications for Ireland", Prl 1110 (1970), See Appendix 3 "The State of Preparedness of Irish Industry".
8. I made a documentary film in 1972 on the decay of central Dublin for private viewing by national and civic figures. The reaction was one of polite indifference.
9. This became a controversial issue in the mid- to late-seventies when several economists supported breaking the link with sterling.
10. Notably under the auspices of the ICEM.
11. *The Irish pound*, Frank Whitson Fetter (1955) p. 16. The British currency system was adopted in Ireland in 1826 (Fetter, page 60).
12. Dublin: Stationery Office, 1958.
13. IEA *European Document Series*, No. 17, Series 1997, page 62.
14. "The Accession of Ireland to the European Communities" (Prl 2064).

POLITICS

CHAPTER 4

The French Are On The Sea

Tom Garvin

Ireland's membership of the European Union has existed now, in one form or another, for quarter of a century, and possible membership of such a union was a live issue in Irish politics certainly from the date of the 1956 Messina summit, if not earlier. The European Union has become so much a fact of Irish life that we find it difficult to imagine Ireland without Europe. No one under the age of 35 can have any real grasp of what it was like to have no European integument of the kind we now take for granted. For this reason, among others, European Union membership has tended to be discussed at a popular level as involving mainly a new version of pork-barrel politics, sometimes genially termed "grantsmanship". The European Union has been good for us, it is argued sometimes, because it has paid for new roads, for grant-aided scholarships and professorships, provided subsidies to make transport between the countries of the Union cheaper and faster, and has aided tourism.

On the other side, Eurosceptics have tended to discuss membership in the same way, but looking at the glass as though it were half-empty rather than half-full. Europe has encouraged an historically deep-rooted dependency culture, it is argued, aggravating clientelist mentalities and discouraging local initiative and national initiative in favour of reliance upon outside money from Brussels. Europe has finally killed off the old Sinn Fein Griffithian and de Valeran ideology of self-reliance and self-respect in favour of a new version of the old slave-mind psychology; we have exchanged the British Empire for a new European Empire.

THE EUROPEAN PHENOMENON: AN HISTORICAL PERSPECTIVE

The two views I have just sketched, or even caricatured, are really the same view looked at from different perspectives. Actually they are both deeply impoverished ways of looking at the Irish experience of Europe, and I would like to offer in this contribution a quasi-historical and *longue-duree* perspective on Ireland and the phenomenon of European unification.

First of all, and most obviously, Ireland is a peripheral island on the edge of the European continent. Like its sister island Britain, Ireland has had historical and cultural ties with the British Empire and the United States which are at least as intimate and enduring as any connection with the great European countries of France, Germany, Italy and Spain. Willy-nilly, a small, historically peasant and lately free-farmer, mainly Catholic culture has been caught up in a mainly Anglo-Saxon and Protestant civilisation, dominated over the past two centuries by two English-speaking super-powers, England in the nineteenth century and America in the twentieth. These two countries can claim to be the planetary dominant cultures of the last two centuries, and their common language, English, is now the world's lingua franca. Catholic Ireland was for a long time the only English-speaking Catholic country, and the only Catholic stable democracy in the world. Analogies elsewhere can be found to Ireland's cultural status as a "lone country" to adapt Samuel Huntington's term: Catholic Quebec in Canada, Muslim Albania in Europe and Jewish Israel in the midst of Dar al-Islam spring to mind.

Cultural predicaments of this kind are not reducible to economics, and present real dilemmas for policy-makers. In our case, we Irish had to marry together cultural systems which many looked upon as antithetical: Tridentine authoritarian Catholicism, of an isolated and besieged type, and Anglo-American liberal democracy. Furthermore, we had to try to create such a marriage in the early nineteenth century under apparently impossible conditions: a society rushing headlong into a catastrophe because of monocrop dependency, a deeply undemocratic society ruled by a small and unsympathetic ascendancy of extravagant wealth and anti-democratic provenance, and a Catholic Church both beloved of the people and itself profoundly elitist.

The first attempt at marrying the two traditions of Irish Catholicism and Anglo-American liberal democracy was that of Daniel O'Connell, and it is significant that O'Connell became immediately recognised in continental Europe as one of the key founding fathers of what is now known as Christian Democracy. Not only did O'Connell argue for a democratic Catholicism, he also argued for the abolition of black slavery and the emancipation of Jews in European societies that still discriminated against them. It is not often that Irish democratic political leaders as different as John Redmond, Charles Stewart Parnell, Eamon de Valera, William Cosgrave, Sean Lemass, Jack Lynch and Garret FitzGerald are looked upon as all equally cultural descendants of the Great Dan, but I would insist that they are, their democratic culture coming from the same source. The republican versus Home Rule division was by comparison superficial and one of a generational character rather than an ideological, really a difference over means than over ends. Sean O'Faolain pushed something like this line in his marvellous biographies of Hugh O'Neill (*The Great O'Neill*) and Daniel O'Connell (*King of the Beggars*) in the 1930s; to less than total popular success. I realise this claim to O'Connellite ancestry for all kinds of people is a large one to make, but bear with me briefly.

There is an extraordinary cultural continuity in Irish attempts to create what might be described as a foreign policy. It is not necessary, but might be useful, for us to go back to the Stuart and Jacobite tradition of seeking help from Royal Spain or the republican wish to get French, American or German help, depending on the historical era. It can certainly be argued cogently that Irish leaders have persistently, and over a very long period, attempted, sometimes with ludicrous or tragic consequences, to achieve a link with foreign powers which might alleviate or counter-balance the overwhelming cultural and socio-economic embrace of Britain. The Stuarts with Spain and France; Theobald Wolfe Tone with revolutionary France; the Fenians with the victorious American Union after the American Civil War; Pearse and his comrades with Imperial Germany; Collins with the emergent Dominions of a crumbling British Empire; de Valera with the United States and the League of Nations in a tragic period of depression, world war and genocide, when little was open to a small, weak emergent country but to keep its head down and hope for the tempest to spend itself.

After 1945, the little state of Eire, later the Republic of Ireland, had to pay the price for its neutrality in the Second World War. Justly or otherwise, it came to be seen in the councils of Washington and of NATO as a wayward, unreliable and unimportant little country which was at odds with Britain and which had had, at best, an ignoble and unhelpful role in the period 1939-45. As late as the early 1990s, this particular desertion of the ancient Irish tradition of search for an outside ally was remembered to our disadvantage by the Anglophile establishment in the US State Department. It took two decades of brilliant Irish diplomacy on the part of Sean Donlon and his colleagues, together with the initiatives of Jean Kennedy Smith and Bill Clinton, finally to expunge that legacy.

This is the true prehistory of the modern Irish engagement with Europe: a half-remembered but very deep longing for an alliance, a friendship that was non-imperial and psychologically satisfying, combined with a culturally determined wish to be self-sufficient and to be true to no one but one's collective self. I am not trying to demote economics in favour of political culture, but I do believe that the role of long-distance cultural syndromes has been vastly underrated by many commentators. This is so despite the fact that the central role of similar traditions is recognised as operating elsewhere. Most countries have asked of Europe "what is in it for us?" in a much broader sense than the purely economic.

Germany and France embraced the agreements that were the ancestors of the European Union not for reasons of altruistic internationalism, but because both countries were terrified of a "fourth round" of warfare between them, following on from the bouts, as they were seen, beginning in 1870, 1914 and 1939, and ending in the tragic undoing of both countries. Germany had been beaten twice, inconclusively in 1918, conclusively in 1945. France had been beaten conclusively in 1870, scored little better than a draw in 1918, and had collapsed ignominiously in 1940. Almost worse, it had been beaten in Indochina by the Vietnamese in the early 1950s and again by the Algerians in the late-1950s. Another reason for the acceptance of "Europe" was the fear both Germany and France had of the communist menace of the time, a menace seen by each country as both internal and external. Not only was the victorious war-machine of the Soviet Union actually inside Germany, the Soviet alliance had a fifth column inside Western European countries in the form of mass political parties and many quiet sympathisers in high places. Germany had to remake its entire political culture after 1945, and "Europe" was a key device in its de-Prussianisation.

Benelux was a clever and rational pooling of resources by the weak countries of The Netherlands, Belgium and Luxembourg, in many ways a pioneering experiment in European integration. Spain and Portugal joined later so as to shake off the historical fascist "monkeys on the backs" of these two post-imperial but European peripheral countries; we must remember that a qualification for entry to the Union was the existence of democratic and liberal political institutions. General de Gaulle's patriotic democracy of 1958 impressed Franco's civilised right enormously. In effect, the European Union accelerated the democratisation of Francoist Spain and, possibly, Salazarian Portugal. Greece joined because of the perceived continued menace represented by its hated ex-imperial master, Turkey. Somewhat similarly, Ireland was eager to join because of its unequal relationship with local super-power England, and Denmark came in because Britain, its main market, was going in, and it went in despite its inherited fear and hatred of Germany.

In the Irish case, Europe offered a reality which had always been fantasised about: a powerful entity that was perceived as benign, was not English and was not controlled by England. Parenthetically, I use the term "England" advisedly, because what was being seen as happening was the final, internationally ratified subordination of an old imperial-England in a new, post-imperial and Americanising world. It was also a post-European world.

Similarly, Finland joined because of fear of Russia, Sweden because the point of her neutrality had evaporated, and the countries of what was once termed "Central Europe" are clamouring to join because of dreams of post-Communist wealth and fear of Russian revanchism. All joined, or wish to join, Europe in what they each saw or see as their self-interest, not because of some vision of an ideal, united Europe.

The central point I am making is that "Europe", like the mysterious, handsome and privately uncaring mute in Carson McCullers's *The Heart is a Lonely Hunter*, is all things to all people. That means, in our context, that it has to be all things to all nationalities and sub-nationalities if it is going to succeed. The nationalisms of the nations of Europe have been persuaded that "Europe" is in their national interest, but there is no European "nation" and there has always been something slightly artificial about "the European identity". One could argue persuasively that the only political and popular culture that Europeans actually share is American, and the national language of this Europe is American English. As Benjamin Barber has pointed out in his brilliant polemic *Jihad versus McWorld*, popular entertainment in the core countries of modern Europe and elsewhere in the world has been possibly irretrievably Americanised, and has become part of what we are, like it or lump it. "Europe" as a focus of cultural or national identity is a delicate plant, caught between the lusty old weeds of traditional European state nationalisms and the creeping, ubiquitous kudzu of American electronic entertainment.

Here in Ireland, we have an ironic advantage; the result of a century of nationalist and official attempts to deanglicise the culture has actually left us even more open to Americanisation, mainly by weakening our painfully acquired grasp of English culture while putting little in its place. The regaelicisation of Ireland failed long ago, but left us with a weakened understanding of our English-language heritage. Partly as a result, Ireland is probably the most thorougly Americanised country in Europe, with Britain as runner-up in this doubtful sweepstakes. This fact qualifies us to run the increasingly Americanised Europe of McWorld. Interestingly, Irish civil servants, political leaders, sellers of cultural services and businessmen in general instinctively recognised this long ago.

THE IRISH EXPERIENCE OF EUROPE

To understand the Irish experience of Europe the comparative technique of contrast is a useful and appropriate one: what was Ireland like without "Europe"? That is, the Ireland of before (say) 1960 or thereabouts when the options of intra-European free trade became serious ones rather than simply theoretical ideals in a nationalistic and protectionist world still not quite recovered from the great Depression and the Second World War.

Ireland in the period between 1945 and 1960 was a quiet place. A sullen acceptance of the stand-off between the two parts of Ireland prevailed. De Valera's Fianna Fáil dominated political life, even when the party was out of office. The Catholic Church had immense political, social and cultural power. The Gaelic Athletic Association dominated much of sporting and social life. Forty per cent of the population earned its living from farming, often of an underdeveloped and under-invested type. The general ethos was small-town and rural, country life being celebrated as being superior to, and anterior to, the lives of people who were forced to live in big cities. Domestic happiness was extolled, and an often extravagant public piety was taught and practised.

A national Catholic tradition of cultural defence was ensconced in power, and that defence was seen in particular as one of resistance to the English-speaking world outside, a world of disbelief, scepticism, anti-Catholicism and greed. Much of this nationalist "broad front" had been constructed in the nineteenth century by an alliance which I have elsewhere determined to be an alliance of "priests and patriots". It has since crumbled, as everyone knows, under the onslaught of international television, radio and film, the onset of urbanisation and secularism within Ireland itself, and also because of the public sins of both priests and patriots. The priests suddenly became human beings, visibly possessing the same failings as other ordinary human beings; an avalanche of sexual and financial scandals descended on the Catholic Church, in part because of the revolution in the mass media, which meant older conspiracies of silence became unsustainable. The patriots, on the other hand, decided that Northern Ireland was unfinished business, and for 30 years attempted to force a united Ireland on an unwilling population by murder, maiming and intimidation, accompanied by an appalling tirade of lying propaganda in Ireland and Irish-America that was reminiscent of the best work of Joseph Goebbels or the Soviet propagandists. The ceasefire of 1994 marks the final recognition by the patriots of their own moral and political bankruptcy.

All of this, I would argue, happened more or less independently of "Europe", and would, in some form or other, have happened anyway; revolutions die eventually, and usually take about a century-and-a-half from their birth to their demise. The Irish revolution which created the alliance of priests and patriots was born in Langari's Timber Yard in what is now Fenian Street in Dublin in 1858, and ended in the car-bomb at Omagh in 1998: 140 years.

What Europe has done is offer everyone a way out of the historical trap in which Ireland was caught, and several intelligent Irish leaders saw this long ago, in particular Sean Lemass and a coterie of civil servants, politicians and academics in the 1945-1963 period. The Europe foreseen was rather different from the one we now know, but it is startling that, while Britain disdained to go to the Messina meeting, Lemass, in opposition, was pleading with the Irish government of the time to go. Fianna Fáil was eager for Europe at the start, as were the younger people in Fine Gael. Only Labour, with its English cultural connections and Marxist style of thinking, stayed aloof. The Europe foreseen was one of France, Germany and Scandinavia, excluding the Catholic and Mediterranean tier of Italy, Spain and Portugal.

Europe promised free trade above all. Ireland's monocrop dependency on Britain remained substantially intact in 1960. At the time of independence, Irish trade was virtually totally with the United Kingdom, and consisted mainly of cattle on the hoof, sheep and pigs. Manufactured exports consisted mainly of agriculture-derived products, such as beer and biscuits. GNP per capita was probably about one-third of what it is now (1999). Every year about 5,000 privileged young people, most of them men, went into higher education; the present-day figure is over 60,000. Increasingly, undergraduate and postgraduate students elect to have part of their university education in a mainland European third-level institution, a change which, I believe, will be of immense long-term cultural consequence.

Back in the 1950s, a large proportion of the population ceased attending school at age twelve, and functional illiteracy must have been common. Illegitimacy was unknown, because the deterrents against it were fearsome and, incidentally, almost certainly illegal, although sanctioned by both state and church. Nowadays, over one-quarter of children are born extra-maritally, and there is no stigma attached to it. On the other hand, drugs and violent crime were almost unknown, and a certain innocence has since faded from Irish society. A harsh book censorship ensured a simple-minded and unintellectual public cultural atmosphere. "Intellectuals" were regarded as pretentious, false and "pseudo", even when they said something intelligent, as they occasionally did. An almost Soviet fear and hatred of independent thinking pervaded the culture. People spoke their minds in secret, or not at all; it was less than a totally free country. People lost their jobs because they did not practise their religion, or practised the wrong one. Journalists who tried to investigate powerful people were pushed out of the country, and this fact was never made public. Unmarried mothers were pushed out to England, as were social deviants of all kinds. A fear of authority was also pervasive; authority was seen as being arbitrary; brutal and unpredictable, and to be evaded if at all possible.

Bullying parents, priests, teachers and employers were common and there was little recourse from such power-holders. Teachers, parents and even professors could behave then in ways which would, nowadays, certainly ensure that they ended up in court or even jail. I offer these contrasts, chosen almost at random, to emphasise the enormous and pervasive wave of change that has occurred in Irish society and social culture in the last 40 years.

Free trade meant more trade, and it also meant that a wider variety of goods could be manufactured for a wider variety of consumers. Britain, the economic powerhouse of fifties' Europe, faded fast in the 1960s in the face of the challenges of Germany, France and later Italy. Irish economic dependence on Britain faded in the 1970s, and nowadays only a third or less of Ireland's trade is with Britain. At the time of independence, nearly 60 per cent of the population derived their income from farming; the equivalent proportion now is about ten per cent. Furthermore, the proportion of small, subsistence farms has fallen, and there is a general tendency for large, commercial farming to win out over traditional modes of farming. Of course, Europe's Common Agricultural Policy has had a lot to do with this change in the last 25 years; a continuation of the British cheap-food policy would have meant a much poorer farming sector in Ireland.

Again, however, I think this general tendency towards modernisation and urbanisation would have occurred anyway, but it very probably would have been far slower under the old British-Irish customs union which was evolving in the 1960s. A far more profound consequence of Europe was the de facto reunification of Ireland for administrative purposes, a reunification which is still in train. The Irish border has become increasingly irrelevant as far as ordinary social and economic life is concerned, and this process is liable to accelerate in the near future. European parallels with the Irish problem exist, and European solutions are on offer. The first successful solution to a post-1918 boundary problem was that of

South Tyrol/Alto Adige, and a similar set of solutions is on offer in the Basque lands. In these islands, Europe symbolises the end of empire and, therefore, the obsolescence of the ancient English-Irish quarrel. I would argue emphatically that that has been the true European achievement in Ireland, an achievement which far outweighs the undoubted benefits of the Common Agricultural Policy, the Brussels cornucopia of grants or even European free trade. The odd thing is, we have scarcely noticed that the 800-year war is over, dying quietly and unmourned sometime between 1972 and 1998.

The proposition that there is life after England may seem trite to people living in the late 1990s, but was one of enormous liberation 35 years ago, and for a long time not fully believed. The cultural consequences of this particular end-game and conclusion are not yet obvious, but will be profound. Freed of their historical obsession with England, Irish people, north and south, will be free to reinvent themselves, as the better of their political leaders, nationalist and unionist alike, have wanted them to do throughout this century. I do not know what Irish people will decide to do in this different world, but I think it will be interesting, and Europe will be an important part of it.

CHAPTER 5

Sharing Sovereignty

Martin Cullen

I would like to thank Professor Garvin for his illuminating outline of Irish political perspectives of our membership of the European Union. I think Professor Garvin rightly situates this in our historical perception of Europe as a place of alternative belonging to the dominance of British culture, which we saw as the sea we swam in for a very long period of time. On the other hand, I believe our perception of the United States has been considerably more one of deliberate identification, given our deep historical links through emigration, than of a parallel civilisation to that of Britain which had to be counterbalanced by European influences. Indeed, I think that our relationship with the United States is, if not unique, exceptional and remarkable in that it has deepened and broadened in political and economic terms, even while we have done the same within Europe. We have avoided any suggestion of a "zero-sum" game in developing these relationships and this is one of the many successes of our participation in Europe.

BACKGROUND TO IRISH MEMBERSHIP

I think it is true to say that for the first 40 years of our independence, whether warmly or not, Ireland's perception of its relationship with the outside world was seen by ourselves, and by others, substantially through the prism of a relationship with Britain.

Ireland was, it should be noted, a founding member of several post-war Europe organisations, such as the Organisation for European Economic Co-operation (OEEC) – later the OECD – and the Council of Europe. However, it is a measure I think of our remoteness in the perspective of our international political and economic relationships, that Ireland did not consider joining the European Coal and Steel Community (ECSC) in 1951, or the European Economic Community and the European Atomic Energy Community when they were established in 1957.

Since the mid-1930s, Irish economic policy had been based on high tariffs, quantitative trade restrictions, import substitution and wariness towards foreign investment. No real alternative appeared to exist to a heavy dependence on the British economy for which we were a cheap source of labour and food. From 1958 onwards, however, as Irish governments became more conscious of the shift in economic weight taking place between the UK and Europe, policy was redirected towards the internationalisation of the Irish economy. Henceforth, growth was to be built upon foreign investment and the development of an export-driven economy.

It must surely be acknowledged that such an orientation foresaw that the UK would, willingly or reluctantly, strengthen its trade relationship with the rest of Europe as a replacement for an economy which had previously oriented itself to a very disparate empire which was coming to an end. I doubt very much that our efforts at opening up our economy would have taken the shape they did without the example of a European institution, the then EEC, which went in ambition far beyond the UK model of a European Free Trade Area.

Ireland applied to join the European Community in 1961, but the block to Britain's entry at that time thwarted Ireland's membership ambitions and it was not until the late 1960s that the prospect of Irish membership revived. In the meantime, the Irish economy had significantly moved away from its reliance on protectionism towards a more open and trade-oriented approach.

THE IMPACT OF EU MEMBERSHIP

I will readily admit that drawing up a balance sheet of Ireland's EU membership since 1973 is complicated by the difficulty in distinguishing between the impact of EU membership and of other influences, such as domestic policy decisions and international economic developments. The most directly-quantifiable impact of EU membership has been in the economic sphere, and, despite Professor Garvin's historical, cultural and political approach, I make no apology for suggesting that our economic development since accession has shaped our political perspective within the Union.

A decision to open your real economy to the international market is generally irreversible, as many of the countries of eastern Europe are discovering. The dynamic created leads to domestic political choices which cannot ignore conditions internationally, and the nature of the EEC, with its precedence over domestic legislation in areas of its competence, underlined our irrevocable commitment to shape our economic and, I would submit, our political debates to include a wider concept of our independence and how our sovereignty might be exercised internationally.

The Economic Impact

I will not dwell on statistics in assessing the economic impact of our membership but some major points should be taken into account. The guaranteed prices of the Common Agricultural Policy (CAP) produced a significant rise in Irish farm incomes from 1973 onwards. The CAP also increased output in sectors such as livestock and milk. Progress towards the creation of an advanced agribusiness/food sector has developed rapidly in recent years.

Direct EU funding in the areas of regional, social, and structural policies has been of major benefit to Ireland. Total net receipts to Ireland in the period 1973-95 amounted to more than IR£21,000m. These resources have been spent in restructuring agriculture, providing skills training to the unemployed, sustaining local development and employment initiatives, and developing the state's national economic infrastructure. A 1994 Economic and Social Research Institute (ERSI) report estimated that the total cumulative impact of structural funding accounted for an increase of 7% of GNP and that the rate of return on the EU's investment was also approximately 7%.

This funding has also contributed to narrowing the gap between Irish per capita GDP and the EU average. In 1973, Irish per capita GDP stood at 58% of the European Community average. In 1997, estimates suggest that it may have risen to around 90% of the EU average. Significantly for the future, patterns of Irish trade have been transformed as a result of membership. In 1970, 66% of Irish exports went to the United Kingdom market with a mere 12% going to what is now the rest of the EU. By contrast, in 1995 the UK took 26% of Irish exports and the rest of the EU 47%, and the EU percentage is rising annually.

These economic facts inevitably bring about political choices and arguments, but I would submit that these arguments are now imbued on all sides with acceptance that Ireland is and will remain a member of the European Union and a player in its development.

The Political Impact

While the economic impact of membership is readily quantifiable, it is arguable that the political implications are less statistically measurable but actually more profound on both a national and international level. On an international level, membership has given Ireland the means and the opportunity to influence the evolution of the European Union and its policies. This was evident, for example, during Ireland's European Community Presidency in 1990 which presided over EU discussions concerning the unification of Germany. Ireland's EU Presidency in the second half of 1996 and the chairing of the Intergovernmental Conference (IGC) to negotiate the Treaty of Amsterdam, again gave the country a key role within the EU at an important stage in the Union's evolution.

A fear which existed at the time of our accession, and even after, was that Ireland as a small and peripheral nation would be swallowed by a huge European process in which our interests and identity would be hardly noticed. I would submit that the opposite is what has actually happened. Through a careful mix of knowledge of the system of European negotiation and a tight focus on national priorities I think it can be said that successive governments have "punched above their weight" and have achieved a remarkable profile for Ireland within the Union. We are, I believe, known among our EU partners as a reliable and efficient partner in whose hands sensitive issues will be dealt with expeditiously and sensitively. We demonstrate, backed by public opinion, enthusiasm for the process of European integration with a realistic awareness of what is achievable among the diverse interests of our partners.

I think, ironically, that far from being a disadvantage, our success here may owe something to our small size which cannot give rise to a vast bureaucracy and which then allows decisions to be made quickly and excellent coherence to be maintained in a negotiation. Ireland has also, since 1973, been fully involved in consultation and co-ordination among EU Member States on foreign-policy issues.

Active participation in European Political Co-operation (EPC) and subsequently in the EU's Common Foreign and Security Policy (CFSP), which was established by the Maastricht Treaty, has given Ireland an opportunity for a more wide-ranging engagement in international affairs, while maintaining its traditional foreign-policy values and aspirations. Irish concerns have been reflected in the development of the CFSP objectives in areas such as human rights and disarmament. Ireland has participated actively in the formulation and implementation of EU policies including, in recent years, on such major international issues as the former Yugoslavia, the Middle East peace process, Rwanda and Burundi.

There are of course different perspectives and priorities among Member States in relation to common foreign and security policy and, with a majority of Member States being members of NATO and the Western European Union, the question of defence co-operation is one which can arise in this context. I do not wish to open a field of discussion in this area but I would say that it has been a position of

Ireland's since accession that the concept of security embraces far more than the narrow perspective of defence and military alliance. I think events in Europe have borne this out and that the provisions in the Amsterdam Treaty relating to the Petersburg tasks – humanitarian and rescue tasks, peace-keeping tasks and tasks of combat forces in crisis management – illustrate that this thinking is now widely shared by our partners. As with other matters, Ireland's perspective on the development of a security architecture for Europe is well understood by our partners through our able and active participation in debate, and we will participate as equals in its construction.

I would suggest that participation in this field and elsewhere has developed and strengthened Ireland's capacity to engage with the "outside world" while also demonstrating to the Irish electorate that the world is multi-polar and interdependent in ways which our "ancient struggle" could never have achieved.

The history of post-war Britain would no doubt have illustrated in any case its relative decline from imperial power to a European state which, like the rest of us, must negotiate to survive. However, our perception of this would, I submit, have been very much slower to form, and very much less self-assured, had we not had the European Community.

The agonising steps towards and away from closer integration which Britain has gone through in the past two decades have, in my view, become of less and less importance to us as the dynamic of our own European participation has taken hold. That we can, for example, face the prospect of entry into EMU without Britain with equanimity and indeed confidence is testimony to the economic and political water which divides our European experience from that of Britain. I would add, in the international context, a further point about our relationship with the United States. While at the outset of our membership of the European Community it was possible to argue that much of the US interest in investment in Ireland was as an English-speaking base with access to the European market, I believe the perspective has changed.

Our huge success in attracting high-tech and information-oriented industries and services is both a product of, and cause of, an extra-ordinary Irish achievement in deepening our relationship politically, diplomatically and economically with the United States, while at the same time embracing European integration. I believe our successful membership of the European Union has massively reinforced our efforts in the US to seek closer economic and political ties, with the most obvious political benefits evident in Northern Ireland.

Indeed it is worthy of note that, within Northern Ireland, both the United States Consulate and the offices of the European Commission have always been able to play a very valuable and constructive role in bringing the communities together and providing a wider perspective on issues. Successive Irish governments' extraordinary ability to harness the goodwill, influence and practical assistance available from the US and Europe has been of enormous value in the search for a lasting peace in Northern Ireland, and has also greatly increased our profile and our reputation for effectiveness, in both continents.

At a national political level, the shape of a vast array of Irish public policy has been affected by EU membership. Equally, pay legislation, environmental protection policy, consumer-protection law, competition law, health and safety statutes, social policy, education and cultural policy have all been influenced by decisions taken by Ireland and its partners at European level.

Irish public attitudes towards the EU are generally very positive, if not necessarily focused on individual issues or policies. In May 1972, membership of the EC was supported by 83% of Irish voters in a turnout of 71% of the electorate. Just under 70% of Irish voters have subsequently approved both the Single European Act in 1987 and the Treaty on European Union in 1992, and 62% voted in favour of the Amsterdam Treaty in May 1999.

Poll data suggest that Irish support for integration is unmatched elsewhere in the Union, with over 80% agreeing that EU membership is good for the country (compared with an EU average of 56%). On the other hand, Irish voters are just above the EU average in their actual knowledge of the Union, with 65% describing themselves as being not well informed about the EU. I think that if we are to move away from what one might call "soft-focus" approval of the EU, inspired very much I think by the political and historical background outlined by Professor Garvin in his chapter, then we must do a job of work in visibly connecting the interests of the average citizen, such as jobs, inflation and security, with those of the Union.

In terms of EU policy development, Ireland's approach may be said to have been that of a dedicated realist, given our nominal position as an equal in the Council of Ministers but our very small size as an economic participant. Reform of the Common Agricultural Policy, competition policy, the shape of regional and social policies and the development of structural and cohesion funding might all be said to owe something to Irish energies and ideas. Within the Union's decision-making processes, the Irish contribution has consistently been one of constructive engagement.

It is no idle boast to say that, in areas where our and others' vital interests are concerned, Irish ministers and officials enjoy a reputation for successful brokerage and negotiation rather than brinkmanship and obstructionism. On broader institutional and political issues, successive Irish governments have been anxious to stress their supportive approach to European integration.

CONCLUSION

Ireland has changed much as a result of EU membership and has contributed to change within the EU. On three occasions, the Irish electorate has given strong support to the country's participation in the further evolution of European integration. Conscious of its political and economic advantages for Ireland, successive Irish governments have shown a strong commitment to the integration process.

Ireland has been a full participant in the process of European integration for a generation. We have benefited enormously from membership of the European Union and have, at the same time, contributed comprehensively to the Union's development. Irish people increasingly see the European Union not simply as an organisation to which Ireland belongs, but as an integral part of our future. We see ourselves, increasingly, as Europeans. Ireland's membership of the European Union has always been about more than free trade and financial transfers, important as these may be. The period of our membership of the Union has coincided with an increase in national self-confidence, a strengthening of our identity and an increase in our international profile.

I would suggest that this increase in self-confidence, strengthening of identity, and increase in international profile are more than a coincidence. They represent a fruition of what was begun in the 1950s and have been a matter of consensus ever since. The concept of "ourselves alone" has no meaning in the economic sphere given the levels of interdependence and interchangeability which exist in trade in goods and services internationally, and this fact has inexorably had an effect on a political perspective already disposed, as Professor Garvin illustrates, to embrace Europe.

The political task today, I believe, is to deepen the roots of this growth of Europe in our imagination. This involves a challenge to our ability to adjust and adapt to a changed European and international environment. While in the past, our perspective on the European Union has been largely that of a small, poor, peripheral country benefiting from the generous economic flows from the CAP and the Structural Funds, in the future we are not likely to benefit in such an obvious and direct way from EU policies. We must now look to the broader perspective, in which our participation in the Union will be more complex but perhaps no less valuable to our own development.

SOCIETY
AND
CULTURE

CHAPTER 6

Strengthening Irish Identity
Through Openness

Liam Ryan

This chapter is a bit like Caesar's Gaul – divided into three parts. And this is no bad place to start. Caesar was a great unifier and he had cultural as well as political ideals. He never got as far as Ireland, as was pointed out once by an Italian journalist who, after some un-Roman disorders following a soccer match in Belfast, reported that it was quite obvious Julius Caesar had never been there. Things might have been different if the Roman general Agricola had followed through on his idea in 81 AD. He looked across at us from a hill in Cumberland and thought we might be brought within the Roman *imperium* with just one legion. The first of many optimists!

The three parts will consist of something on European identity, something on Irish culture in relation to Europe, and something on the social impact of EU policy on Ireland.

EUROPEAN IDENTITY AND IRISH IDENTITY

Irish society has changed more over the past 25 years that at any time in its history. And the rate of change has been telescoped into a much shorter time-span than similar changes that have taken place elsewhere. What took over 100 years in Britain and in much of Western Europe has all happened in Ireland in the space of a generation. Of course, not all of this is attributable to EU membership. We had already begun to taste the good life under Sean Lemass who assured us that even better times were to follow: "The years ahead", he said in 1996, "will be a great time to be alive and to be young and to be Irish". Charlie Haughey, too, shared in the general optimism and euphoria of the 1960s when, as Minister for Finance in 1969, he proclaimed that: "Ireland has now solved its economic problems and all that remains is to share the wealth more equitably among the people". Charlie was always good at persuading people to share their wealth!

What we joined on 1 January 1973 was a Common Market and our motives for entry were singularly uncomplicated. The decision to join was arrived at on the basis of mundane self-interest, individual and national. It is, however, worth noting that some cynics at the time suggested that it may well not have been a vote to join something as a vote to get to hell out of whatever we were in.

But already there was talk of loftier motives. The great European statesmen of post-war reconstruction – Monnet, Schuman, de Gasperi, Adenauer – were invoked to claim that the EEC had a nobler destiny. It would be a realisation of the European dream, a new Christendom even. And Ireland, it was suggested, could contribute to this exciting grand design. The Catholic bishops waxed eloquently about Ireland's place in Europe – had we not illuminated the darkness of Europe in the long ago through our saints and scholars – and went on to declare that "our national life at every level: religious, cultural, intellectual and social: will be profoundly affected by the step we are about to take". Their lordships referred sentimentally to our fellow-Europeans as "old friends", gratefully remembering our past contributions and ready to welcome us back. (*The Irish Times* 29.12.72).

However, in spite of much talk about a "common cultural heritage", the ideal of a common European identity has remained high in aspiration but low in priorities within the EU. When we ask what has been the cultural impact of the EU in Irish society, there is a prior question to be asked: to what extent is there a cultural awareness at all in the concept of "Europe" as conceived at present in the "European Union"? Is it conceived as a cultural union, as distinct from a merely political or social union. Or, in economic terms, is Europe conceived of as a "common culture" as distinct from merely a "common market". One finds very little reference to the former and certainly no awareness of the values and culture which once made Europe a coherent civilisation, a unity which grew from that peculiar mixture of the Greco-Roman and the Judeo-Christian. Perhaps there may no longer be validity in the image of Europe as a central cultural trunk with a diversity of branches, and fed from the triple roots of Greece and Rome and Jerusalem.

A programme I once saw on the European University Institute in Florence started only at the Renaissance, as if the Roman Empire, Christianity and the High Middle Ages had never happened. Yet this was the period, a very long one, when "Europe" really was a unity both politically and culturally, whereas the Renaissance is precisely the period when it began to break up.

Vaclav Havel has repeatedly called on the EU to develop a new and genuinely clear articulation of what European identity means. In accepting an honorary degree from Trinity College Dublin in June 1996 he called on the EU not to shrink from "the transcendental aspect of its own endeavours" and to "rediscover, consciously embrace and in some way articulate its soul or its spirit, its underlying idea, its purpose and its inner ethos". Two years previously, when addressing the European Parliament in Strasbourg in March 1994, he was even more direct:

> Into my admiration, which initially verged on enthusiasm, there began to intrude a disturbing, less exuberant feeling. I felt I was looking into the inner workings of an absolutely perfect and immensely ingenious modern machine. To study such a machine must be a great joy to an admirer of technical inventions, but for me, a human whose interest in the world is not satisfied by admiration of well-oiled machines, something was seriously missing. Perhaps it could be called, in a rather simplified way, a spiritual or moral or emotional dimension. My reason had been spoken to, but not my heart.

Perhaps Vaclav Havel is seeking too much. He readily admits that the idea of European unity did not simply fall out of the sky nor was it born on the drawing boards of political engineers. It grew out of an appreciation of something in common that had been there before, some unspoken common ground, perhaps something obvious that everyone takes for granted. It grew out of an understanding that "Europe" was a fact of life, and from an appreciation of the possibility that, for the first time in history, its unity and order could grow out of the free will of everyone, and be based on mutual agreement and a longing for peace and co-operation.

What is at issue here is the age-old problem which fascinated the founding-father of all European philosophy, Plato, namely the relationship between the particular and the universal. What exists is always the particular, and it is in the nature of what is living to diversify. Just as politically, the aim of the European Union is not to become a monstrous super-state in which the autonomy of all the various nations, states and regimes of Europe would gradually be dissolved, so the idea of a unity of European culture must be understood as allowing for and even demanding the uniqueness of regional variations. The unity is to be in diversity, not in uniformity. A universal European culture will be found only in the particular cultures that constitute Europe – there is no European centre where it exists. As T. S. Eliot stressed in *Notes Towards a Definition of Culture*, two conditions are required for the health of the culture of Europe, that the health of each community culture be unique, and that the different cultures should recognise their relationship to each other:

"there can be no European culture if the several countries are isolated from each other .... There can be no European culture if these countries are reduced to identity."

In short, we do not achieve universality in art and culture by a rocket-launch into the European. It is to be found only by digging down deeper into the ground we stand on. In other words, an Irish Ireland, if we think it exists, not only has nothing to fear from Europe, but it had better exist if we want to be culturally European. Yeats was intensely aware of it, not just the poet but also the painter. Jack Yeats's paintings command five- and six-figure sums today precisely because he never went the rounds of the schools and the styles that change every decade. James Joyce, convinced that "the Celt has contributed only a whine to Europe", took issue with what he saw as the simple nativism of Yeats, and took flight to absorb the cultural masterpieces of the centre rather than the periphery. But he too achieved success only by digging deeper into the ground that he had left behind. Both Joyce and Yeats would agree that exposure to the ways of life and cultural products of other nations is necessary. Indeed, this was an insight held in common by Tom Kettle, James Connolly and Frantz Fanon: to develop a national consciousness one needs as a prerequisite an international awareness, and to grasp one's own identity one needs to understand the identity of other peoples. In Tom Kettle's words: "If Ireland is to become truly Irish, she must first become European".

In what sense, if any, have we become more truly Irish or more truly European since joining the EEC in 1973?

THE CULTURAL IMPACT OF THE EU ON IRELAND

We have been arguing that a cultural European unity is necessary if Europe is to be more than a super-state or a common market. Necessary too is an equilibrium analogous to the political equilibrium between the European and the regional. European culture too has always had, and must have, a local habitation and a name. Conversely, of course, the local must not become so localised that it becomes merely a provincial agent of fragmentation and disintegration.

There is ample evidence to suggest that Ireland has learned, since our "entry" to Europe, that we make a contribution to Europe only if we bring to it our own character, our own values, our own identity. At the same time, we have realised that no nation as small as Ireland, no nation however large, can hope today to retain its uniqueness through isolation. For well over half-a-century after Independence, Ireland sought to preserve its identity through isolation.

Protectionism became the order of the day; economic protection, social, cultural and especially religious protection. We enthusiastically adopted Plato's maxim that if one wants to prevent change, one must keep the stranger out. Today, we realise that openness is more conducive to keeping us Irish, that Europe is the context in which we can be more comfortably ourselves. We have come to realise that Ireland will succeed in retaining what is distinctive and particular by being part of a European Universal, a coherent cultural tradition, still perhaps fragmented but one which retains some of its inspiration and influence.

It has often been suggested that, in establishing the EU, Europe might be reverting to a medieval pattern, an empire with its regions, and that the modern nation state had become too small or too large for most modern purposes: that it was too small for economic survival, for defence, for energy, even for fighting crime, and too large for purposes of true community and democratic decision-making. However, within the EU, the nation state has not surrendered its place in the sun nor is it likely to do so. What has happened is that within the EU, by very definition, every nation, every culture and language have become minority nations and cultures and languages. And this has been especially beneficial to the smaller nations.

Being a member of the European Union enables member countries to achieve collectively far more than they can on their own. For a small country such as Ireland there is the advantage accruing from being at the centre or sources of anything. It is from the centre and the sources that we get understanding and appreciation. And on the hypothesis that there is something identifiable as European civilisation and culture, and that it has a value, the closer we are to the sources, the mainstream, the better will be our understanding and appreciation, and the greater our enrichment.

It is quite possible that the great increase in religious vocations in the decades after Independence had something to do with the fact that from the 1930s to 1950s Ireland as a nation became a closed introspective society out of the mainstream of modern life and politics. During that period, the Catholic Church was one of the few institutions in Ireland offering an ideal. The Church was looking out at the world and calling on young men and women to do something about the paganism and the poverty in which most of humanity lived. The sheer idealism that once inspired young Irish people to go and convert the peoples of Africa or China now no longer exists. Nowadays the wheel has come full circle. It is now the nation that is looking out at the world and taking its place among the nations of

Europe, while the Church has become introspective and unsure. At times, though, one is tempted to see a parallel between the Church's attitude to the Second Vatican Council and the State's attitude to the EU. Both Church and State busy about implementing directives but with neither comprehending the spirit. It need scarcely be stated that the true test of Ireland's love affair with Europe will come only when we are asked to be contributors rather than recipients, when we must put away the begging-bowl and reach for our cheque-book instead.

Fintan O'Toole, the *Irish Times* columnist, has argued that there are three important ways in which Ireland has become less European in cultural terms since entry into the EEC in 1973:

1. that Roman Catholicism in Ireland has become less consciously European
2. that the rapid collapse of Irish classicism since Vatican II has undermined our connection to a common European culture
3. that the romance of Europe as a place of exile for Irish artists and writers is much diminished because Ireland itself has become a more liberal society.

On the first point O'Toole argues that ultramontane Catholicism was Ireland's strongest Eurocentric influence, linking us to France, Spain and Italy. But now the Irish seminaries in Louvain, Paris and Salamanca have closed and Irish Catholicism is now more linked with the Third World, with Latin America or Africa than it is with a European ideal.

It is true that Church leadership in Ireland tends to see EU membership as an opportunity but more often as a threat. There is a tendency to see Irish Catholicism as a last bastion of Christianity, an outpost in danger of being dragged down by a post-Christian Europe. Who knows whether a European Parliament with real teeth might impose secular values on Ireland? In brief, EU intervention might be a good thing when the subject was milk or beef, but not good when the subject was rights for homosexuals or abortionists. There has always been a question that Ireland might revert to European levels and averages from our high levels of religious beliefs and practices, and even from our unique birth rates and demographic patterns. In short, that, as a result of EU membership, the average Irish man or woman would become more secular, more materialistic, more permissive and more individualistic.

The first point to make is that either this has not happened or, if it has, it has not been solely as a result of EU impact. The second point is more important. Pessimistic interpretations like this are not new. Each generation tends to see the one that comes after it in a less kindly light. As an example, one can take Canon Sheehan's depiction at the beginning of this century of a Fenian convict returning home after 20 years in jail and appalled at the changes that have taken place.

> The old, free open-hearted spirit that made them so lovable is gone and, in its place, has come in a hard grinding material spirit. Each man's interest is now centred on his bounds ditch – he cannot and will not look beyond. He has come into his inheritance…. It has passed into an article of faith that the whole business of life is to succeed, no matter by what means. Natural affections are extinguished, and the whole mind of the country is directed in one way, to become a little England or America.

Indeed, one of the hopes expressed about the consequences of our entry to Europe – that Europe would provide a cultural counter-balance to our dominance by mid-Atlantic culture – has not happened. In films, TV, in popular culture, in the impact of the media generally, EU membership has not counter-balanced the American or British influence. An enlightened person of 25 years ago might have hoped that the Anglo-American cultural dominance of Ireland might have been broken. It has not happened.

Fintan O'Toole's second point about the decline of the classical tradition and its impact on the European cultural tradition in Ireland is scarcely valid. In so far as Latin has disappeared from our schools and from our liturgy, its influence as a factor for Eurocentrism has been more than compensated for by what EU membership has opened up to the youth of Ireland. A new emphasis on European languages in our schools, third level students all over Europe either on Erasmus schemes or as migratory workers, travel and mobility and school tours are a feature of even the poorest children's experience. A teacher in one of the schools serving a large housing estate in West Clondalkin, Dublin tells me that more than half of her class have spent their summer holidays in Spain.

And for those who think that the youth of Ireland, no less than the nation of Ireland, have been corrupted by the fleshpots of Europe, it might be salutory to recall Aristophanes' description of the youth of Athens around 400 BC and to realise that the more things change sometimes the less they change. Aristophanes complained that:

> The young men are hanging around the marketplace and the

baths engaging in idle conversation. While the training grounds are empty, the baths are crowded. The young indulge in excessive eating and drinking, lovemaking and games. They dress slovenly and let their hair run long. They have no manners at table but snatch food away from under the eyes of the old. They make no attempt to harden themselves and, accordingly, their physical condition is bad showing a typically weak chest, a pale face, narrow shoulders, but they have a big tongue and a loud mouth.

I have suggested that our motives in joining the Common Market in 1973 were not totally economic in nature. They also had a long pedigree in our desire to transcend the bounds of geographical insularity, post-war isolation and the confines of protectionism. There was also an acute awareness that a nation that was left behind economically would most likely be left behind socially and culturally also. But how genuinely has the broadening of our social and cultural horizons been? The growth in the learning of foreign languages undoubtedly lessens our parochialism but it also serves to highlight the increasingly anachronistic position of the Irish language as a socio-cultural phenomenon supported by the State. Whatever one's opinion on the controversy of compulsory Irish taking up school time that might be better devoted to the imparting of skills for the marketplace, the ending of the profound tokenism to the language in Ireland and its knock-on effects, such as the *Gaeilge artifísealta* of public-service Irish, cannot of itself be a bad thing.

John Hume has long been a believer that greater Europeanisation will provide a context for refreshing and revitalising the Irish language. Despite the commitments made in the Constitution, the promotion by government, the work of schools and the efforts of Irish enthusiasts, the hopes for the language have not been fulfilled. Within the narrow confines of Ireland it would always continue to lose out to the more international English. But as John Hume argues:

> It is in the broader European context that the Irish language could find the recognition of its real linguistic significance and cultural value. There it can be valued with other, lesser used, minority or regional languages or dialects in a Europe which wants to preserve the diversity of its culture.

Cultural differences are naturally embedded in linguistic divisions. The process of European integration began with four languages among the original six members. There were six languages when the

Community grew to nine countries, nine languages when it grew to twelve countries, and eleven language when it grew to fifteen countries. These are just the official languages. The fact that there are so many regional and minority languages and cultures in Western Europe make their position an unavoidable question for those shaping European policies.

There is some evidence that the Irish language, as the most widely used of the Celtic languages, is beginning to thrive better in a European open society than it ever did in an Irish glass-house. John Hume is optimistic:

> The energy and enthusiasm which different MEPs are bringing to bear on this issue, and the appreciation and interest they show for minority languages and cultures other than their own, have served to convince me that Europe provides a beneficent environment for lesser used languages such as Irish.

The problem caused in the Gaeltacht by modernisation, tourism, emigration and the influx of English speakers is not unique to Ireland. Neither is the debate on the role of TV and radio in relation to minority languages. Such issues in Ireland now have a European dimension. Agencies and voluntary groups working for the Irish language have learned from the experience, bad and good, of other linguistic groups. And, similarly, those other groups have learned from the Irish experience.

Put simply, membership of the EU, has given minority cultures and languages a new self-assurance. In the European context, they can provide more than mutual encouragement. They can combine to demand better recognition and supportive policy, but above all else they can begin to come out from under the shadow of the dominant culture in their State.

SOCIAL IMPACT OF EU MEMBERSHIP ON IRELAND

In order to assess the social impact of EU membership on Ireland, it is relevant to ask: what sort of Europe did we want? And what sort of Europe do we have? Twenty-five years after entry we can say with some certainty that we do not have a highly centralised, autocratic and bureaucratic Europe with identikit citizens sharing a homogenised culture. The strong survival of the nation states have seen to that. Neither do we have a Europe of independent nation states, each self-centred and pursuing its own political and material interests. Rather what we have is a Europe more tightly-knit in its unity, which values its regional and cultural diversity, while working to provide for a convergence of living standards. Of course, the aim of the EU is for greater economic growth and more competitiveness through partnership, which enhances the social solidarity of the EU at the same time.

The great fear at the time of our entry to Europe was that the EEC would create a dual society with economic, social, political and even cultural power located at the core and disadvantaged groups of small nations located at the periphery. Anti-marketeers, as we may call them, warned at the time that Ireland's membership of the EEC would prove to be a millstone rather than a milestone, a wrong turning rather than a great leap forward. So far this has not happened. It is the policy of trying to ensure convergence of living standards throughout the EU that has had the greatest social impact on Irish society.

The social impact on Irish society has come from five main sources:

1. Legislation (Directives) has had a great impact on equality policies in Ireland. It is safe to say that these policies have been almost entirely Europe-driven.

2. Funding: The ESF, ERDF and Structural Funds have all had a major impact on the infrastructure, on training through the medium of FÁS, on education through the Regional Technical Colleges (now Institutes of Education), have greatly raised our living standards, but ironically while trying to prevent a dual society in Europe, we may unwittingly have perpetuated a dual society in Ireland. This is especially true of the CAP.

3. EU Administrative Systems: Through political dialogue and civic dialogue most Irish administrative systems are plugged into EU systems. Now this is complemented by the so-called "social dialogue" between workers and employers, between voluntary and special interest groups and others. There is now a EU dimension to most social and   administrative activities.

4. EU Language and Terminology: Here I have in mind terms such as "social exclusion", a phrase which did not exist ten years ago, but which has had a profound influence on social policy throughout the EU. Change the terminology and you change the context; change the context and you change the problem.

5. The Smaller Programmes such as Combat Poverty, Women's programmes, Disability programmes, etc. The money for these may have been small but in terms of ideas and discussions they enjoyed a major input from Europe.

All these five points of contact have had a direct impact on social policy and social life in Ireland. They have had not just a financial impact but have also had policy and social implications. The conclusion seems warranted that EU intervention across these five areas simultaneously reduces inequality in Irish society and at the same time creates inequality and perpetuates it.

In attempting to understand how these five areas of intervention impact on Irish society, it may be useful to begin with what we may call the Economic and Social Research Institute (ESRI) thesis developed by Breen et al. in *Understanding Contemporary Ireland* (1990), namely that the Irish class structure today is a product, to a large extent, of the interventionist Irish State and the strategy of development it adopted from 1958 onwards. According to this thesis, Irish society is itself a product of public expenditure, and such expenditure supports an unusually high proportion of the Irish class structure. More particularly, the ESRI team argue that the way the State raised resources, and the way it distributed these resources across different social groups, contributed greatly to the growth of inequality in Ireland. And having created inequality, the State continues to perpetuate it.

In this context, it is legitimate to ask whether the massive influx of EU funds to Ireland serves the same function? Does the allocation of these continue to create and perpetuate inequality or help to reduce it? The answer appears to be that European funds do both, simultaneously reduce and create inequalities.

This is most in evidence in the case of the CAP and its associated farm price-support systems. Even before the CAP, one feature of Irish policies has been the contradictory strategy adopted in relation to farming. On the one hand, it has been the stated aim of governments that farming should modernise and become efficient and economic. On the other hand, there is a reluctance to disturb the rural social structure, so the policy is also to keep as many farmers as possible on the land. This has resulted in producing a dualism in Irish agriculture, something now being perpetuated by the CAP.

One of the central goals of EU farm price-support schemes has been to help to equalise farm and non-farm incomes. However, one unforeseen consequence of the policy has been to widen the gap in income and wealth between large and small farmers. This suggests that the price-support system does not restructure agricultural production in any significant way, but merely reinforces existing trends, which seem to be determined by the forces of the market rather than by State or EU intervention. Price increases and supports benefit the larger producer: the more a farmer produces the more the volume of price support received. What happens when the EU decides that it can no longer pay large subsidies to keep production flowing to non-existing markets is another day's work. One other feature of the CAP is worth noting. It is the one area of EU policy where the bureaucratic centre of Brussels completely dominates national policies. We may have done better or worse in devising our own policies; the fact is that we did not. Brussels had made it unnecessary.

In contrast to the CAP policies which in attempting to equalise farm and non-farm incomes inadvertently create a polarisation between large and smaller farmers, EU anti-discrimination directives have provided a charter for the economic equality of women in all member countries. This has been of particular importance in Ireland where the economic dependence of women still resembled the pre-World War II pattern in 1973. The 1970s saw the beginning of a major drive by the EU Commission to place the economic equality of women firmly on the agenda. Between 1975 and 1986, five anti-discrimination Directives were adopted, which as well as supporting social change towards providing equal opportunities for women and men, aspired towards the harmonisation of working and living conditions within the EU. Ireland, like all Member States, was obliged to pass the Directives into national law and to provide to citizens effective means of redress. The Directives provided rights to:

* equal pay for equal work
* equal treatment for women and men in employment
* equal treatment for women and men in social security payments
* equal treatment in occupational social security schemes
* equal treatment for self-employed women and men.

As these EU Directives were implemented in national laws, policies for equality of opportunity became a permanent feature on the political agenda of the European Union.

Unlike CAP policy and Anti-Discrimination policy which have been handed down from Brussels in the form of binding Directives, policy to combat social exclusion has evolved from a very harmonious co-operation between the EU and national governments. The gradual permeation of EU economic policy by principles of social policy grew out of the Anti-Poverty Programmes. These in turn led to the close links between unemployment, especially long-term unemployment, and social exclusion. And this in turn led to social cohesion being made a priority objective of the EU alongside economic growth. This was placed firmly in the context of the reform of the Structural Funds, and Member States were asked to formulate National Development Plans in order to clarify precisely the obstacles, the strategies and their plan's objectives. This resulted in Ireland adopting a disciplined programmatic approach to tackling unemployment and social exclusion. Ireland's objectives in combating social exclusion, as formulated in the *National Development Plan 1994-99* were accepted as EU policy objectives for Ireland. This close co-operation between EU and national policy formulation has produced impressive results. I mention just two:

1. Across Ireland there has been an almost nation-wide programme of locally-driven projects tackling social exclusion and unemployment funded by the EU. The numbers involved in these programmes are equivalent to 75 per cent of the numbers recorded as unemployed in April 1997.
2. The role of the EU in helping Ireland to tackle social exclusion was not just about the transfer of funds but also about how Ireland benefited from the systematic discipline and accountability imposed by the EU. It required both the EU and Irish authorities to be precise and specific about what the problems were and how the programmes would alleviate them.

It should be noted that the great strides forward in economic and social development in recent years in Ireland have not been solely due to receipt of EU funds. The growth has also come from enlightened national industrial policies, from educational promotion, from taxation policies, etc. With the expected diminution of EU funding after 2003, it will be essential that the same strategic and disciplined approach be applied to the expenditure of national funds as has been applied to EU funding over recent years.

CONCLUSION

In assessing the changes brought about by Ireland's membership of the European Union it is well not to engage in the dangerous and uncertain procedure of the "imaginary experiment" – trying to picture what the consequences would have been for Ireland had we not gone "into Europe" in 1973. In any event, such an examination of the gains and losses of European Union membership has already been more than adequately done in Patrick Keatinge (ed.) *European Community Membership Evaluated* (1991).

Clearly, in our first 25 years of EU membership, the prophets of doom have been proved wrong. Predictions of economic ruin and loss of cultural identity have so far all failed to materialise. Claims that we were selling our heritage for a mess of very bad pottage, or that the centre would dominate economically and culturally while the periphery languished, have also been proved wrong. In fact, Ireland has got some very good pottage, and it will continue as long as countries such as Germany pick up the tab for the peripheral but sometimes useful freeloader. It may well be that we have had too much of the begging-bowl mentality, though when one considers what the larger states of Europe have inflicted on the smaller ones over the centuries, the debt of compensation has not yet been adequately paid.

The EU began as a Coal and Steel Community in 1957 and became the EEC in 1959. Throughout its first 25 years the word "community" was dominant. We have asked in what sense do Ireland and the EU make up one community, in the original meaning of that word. The Latin word *societas* meant not just a social entity but also a cultural entity. With very real prospects of further enlargement to the east, the question remains how enlarged can a so-called community become while still being in any authentic sense a *societas* in its original meaning.

Perhaps the final irony of our EU membership lies in this. For Ireland, membership is about modernisation, employment, jobs and markets, economically and socially catching up with the rest of Europe. For many Europeans, Ireland is the island of Heinrich Böll's *Irish Diary* – quaint, unspoiled, a land of romantic peasants, of postcard people full of the petty pleasures, prejudices and simple virtues of an island people. Ireland has come a long way since Honor Tracey wrote of "this boggy little piece of land with few inhabitants, lying forlorn in the ocean, washed by rain and curtained by mist, in grave danger of being overlooked by the outer world were it not for its frequent and lively toots on the horn". Did somebody hear a Celtic Tiger growl?

CHAPTER 7

Recasting the European Social Model

Peter Cassells

From my work with the Irish Congress of Trade Unions, from the early 1970s onwards, on economic and social policy, I have got a worm's eye view of the impact of European social policy on Ireland. What struck me at first, was the strange version of social policy being pursued at the level of the European Community, as it was then known.

I was fully aware of the European Social Model as operated, in particular, in Germany and the Scandinavian countries, under which social solidarity operating through the state cared for large numbers of citizens, guaranteed individual rights and provided essential services. This model was linked to the Social Market Economy in which the free market was closely supervised by an administrative state with the social partners integrated through institutional participation at all levels. In Ireland, social policy was generally understood to mean policy on social welfare, health, education and housing, and was more influenced by Catholic social thinking than European social democracy.

Within the framework of the European Community, however, social policy in the 1970-80s was confined to helping less developed regions, through the Social Fund, with their training and restructuring needs arising from coping with free trade. Also, in a very French meaning of the phrase, it covered working conditions but only where they might lead to a distortion of trade, e.g. through a failure to provide equal pay or to invest in health and safety.

Ireland's first encounter with European social policy, narrowly defined, occurred shortly after EC membership on the question of equal pay. At a tripartite meeting in Brussels in October 1973 on a European Council Directive on Equal Pay, which provided for implementation of the right to equal pay no later than 31 December 1975, the Irish government representative implied that the date set in the Directive might not be acceptable to the Irish government. The Treaty of Accession of Ireland did not provide for any exemption or for any transitional period for the implementation of equal pay.

The Anti-Discrimination (Pay) Bill, 1974 was published by the Minister for Labour, Michael O'Leary, TD in February 1974 to transpose the European Directive into Irish law and provide for full implementation of equal pay by 31 December 1995 in accordance with the European deadline. However, on 17 December 1975, following pressure from employers and strangely the General Secretary of the Irish Shoe and Leather Workers Union, Michael Bell, the Taoiseach, Liam Cosgrave, announced that employers would be allowed to claim inability to pay and that the Government would seek a derogation from the Commission for those employers.

Following a formal complaint from the Irish Congress of Trade Unions, the European Commission rejected the government's application for a derogation and on 5 May 1976, the Minister for Labour had to inform the Dáil that the Equal Pay Directive would be implemented in full. This legislation not only transformed the workplace for Irish women but also gave a strong underpinning to the demands from women's organisations and unions for major changes in the role of women in Irish society – changes, which still reverberate with us today.

The public confrontation between the European Commission and the Irish Government, with the Commission's legal authority winning out, also ensured that, throughout the 1970s and the early 1980s, important European directives on health and safety, collective redundancies and acquired rights were transposed into Irish law. These directives improved employment conditions for Irish workers, though to be fair to the Minister for Labour, Michael O'Leary, other important improvements, such as protection from unfair dismissal and increased holidays, were initiated by himself rather than by Europe. Also, through the European Social Fund, the skills of Irish workers were improved by AnCO (later FÁS) and the level of technological education improved by our Regional Technical Colleges (now Institutes of Education).

Despite these improvements, the European Community continued to be seen as mainly about free trade, a larger market and agriculture. This perception was fuelled by the increased wealth bestowed on farmers through the Common Agricultural Policy and their reluctance to pay tax on that wealth. While the Commission had adopted a Social Action Programme, including an anti-poverty programme, under the leadership of Dr Patrick Hillery, the first Irish Commissioner, it lacked the powers and instruments to deal with unemployment, industrial policy, urban deprivation and the position of workers in traditional sectors who lost their jobs through restructuring arising from increased competition. It also had no role in education, health or other social services. Indeed, the 1980s saw an obsession with what became know as "Eurosclerosis" and a growing emphasis on competition, deregulation and free trade as the British Government, under Margaret Thatcher, sought to confine the European Community to a free trade area without any economic, social or political controls.

The momentum to expand social policy at European level, both in its narrowest and broadest form, changed and grew apace, with its consequent impact on Ireland in the late 1980s and early 1990s. This can be seen from:

* the adoption of the Community Charter of Fundamental Social Rights of Workers (the Social Chapter) in December 1989
* the Maastricht Treaty, which provided for qualified majority voting on workers' rights and also revamped Article 118 of the Treaty which introduced a detailed consultative procedure between the Commission and employers and unions on social policy to enable the social partners to conclude agreements at European level (these agreements have led to the introduction in Ireland of parental leave and of important rights for part-time workers and those on fixed-term contracts)
* the publication in 1994, of the White Paper on Growth, Competitiveness and Employment, which broadened the debate on economy policy beyond the narrow confines of monetary issues, deregulation and cutting wage costs, to the inter-linked issues of investing for the future, competitiveness, innovation and positive flexibility. The White Paper, while endorsing the European model of development, recognised that it required renewal and adjustment and that European countries must compete with the best in the world through high productivity, high levels of quality and high standards
* the Amsterdam Treaty, which included a new Title on Employment, linked to National Employment Action Plans, and a new article on non-discrimination, which empowered the EU to take action to combat discrimination based on sex, race, religion, age, disability and sexual orientation, and provided for co-operation between the Member States to fight social exclusion.

What gave rise to this significant change in social policy in Europe, which in turn had an impact, in particular through the White Paper on Growth, Competitiveness and Employment, on the development of social partnership in Ireland? Firstly, the drive to complete the European Single Market exposed serious economic and social disparities between Member States, which not only impeded the free movement of labour but also raised fears among the richer countries of social dumping. This led to conclusions at European Council summits in 1989 that:

> completion of the single market cannot be regarded as an end in itself; it pursues a much wider objective, namely to ensure the maximum well-being of all in line with the tradition of social progress which is part of Europe's history. . . . Social aspects should be given the same importance as economic aspects and should accordingly be developed in a balanced fashion.

Secondly, some European leaders, in particular Jacques Delors, recognised that the growth in unemployment and Europe's failure to create jobs had left many people alienated from Europe's institutions and policies. Delors accepted that the Maastricht project for economic and monetary union did not sufficiently address the "real economy" and its problems, and he posed the fundamental question of "whether there is a European disease that is undermining our strength, sapping our competitiveness and weakening our resistance to the rampant virus of unemployment?" He not only dragged the problem of cyclical, structural and technological unemployment in the EU to the centre stage of its policy-making, he also questioned whether Europe was ready for the future, in particular for the Information Society.

All countries in Europe are going through a period of rapid economic, industrial, social and political change. While there is nothing new about change itself, the rate and depth of the change now taking place is of a dimension different from virtually anything seen previously.

These changes, as we know, are happening because:

* People are changing, leading more complex lives, concerned about personal development, seeking a better balance between family and workplace responsibilities, and demanding greater choice, higher standards and more flexibility in the delivery of services.
* Information technologies and advances in organisation skills have made possible the development of a system of production based on knowledge and information processing – thereby fundamentally altering the nature and structure of work.
* The increasing integration of the economies of the world, the emergence of global companies and the dramatic growth in international financial markets mean that the movement of

finance or a fluctuation in currency can be more important in determining a country's, or a company's, cost competitiveness than labour costs.

* Workplace innovations, including changes in the composition of the workforce, a rise in the knowledge and skills content of jobs, and the emergence of new forms of work organisation are radically changing the world of work.

These changes pose major challenges for European and Irish social policy.

Commenting on this transition, in the EU White Paper on Growth, Competitiveness and Employment (1994) Jacques Delors pointed out:

> this decade is witnessing a forging of a link of unprecedented magnitude and significance between the technological innovation process and economic and social organisation. Countless innovations are combining to bring about a major upheaval in the organisation of activities and relationships within society. Throughout the world, production systems, methods of organising work and consumption patterns are undergoing changes which will have long-term effects comparable with the first industrial revolution.

I believe that the scale of the transformation required to support the repositioning of European society, and in that context Irish society, has, however, yet to be grasped. The multiple innovations in technologies, values and structures will bring profound changes in the way we live our lives, just as the earlier industrial revolution changed the world in its time. When we think of the industrial revolution we tend to think of technical inventions and forget that industrialisation radically transformed the whole organisation of society.

Europe's difficulties in adjusting to these changes has led some politicians and employers to blame the European Social Model, to make comparisons with the United States and south-east Asia and to call for Europe to adopt a more radical neo-liberal approach. To me, these comparisons are distracting and futile, and of far more importance is deeper research and agreement on how we anticipate, support and underpin the structural changes needed to rapidly modernise the European Social Model for the 21st century. It may be, as pointed out by Professor Rory O'Donnell, in his Jean Monnet inaugural lecture (29 April 1999), that Northern European neo-corporatism and the institutional arrangements in the once-successful continental countries no longer provide the answers, and that Ireland's approach to social partnership, with the emphasis on problem-solving and where consensus and a shared understanding are more an outcome of the process than a precondition, is more suited to current economic, organisational and technological circumstances.

Given the lessons to be learnt from our innovative and, at times, unorthodox approach to social partnership and from the way we have balanced the European approach with the culture of American inward investment, it may be that Ireland could play a leading role in modernising the European Social Model to tackle, in particular, two major challenges:

CHALLENGE NO. 1

To Create New Forms of Collective Structures that Promote and Support Individual Differences

Modernising our European Social Model to create new forms of social cohesion and collective structures that promote and support individual differences and the desire for diversity in ways which do not demand conformity and sameness, is one of the most significant challenges for Europe.

We should not underestimate the challenge this poses for:

* the provision of services, in particular public services, as individuals demand more choice and a say in how these services are delivered
* the organisation of work, as individuals demand more emphasis on career paths, personal development, better reward systems and more education and training
* working time, as individuals demand more flexible contracts and a better balance between workplace responsibilities and family responsibilities.

Indeed, many aspects of government, industrial relations and social policy today lag far behind people's perceived needs. It may be that many of the protections, which were rightly put in place in the era of mass production, are now barriers to individual development in a more flexible society.

CHALLENGE NO. 2

Modernise our Economies and Labour Markets

The biggest failure in Europe today is the inability of many governments, unions and employers to jointly modernise the European Social Model to take account of:

* the shift from heavy industry and mass production to knowledge-intensive jobs with a higher skill and informational content
* the growth in long-term unemployment and social exclusion as low-skill, lower-productivity jobs are eliminated and workers who have lost their jobs are unable to take up the new higher-skill opportunities
* the need to strike a new balance between flexibility and security with the emergence of more flexible working arrangements and contracts
* the changing gender balance in working life with women accounting for the entire growth of Europe's workforce over the last ten years.

Our labour markets and our social protection systems must be revamped to:

* give workers access to life-long learning and to forms of work organisation that recognise people as the key resource in a knowledge-based economy
* give the unemployed a guarantee of employability and access to skills through active social protection systems that invest massively in retraining and re-skilling, and provide incentives to work. We should recognise that work and income liberate while dependency imprisons.
* enable workers to combine working life with family responsibilities through childcare, care of the elderly, parental leave, career breaks and a social protection system that accommodates more flexible working arrangements.

Hopefully Ireland, so long a taker from Europe, is now in a position to contribute positively to the modernisation of the European model as we seek to cope with the profound technological, social and demographic changes taking place.

THE ECONOMY

CHAPTER 8

Twenty-five Years 'A Growing'

Dermot McAleese

INTRODUCTION

The Irish economy has undergone profound changes since 1972. Most of these changes have been for the better and have resulted in higher living standards, better education, improved health and other indicators of material well-being. Ireland's Gross Domestic Product (GDP) per capita has progressed from 58% of the EU average in 1973 to 106% in 1998, overtaking the UK in 1996 (Table 1). While the GDP indicator exaggerates the extent of economic improvement, alternative indicators tell a similar story. Thus GNP per capita on a purchasing-power basis, a more reliable indicator of living standards, shows the Irish figure rising from 64% to 87% of the EU average during this period.[1] A truly dramatic spurt towards convergence has occurred since 1994 (Figure 1). The debate on convergence, however, alerted us to the danger of not being prepared for more intense competition and strengthened the case for domestic policy change. In this way, the debate led by Rory O'Donnell and others made a significant contribution to Ireland's successful integration in the EU.

As the economy has become more prosperous, it has also become more open to external influences in terms of the conventional measures of globalisation: foreign trade ratios, growth of foreign investment, extent of intra-industry trade. These external influences have exerted a positive impact on economic growth. The potential benefits of openness are particularly significant for small countries. Small economies that have adopted outward looking policies have tended to outperform closed economies (International Monetary Fund, 1993). The Irish economy has benefited disproportionately from R&D spillovers from more developed economies through foreign investment and buoyant capital and intermediate imports (Coe and Helpman, 1995). To understand Irish economic growth, therefore, one must study how EU membership has deepened, assisted and accelerated Ireland's integration into the wider economy.

Of course EU membership was not absolutely essential for integration with the European economy. Non-member European

TABLE 1: The Catching-up Process in the EU (GDP per person)

	Ireland	Spain	Greece	Portugal	U.K.	Germany	Netherlands
1973	58.5	75.1	62.7	57.3	103.3	115.0	107.6
1980	63.5	70.7	64.0	54.8	96.8	117.1	105.4
1985	64.8	69.8	62.4	53.1	99.6	117.6	103.0
1990	71.0	74.5	58.4	59.2	100.1	116.0	100.9
1993	82.7	77.8	64.5	69.1	98.9	108.0	103.6
1994	88.0	75.8	64.7	67.1	98.4	109.7	104.5
1995	95.2	76.1	64.3	67.1	98.3	109.2	104.0
1996	100.7	76.6	64.6	67.8	98.9	108.3	104.7
1997	103.9	76.9	64.6	68.2	99.6	108.9	104.9
1998	106.3	77.3	64.5	68.6	99.6	109.0	104.8

Notes:
1. GDP figures are computed at current market prices and PPS per head of population: ERUR 15 = 100.
2. Irish GNP/GDP has fallen from 96% in 1980 to 90% in 1985 to 86% in 1992. It remains at 86% in 1998.

Source: European Economy, "Broad Economic Policy Guidelines", No. 62, Brussels, 1997.

countries have seen the same broad pattern of evolution as that experienced by the Irish economy. We must focus on the 'added value' of membership – the extent to which membership enhanced the scope, speed and beneficial impact of Ireland's economic integration in Europe. This added value derives from the way membership of the Community affected not just the agriculture and manufacturing sectors but also the services sector and the conduct of economic policy. The Maastricht criteria, for example, exercised a dominant influence over Irish macroeconomic policy during the 1990s. Evaluators of the impact of membership must also keep in mind how one's assessment of the effects of the EU can be influenced by the particular economic conjuncture at the time of writing. At present (1999), convergence of Irish living standards to the European average is the dominant fact of economic life. But only a short while ago our self-image in the EU was that of a small, poor, peripheral country struggling hard against the forces of economic divergence. As can be seen from Figure 1, Irish GNP per capita actually declined relative to the EU between 1972 and the mid-1980s. European integration offers opportunities for more rapid economic development, not a guarantee of economic success.

Many economic effects of integration are difficult to quantify. For

FIGURE 1: Ireland Compared to EU:
GNP per head at PPPs 1960-2000

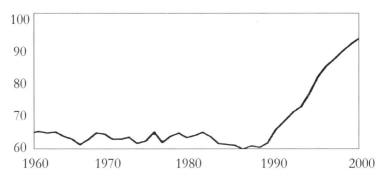

Source: Honohan (1997), p. 36

that reason, they tend to be glossed over.[2] For example, the relentless exposure of the economy to the effects of external competitive forces can affect national lifestyles and behaviour. Integration can lead to less job security, weaker trade unions and greater vulnerability to external economic fluctuations, albeit from a higher income base. Also, the significant decline in the discretionary powers of national governments can have important political and social implications.

The plan of this paper is as follows. First, the expected economic effects are outlined and then contrasted with the actual outcome. Since the actual outcome is influenced by many factors besides the EU effect, the conclusions have to be taken as suggestive rather than compelling. Second, we consider the impact of the single market. This involved liberalisation of the services sector, the far-reaching effects of ensuring level playing fields, structural funds' programmes and enhanced capital mobility. These aspects of membership were not debated much at the time of accession but have turned out to be extremely important for the economy. Third, the break with sterling and the EMU debate is analysed. Fourth, the negative aspects of membership are discussed. Finally, the extent to which EU economic policy has been affected by Irish membership is examined.

IMPACT OF THE EU – EXPECTED EFFECTS

The expected effects can be analysed under four headings: market access, the Common Agricultural Policy (CAP), safeguards and transitional assistance.

Market access

Membership of the Community meant free and, more importantly, secure access for Irish exports to EC markets. It was estimated that the abolition of the common external tariff on Irish exports (excluding UK) would enhance the profitability of exporting to this market by between 110 and 150% (McAleese and Martin, 1972). This constituted a significant incentive to exports. Against this had to be weighed two negative effects: a) the loss of our preferential position in the UK market and b) the exposure of Irish business to the full rigours of European competition.[3] Trade diversion effects (i.e. substitution of low-cost third-country suppliers by European suppliers) were not seen as a problem, mainly because EU tariffs were low on raw materials and intermediate goods of relevance to Ireland.

Free trade was expected to benefit the manufacturing sector for three reasons: (a) competition from Member States would force domestic industry (export and import-substitution sectors) to be more efficient; (b) export industries would gain economies of scale through larger sales' volume to the European market; and (c) dynamic efficiency would be enhanced by speeding up the pace of technological diffusion.[4]

Trade liberalisation led to the expected increase in exports. Ireland's export performance since accession bears comparison with the most successful of the Asian Tigers, especially in manufactured exports. By 1995, manufactured goods accounted for 74% of total exports by comparison with only 20% in 1961. The geographical pattern of exports also changed. From accounting for 75% of Irish exports in 1960, and 61% in 1971, the UK market share has fallen to about 25% (Table 2). Accession encouraged market diversification

TABLE 2: Irish Trade by Area 1960, 1972 and 1995

Area	Exports			Imports		
	1960	1972	1995	1960	1972	1995
UK	75	61	28	49	51	36
Rest of EU	7	18	40	15	19	20
Total EU	*82*	*79*	*68*	*64*	*70*	*56*
Others	18	21	32	36	30	44
Total	100	100	100	100	100	100

Source: CSO, *Trade Statistics of Ireland*, Stationery Office, Dublin, various issues.

away from the UK towards the faster growing continental economies. The general belief then, and now, was that this would improve export growth. The reduction in Irish links with, and dependence upon, the slow-growing British economy was seen as having a 'liberating' effect on the Irish economy (Johnson, 1997, p. 179).

However, contrary to expectation, UK import demand was not particularly slow-growing. True, it grew slower than other markets for the five years immediately after accession, 1972-77, but since then UK import demand has grown faster than the EU average (O'Donnell, 1998). Because of the large proportion of Irish exports destined for the British market up to the 1980s, this rapid growth of UK imports contributed a strong positive market effect to Irish exports instead of the negative effect expected at the time of accession.

Imports also increased rapidly. Some of these imports were substitutes for domestically produced goods and involved shutdowns, loss of employment and other costs of structural adjustment. The key issue centred on the extent to which erosion of indigenous industry's domestic market share could be compensated for by additional exports. If increases in import substitutes were matched by expansion of exports in the same industry sectors (better still in the same firm), the adjustment process would be relatively smooth, since resources move more easily within industries than between industries. Some indication of the extent of matched

TABLE 3: Intra-Industry Trade in Manufactured Goods with EU 1961-1992

SITC Section	Description	Intra-industry Trade (Grubel-Lloyd indices)[a]					
		1961	1972	1977	1985	1990	1992
5	Chemicals	0.08	0.40	0.40	0.37	0.37	
6	Manufactures, classified by materials	0.35	0.38	0.49	0.40	0.37	–
7	Machinery, transport equipment	0.13	0.24	0.48	0.51	0.48	–
8	Miscellaneous manufactures	0.40	0.59	0.61	0.53	0.47	–
5-8	*Manufactures*	0.25	0.38	0.49	0.47	0.44	0.41

a calculated from 4-digit (1961, 1967) and from 5-digit (1972, 1977, 1985, 1990) OCED data, weighted by current trade values in each year.
Source: Brulhart, McAleese and O'Donnell (1999) and Brulhart and Elliot (1998).

increases in exports and imports is provided by indices of intra-industry trade. Indices of intra-industry trade (IIT) showed a significant expansion of IIT in Irish manufactured trade with Member States throughout the period from 1972 to 1992. The Grubel-Lloyd index rose from 0.38 in 1972 to 0.41 by 1992 (Table 3). Marginal IIT also rose, from 0.17 during 1979-83 to 0.30 during 1988-92. Hence, there was a substantial amount of 'smooth' adjustment as well as of the more difficult inter-industry adjustment.[5]

The textbook story is one whereby exports increase because former import-substitution firms are induced by the price/profit 'signals' of the new trade regime to shift from production for the home market to production for the export market. Irish experience indicates that such textbook transformations of indigenous enterprises were the exception rather than the rule. Even with the fairest trade winds, it proved difficult to transform an import-competing enterprise into an export-oriented one. Few indigenous firms (or foreign subsidiaries established under the protectionist regime) succeeded in making the necessary adjustment. Thus, employment in Irish-owned manufacturing firms fell from 153,000 to 118,000 between 1973 and 1995 (Table 4). New foreign investors in the manufacturing sector, not indigenous firms, generated the export boom. These firms were attracted to Ireland by the prospect of secure access to the EU market, a benign corporate tax system and proactive promotion by the Industrial Development Authority

TABLE 4: Employment in manufacturing and internationally-traded services by nationality 1975-95

| Nationality | 1975 | | 1995 | | % Change |
	Employment	% Share	Employment	% Share	1975-95
Ireland	143,817	65.6	123.314	53.4	−14.3
Foreign	75,453	34.4	107,639	46.6	42.7
of which:					
U.K.	29,748	13.6	13.823	6.0	−53.5
U.S.A.	18,645	8.5	58.828	25.5	215.5
Germany	6,074	2.8	10,968	4.7	80.6
Other European	17,989	8.2	15,429	6.7	−14.2
Other non-European	2,997	1.4	8,591	3.7	186.7
Total	219,270	100	230,953	100	5.3

Source: Ruane and Georg (1997)

(IDA).[6] Between 1973 and 1995, employment in foreign-owned firms rose from 77,000 (33% of total manufacturing employment) to 96,000 (45%). Another curious twist to the story is that, contrary to initial hopes, most foreign investment in Ireland came from the United States, not from the rich regions of Europe. US manufacturing subsidiaries employed 52,000 in 1995 compared with only 18,000 in 1973, equivalent to 24% of all manufacturing employment. The net result was that adjustment was far from painless. Industries did disappear; firms did close down; and many employees in long-established industries lost their jobs. Labour-intensive traditional industries declined and high-tech sectors prospered. Those who obtained these new jobs did well; those who did not fared badly.

Thus foreign investment played a lead role in the adjustment process. Because of its strong export-orientation, it led to another singular feature of Ireland's adjustment: namely the capacity to grow rapidly without running into a balance of payments constraint. Indeed, a remarkable feature of the Celtic Tiger of the 1990s is the continuing surplus in the balance of payments, notwithstanding the buoyancy of import demand.

The Common Agricultural Policy (CAP)

Prior to entry, European food prices were higher than Irish prices, and even higher still than the prices Irish food could attract in the export market. In 1969, the EC guide-price for butter was three times higher than the average export price for Irish butter sold on the world market. By 1972, the price gap had narrowed but the difference was still large: 20% for beef and at least 50% for dairy products. Because roughly two-thirds of Irish food production was exported, participation in the CAP meant a major, historic transfer of income to the Irish farmer from the European consumer and taxpayer. Between 1970 and 1978, agricultural product prices rose 35% in real terms and real incomes per capita in agriculture more than doubled (Table 5). Land prices rose 4.7 fold after correcting for inflation (Sheehy, 1984). This illustrates a well-known principle in international trade: protection can bring significant benefits to certain sectors of the economy at the expense of widely dispersed small losses to many more.

After 1979, however, incomes began to fall. By 1981, land prices were half of their 1978 level. Optimism was succeeded by pessimism. 'Unless something unexpected comes to their rescue', Seamus Sheehy warned, 'Irish farmers must accept in the immediate years ahead

Table 5: Irish Agriculture: expected and actual percentage changes,
1970-78

	Projected	Actual
Agricultural product prices	+32	+35
Volume of Gross Agricultural Output	+33	+35
Volume of inputs	+40	+49
Price of inputs	+6	+28
Real income	+100	+70
Workforce	−21	−20
Real income per capita*	+153	+112
Cow numbers	+30	+22
Milk output	+52	+55
Cattle output	+35	+25

* Income from self-employment and other trading income deflated by consumer price index.

Source: Sheehy (1984)

income levels less favourable than those obtaining pre-EEC' (Sheehy, 1984, p. 102). Incomes did fall as predicted, but recovered thereafter both in absolute terms and relative to the industrial wage (Table 6).

Table 6: Farm income and the industrial wage 1984-1997

Year	Average family farm income IR£	Average Industrial wage IR£	Farm income/ industrial wage (%)
1984	5,370	8,257	65.0
1985	4,482	8,915	50.3
1986	4,327	9,580	45.2
1987	5,779	10,069	57.4
1988	7,197	10,547	68.2
1989	7,282	10,971	66.4
1990	6,682	11,394	58.6
1991	6,053	11,878	51.0
1992	7,172	12,372	58.0
1993	8,075	13,036	61.9
1994	9,063	13,396	67.7
1995	9,644	13,678	70.5
1996	10,920	14,081	77.6
1997	10,798	14,523	74.4

Source: Power and Roche National Farm Survey, various issues: CSO, Survey of Industrial Earnings various issues.

From a national point of view, the important factor was that after 1973 increases in farm incomes no longer had to be underpinned by the Irish exchequer, but instead were predominately financed from Brussels. The gains to the Irish economy from CAP arose under two headings. First, there were budgetary transfers to support minimum prices. Second, there were trade transfers. The latter arise because the European consumer pays a higher price for Irish beef and dairy products than the world market price. The amount of the transfer is computed by measuring the difference between EU and world prices, and multiplying it by the value of Irish exports to Union countries. Over the period 1979-86, the combined gain from the budget transfers and trade transfers was estimated to lie in the range 5.2% to 9.8% of GNP (Matthews, 1988). Estimates published by the Department of Agriculture showed that the combined amount of the budget and trade transfers to farming amounted to 6.5% of GNP.[7] The artificial position of Irish agriculture is apparent when one realises that income arising from agriculture in 1996 was actually £300m less than the value of these transfers.

While the CAP brought about a transformation of living standards in rural areas, it did not lead to the regeneration of economic activity in agriculture. Employment in agriculture declined by 42% between 1973 and 1986 as compared with the EC average of 38% and that decline has continued. By 1998, numbers engaged in agriculture had fallen to 131,000, only 8% of the total labour force. By raising prices, agricultural support gave rise to oversupply, high subsidisation costs and, eventually, officially imposed quotas. Thus, Irish milk production, which had enjoyed a rapid 5% growth in the 1970s, was brought to a virtual standstill by the 1984 milk quotas.

Standard cost-benefit analysis deplores the expense, the economic waste, the haphazard income distribution impact and the adverse environmental effects of the CAP. A telling statistic, much favoured by Commissioner Ray MacSharry, was that 20% of Europe's farmers received 80% of CAP payments. (At present, 30% of Irish farmers receive 70% of CAP farm support.)[8] Another unfortunate consequence of CAP, noted by the National Economic and Social Council (NESC), was its tendency to blind policy-makers to the need for long-term national policies concerning the role of agriculture in the overall development of the economy (NESC, 1989, p.214). CAP may have delayed the development of a market-focused agriculture processing industry. Outside the Community umbrella, Irish agriculture would have been forced to become more efficient, just as Irish industry has been. There would have been less rent-seeking, and something nearer the New Zealand model might have been achieved. The point is not that CAP was bad for the Irish economy – this would be an untenable case – but that it had to change.

The scale and duration of the CAP transfers have vastly exceeded expectations. They provided a long breathing space for structural adjustment to take place.[9] From a historical perspective, the question is how well this breathing space has been used. The amount of livestock and dairy output increased, as expected, but whether Irish food has also established the hoped-for strong brand image and selling position in the European market is a matter of some debate.

Safeguards

Safeguards for 'sensitive' sectors threatened by the prospect of foreign competition attracted much attention and absorbed an inordinate amount of diplomatic energy at the time of accession. The same process was repeated during the negotiation of the Single European Act in the mid-1980s. In retrospect, the effort seems to have been rather unproductive. Despite the spilling of vast quantities of negotiating blood, import-substitution industries, such as motor assembly, footwear, jute, tanning and textiles, have been cut to ribbons by foreign competition. The pessimism of the CIO and COIP Reports' account of the state of preparedness of Irish-owned industry issued prior to our accession proved to be all too far-sighted.[10]

The poor showing of indigenous firms in the 1970s and 1980s in face of competition raises a question mark over whether manufacturing industry would have been able to withstand the full brunt of foreign competition in the 1960s at the time of our first application for membership. Certainly, it was wise to withdraw the application in line with the UK, though a full retrospective cost-benefit analysis of this decision has yet to be undertaken. With hindsight, the most likely effect of the safeguards and exception clauses was simply that it moderated the pace of decline of these sensitive industries. This conclusion would not have fazed Adam Smith, who argued that trade liberalisation should proceed by 'slow gradations' and 'with a good deal of reserve and circumspection'.[11]

Irish policy towards safeguards has tended to be rather conservative and cautious. The Irish authorities have repeatedly sought extended transitional periods and exemptions. As far as third-world-country imports were concerned, Ireland has tended to side with the more protectionist stance of the Mediterranean Member States than with the liberalism of the UK and the Low Countries.

This was particularly evident in the frequent invocation of anti-dumping rules, as well as in resistance to liberalisation of trade in processed foods. With the passing of time, these safeguards have diminished greatly in importance.

EXTENDING THE COVERAGE – THE SINGLE MARKET AND BEYOND

Membership of the Community affected the trade orientation of the Irish economy and its economic structures. As European integration progressed, however, other effects of membership began to impact on the economy. First, liberalisation was extended from the goods sector to the services sector. Second, the focus of integration spread from abolition of tariff barriers (negative integration) to securing a 'level playing field' (positive integration). Third, Ireland became the recipient of large financial transfers to encourage development. Fourth, capital mobility has been enforced in response to the integration of the goods and services markets. (Measures to integrate the EU labour market have been more tentative.) These changes, which were primarily connected with the Single Market programme, came as a 'surprise' in two senses: they were not anticipated at the time of accession, and they were to prove enormously beneficial to the Irish economy.

From Goods to Services

Although the Rome Treaty contained provisions relating to services and factor mobility, these were largely ignored until the 1980s. Telephones, transport, energy and steel and other 'commanding heights' of the economy were run by state-owned companies in most European countries and were not considered suitable for exposure to external competition. Yet, over time, it became apparent that in order to achieve political acceptability free trade would have to be 'fair'. Domestic and Member State competitors would have to be allowed to compete on an equal footing. This was how the drive towards a level playing field originated.

While it would have been entirely logical for Ireland to take the initiative in services trade liberalisation on the grounds of self-interest, no such initiative was taken. Rather the liberalisation of the services sector was forced upon us by Brussels. Irish policy-makers were not inclined to rock the boat in protected public utilities where producers' priorities, mainly the trade unions and management, ruled supreme. Brussels initiatives tended to be resisted. Liberalisation tended to be labelled Thatcherite and automatically condemned, in a rather unthinking manner it must be said. Competition was eventually introduced into airline transport, telecommunications, banks and insurance under Commission pressure. This was something not anticipated in 1973; had it been anticipated, it would most likely have been resisted.

Yet the extension of liberalisation to services has proved to be remarkably beneficial to the economy (O'Rourke, 1994). The ESRI model indicated that Irish GNP in the year 2000 would be 5.1 percentage points higher than it would have been in the absence of the Single Market programme (Bradley, et al. 1992). This estimate may well be too low. Thus, most of the increase in employment in the 1990s took place in the market services sector, not in manufacturing or agriculture. Declines in price were responded to by an upsurge in demand. Barrett (1997, 1998) showed how following the drop in prices to one-quarter of the original level, the volume of air passenger traffic between London and Dublin increased four-fold. O'Malley (1990) concluded that, while indigenous manufacturing industry could do badly from the Single Market, the net outcome would depend crucially on the response of foreign investment. A decade later, it is evident that foreign investment did respond favourably, offsetting any negative impact effects of greater openness. EU membership was also important to the development of the International Financial Services Centre (IFSC). Contacts developed through Community institutions helped to get the project started, and the common institutional framework within the EU made Dublin a credible alternative to other financial centres. With 5,000 people at work there, the IFSC has turned out to be an important employer, as well as a generator of significant tax revenue. Had it not been for the IFSC, employment in the financial services industry would actually have declined slightly over the past decade. Just as manufacturing industry required new foreign investors to take advantage of the more open export markets, so the Irish financial services sector has largely had to rely on new foreign enterprises to generate employment growth.[12]

Level Playing Fields

Removal of import restrictions and customs controls leads to demands for a level playing field from both import-competing firms and exporters. Import-competing firms complain that their governments' high domestic taxes, strict environmental standards, circumscribed state aids and protective labour legislation place them at a competitive disadvantage vis-à-vis competitors in Member States with low taxes and less demanding standards. Exporters also feel aggrieved if they do not receive parity of treatment (in say the award of public contracts) with domestic producers. The 1992 Single Market programme, by attacking non-tariff barriers in the Community, gave a major impetus to such pressures.

In a strict economic sense, the case for a level playing field has little to do with 'fairness'. Trade always seems unfair to import competing producers suffering loss of market share. Yet, if one Member State prefers to impose higher environmental standards than another, there is nothing 'unfair' about the consequent restructuring of its domestic production away from that industry towards others. The industry will argue that it should be compensated for the higher costs of production necessitated by having to meet the higher environmental standards. But this is about as logical as the Irish tourism industry accusing Mediterranean countries of having an 'unfair' climatic advantage over the west of Ireland.

A case for harmonisation can, however, be made on grounds of market failure (Corden, 1998). Such market failure might arise for several reasons: the existence of network externalities (best exploitable if common standards are used for telecom equipment and air-traffic control), economies of scale (common standards allow these to be more fully utilised), and increasing transparency (common rules make markets more open, and hence more competitive). By setting limits to the amount of state aid that can be offered, and by adopting common infrastructure standards, a level playing field can also reduce the costs of investing in another Member State. Another argument for common standards rests on political economy considerations: trade conditions must be fair but must be seen to be fair by the business community.

The search for a level playing field has taken many forms. First, it has given a strong impetus to competition policy. Historically, Irish people have tended to view the free market as the institution that gave us the Famine and rack-renters rather than the spread of opulence envisaged by Adam Smith. Actions taken to enforce competition have tended to be undertaken because Brussels requires such measures. Yet, as Irish competition law has become aligned with European law and the role of the Competition Authority has strengthened, the benefits in terms of lower charges for services, and consequential benefits to users of these services in the traded sectors, have become more widely appreciated.[13]

Second, restraints on state aids have been imposed. One rarely-mentioned benefit of membership might well be the resultant limitation on domestic politicians' discretion in rescuing lame ducks. An Irish government untrammelled by Brussels would have found difficulty in turning off the flow of subsidies to several economically weak but politically sensitive companies and sectors (Irish Steel, Aer Lingus and the beef-processing industry, for instance). It is doubtful if any really worthwhile foreign project was turned away because of Brussels-imposed restraints on the amount of grant the Irish authorities were permitted to provide. In the case of new industries and R&D, Ireland has been allowed more leeway in state aids than might be permitted to the larger and more developed Member States.

Third, government procurement practices also have come under scrutiny. Public procurement typically accounts for 10-12% of GDP in industrialised economies. The degree of procurement bias in favour of domestic producers is notoriously difficult to measure. One way to estimate it is to compare the import propensity of government enterprises with equivalent private enterprises. If one finds that the import propensity of government enterprises exceeds that of similar private firms, this is taken as an a priori indication of bias. Bias of this type has been found in Ireland in a comparison based on data for the mid-1980s (Brulhart and Trionfetti, 1998). The extent of the bias has probably much diminished since then. Extensive procedures have been implemented to ensure fair treatment for out-of-state tenders. This has had the advantage of a steep reduction in the costs of many goods and services supplied to the government, albeit with the disadvantage of making the tendering process more cumbersome and bureaucratic. In theory, Irish exporters should have benefited from corresponding measures in other Member States, although there have been complaints that full reciprocity of treatment is not being provided.

Fourth, taxes have had to be modified. In the case of indirect taxes, this has tended to reduce disparities between Irish and UK tax rates, and to lessen the incentive to smuggle. Restraints have also been placed on our direct tax regime, notably the corporation profits tax, and also on other forms of tax relief to internationally traded activities. So far these restraints have not been unduly burdensome. On externality grounds, there is a clear case for intervention by Brussels to prevent distortionary tax competition and fiscal degradation. As the European market becomes more integrated, the need for co-ordination of tax policy will become more pressing.

Another policy area much influenced by Brussels has been environment policy. Ireland has been surprisingly slow to board the 'green' bandwagon. Indeed most environmental protection measures have been enforced in response to EC insistence. Environmental impact studies, for instance, have been required in order for new projects to qualify for Structural Funds assistance. The Commission pointed out several years ago that taxes on labour comprised 57% of total tax revenues of Member States, as compared with only 6% on activities and products linked to environmental problems. Thus we tax the under-used factor, labour, ten times more than the over-used factor, the environment. Increased energy and carbon taxes will be needed to come to grips with this problem, as well as with global warming.

Financial Transfers and Structural Funds

Integration agreements often carry provisions for economic and technical co-operation combined with modest financial transfers from the richer to the poorer members. None, however, has remotely matched the amount of transfers effected under various EU aid programmes. While modest amounts of aid have been disbursed through the ERDF and the ESF since the early 1970s, a major stimulus came with the Single Market programme and the launch of the Structural Funds programme in 1989 (Table 7). Doyle (1989), O'Donnell (1992) and others made an eloquent and subtle case based on two strands. First they argued that regional inequalities might be exacerbated by the Single European market and EMU, especially in regions where innovative sectors were absent and scope for exploiting economies of scale was limited. And second that 'regional counterbalancing' measures (including fiscal transfers) would therefore be necessary to ensure convergence.

Financial transfers from Brussels have taken two main forms: financial supports from the Common Agricultural Policy and resources received from the various Structural Funds.[14] Agricultural price supports have already been discussed. The other part of financial transfers, the Structural Funds, was allocated in order to promote convergence of living standards in the weaker regions. During the decade 1989-99, Ireland's structural fund receipts amounted to about 2.6% of GNP per annum. This scale of assistance can be compared with World Bank estimates of aid flows to middle-income developing countries of 1% of GNP. Aid to populous poor countries such as India and China amounts to even less than this. Also Structural Funds aid consists entirely of grants, not loans on concessional terms.

The impact of the Structural Funds is difficult to quantify. We know how the money was spent. The difficult part is to estimate the economic return obtained on the expenditure. For this, we need to

TABLE 7: Irish Receipts from the European Union

IR£m current prices	1975	1985	1990	1991	1992	1993	1994	1995	1996	1997	1998*
FEOGA guidance	0.6	56	94	143	147	126	131	143	151	166	177
ESF	4	141	129	371	277	312	277	256	253	271	315
ERDF	2	76	225	342	445	464	176	358	297	356	408
Other	2	19	7	11	11	61	84	116	154	194	168
FEOGA guarantee	102	837	1287	1334	1114	1282	1174	1150	1365	1520	1500
GROSS RECEIPTS	110	1129	1741	2201	1994	2245	1841	2023	2220	2507	2578
Less Irish Government Contributions	10	213	283	348	353	454	506	543	542	513	673
NET RECEIPTS (£m)	100	915	1458	1853	1641	1792	1336	1480	1587	1994	1905
NET RECEIPTS (% GNP)	2.9	5.9	6.4	7.6	6.2	6.3	4.4	4.4	4.3	4.8	4.1

Sources: (a) Central Bank of Ireland Annual Reports 1986, 1991-1996.
        (b) Ireland's receipts by way of grants and subsidies from EU budget, 1973-1998. European Commission, Brussels, 1998.

make assumptions about what would have happened in the absence of the aid. Simulations of this type have tended to suggest surprisingly modest effects. For instance, Bradley (1992) estimated that Ireland's GNP would be 2.7 percentage points (and GNP per capita only 0.8 percentage points) higher by the year 2000 as result of the 1989-93 programme. Later, using the same ESRI macro model, Honohan (1997) estimated that the combined impact of the two EU structural aid programmes spanning the decade up to 1999 would add only 2 percentage points to GNP in the long run. The modest scale of impact is evident from Figure 2.[15]

Perhaps some specific areas of spending failed to yield the return they should have. Tansey, for example, argues that while structural funds from 1989 greatly increased participant numbers on active labour market programmes, 'the evidence that they have significantly improved the national training effort is at best mixed' (Tansey, 1998, p. 133).

Another possibility is that the estimates omit certain important, non-quantifiable effects of the aid programmes – for instance, the Structural Funds programmes boosted confidence and enhanced the acceptability of many of the EU 'level playing field' initiatives that might otherwise have been considered very unpalatable. Also, the

FIGURE 2: GNP per head at PPP with and without SFs

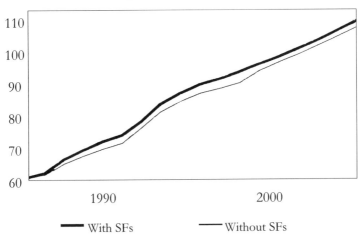

NOTE: PPP = purchasing power parity;
      SFs = Structural Funds (incl. Cohesion Funds)

Source: Honohan (1997)

obligation to account to Brussels for the spending of the funds has led to considerable improvements in the way public-sector investment is planned and monitored. The adoption of multi-annual programming encouraged national authorities to think beyond the single-year planning horizon. As Alan Gray observed, the contribution of the European Commission in influencing Irish planning and evaluation methods 'deserves more than a footnote in Irish economic history' (Gray, 1998, p. 52). The structural funds framework also led to greater co-ordination in activities co-financed

by the Community. Cynics will say that it was all done merely in order
to obtain the EU money, and in part they are right. But mind-sets
have also changed – for the better. Finally, the ESRI model took no
account of the ongoing impact of Structural Funds received prior to
1988, which were quite substantial (see Table 8).
Ireland's status as a large net recipient of EU funds is now in the
process of rapid transformation (FitzGerald, 1998). For one thing,
with higher GNP, Ireland's ongoing contribution to the EU has risen
from £283m in 1990 to an estimated £670m in 1998. If the economy
continues to grow at four times the EU average, Ireland will, before
too long, become a net contributor to the EU. For example, Ireland's
net receipts of EU transfers are projected to fall from £1,910m in
1999 to £827m in 2006, according to Department of Finance
projections.

TABLE 8: EU Transfers to Ireland 1973-98

Year	CAP Price Supports IR£m	Structural Funds IR£m	Total IR£m	SFs % of Total	SFs % of GNP
1973	37.1	0.0	37.1	0.0	0.00
1974	63.8	3.6	67.4	5.3	0.12
1975	102.2	6.9	109.1	6.3	0.18
1976	102.0	17.5	119.5	14.6	0.38
1977	245.1	27.8	272.9	10.2	0.50
1978	365.6	44.6	410.2	10.9	0.68
1979	396.5	132.6	529.1	25.1	1.74
1980	381.1	179.5	560.6	32.0	1.99
1981	304.6	202.2	506.8	39.9	1.86
1982	344.3	257.8	602.1	42.8	2.07
1983	441.7	286.0	727.7	39.3	2.10
1984	644.6	222.1	866.7	25.6	1.50
1985	836.6	292.1	1,128.7	25.9	1.85
1986	884.0	262.6	1,146.6	22.9	1.50
1987	739.6	360.7	1,100.3	32.8	1.90
1988	838.5	323.1	1,161.6	27.8	1.62
1989	963.4	331.9	1,295.3	25.6	1.50
1990	1,286.7	454.3	1,741.0	26.1	1.87
1991	1,334.4	866.8	2,201.2	39.4	3.40
1992	1,113.6	880.4	1,994.0	44.2	3.28
1993	1,281.6	963.5	2,245.3	42.9	3.35
1994	1,173.7	667.7	1,841.4	36.3	2.14
1995	1,150.2	873.0	2,023.2	43.1	2.58
1996	1,364.5	855.0	2,219.5	38.5	2.27
1997	1,519.8	986.8	2,506.6	39.4	2.35
1998	1,500.0	1,077.6	2,577.6	41.8	2.29
TOTAL	19,415.4	10,576.1	29,991.5	35.3	1.73

Sources: Budget documents, Central Bank of Ireland Quarterly Reports,
        Department of Finance.

Capital Mobility

While the Treaty of Rome involved a commitment to freedom of capital movements, little was done to implement this provision prior to the Single European Act of 1987. Capital controls between Ireland and other Member States were not abolished until the early 1990s. Irish pension funds responded by increasing their overseas holdings to over 40% of their total assets of IR£19 billion, and the process of international diversification of Irish investment funds will intensify after the introduction of the euro. Irish banks have also become more heavily involved in global capital market transactions – by mid-1997, their gross liabilities to non-residents amounted to IR£50 billion.

The abolition of capital controls means that Irish capital is free to go to where it can make the highest return and diversify risk. This freedom to borrow and lend abroad has brought economic benefits to Irish individuals and Irish companies by enabling them to diversify their portfolios and maximise the return on capital. It has also intruded on Irish fiscal policy in a helpful way. Any hint of reversion to the irresponsible fiscal policies of the past would lead to prompt capital outflows, higher interest rates for Irish borrowers, and a very clear negative signal to the public about the Government's performance.

Another benefit of capital mobility stems from its counter-cyclical stabilising role in the economy. When the Irish economy is booming and the rest of the world is depressed, there is a net profit outflow from Ireland to the outside world. When the rest of the world is booming and the Irish economy is relatively depressed, exactly the opposite happens. Thus Irish consumers find their spending evened out over the business cycle (Lane, 1998).

A less edifying effect of international capital movement has been to make individual capital transactions increasingly difficult to trace and tax. The Byzantine financial paths described in the McCracken Tribunal Report (1997) illustrated the difficulty in a graphic way. As a result, tax evasion and avoidance of taxation have become easier than before. Governments in high-tax jurisdictions are under pressure to reduce tax rates so as to minimise the incentives to transfer capital to lower-tax jurisdictions.

The danger of a resultant 'race to the bottom', or fiscal degradation, is a cause of concern. Globalisation of the private sector must, sooner or later, be matched by secure closer co-ordination of capital taxation policies among Member States.

THE BREAK WITH STERLING AND EMU

The next step in the integration process is the introduction of the euro and economic and monetary union (EMU). The replacement of the Irish pound with the euro has provoked much controversy – though more among economists than among the public. Curiously, for a touchy nation, there seems to be very little nostalgia or affection for the Irish pound as such – few regrets have been expressed about the forthcoming demise of Mother Catherine McAuley, James Joyce, and Daniel O'Connell from our daily currency.

EMU was preceded by the break with sterling in 1979. Dissatisfaction with the sterling parity was a persistent theme in economic debate during the 1970s. The problem was that sterling had lost the one absolutely essential attribute of an anchor currency: a low inflation rate. When an alternative anchor, in the shape of the European Monetary System (EMS), appeared, it was eagerly grasped. As it happened, the EMS anchor also proved defective. Irish inflation increased sharply during 1979-81, the EMS discipline turned out to be relatively lax, the UK got its inflation under control, and the Irish government ran into a terrible fiscal crisis. Disinflation did not take place until after 1982 by which year inflation of 19.4% was recorded (McGettigan and Kenny, 1996; Lane, 1998). Whether in retrospect the break was a good thing or not for the Irish economy is a subject worthy of further study. Had we retained the sterling link we would have shared the sharp disinflation that accompanied the decline in UK inflation from 18% in 1980 to 5% in 1983. Adherence to an effective exchange-rate index, mentioned as a possible alternative to EMS, would have created difficulties in view of Ireland's dire financial position. What is certain is that without the break with sterling in 1979, Ireland would have lacked the know-how and the institutional self-confidence to contemplate EMU without the participation of the UK.

Three main economic benefits to Ireland were foreseen from EMU. First, trade and foreign investment with the eleven Member States in EMU would be less expensive to transact in a single currency with zero exchange-rate risk. Second, the euro would make it easier for people to compare prices in different parts of Europe. Price transparency will ensure that competition is intensified and prices are kept low. Third, over the long run, the elimination of exchange-rate risk would reduce Irish interest rates (by somewhere between 1 and 2 percentage points). This would stimulate investment and generate faster growth. Proponents of EMU made much of this third factor (Baker et al., 1996; de Buitléir et al., 1995), but the other two could ultimately prove to be just as important. Against this there were some drawbacks.[16] Irish firms would become vulnerable to changes in sterling given Britain's opt-out based decision. Business was badly scarred by the weakness of sterling in 1992-93 as it had been to a lesser extent in 1986, and many firms had extreme difficulty in coping with a rate of one Irish pound equal to 110p sterling. Had the single currency been in operation in 1992, Irish firms would have had to cope with the equivalent of 115-120p sterling per IR£ through much of 1995 and 1996 – something that would have proved a traumatic experience. However, in an EMU situation, Irish business would not also have had to cope with the astronomical interest rates that accompanied past exchange-rate crises.

Another objection was that EMU would result in inappropriate interest rates for the Irish economy. A booming economy ideally needs higher interest rates to cool things down. But, after EMU, the Irish Central Bank will surrender control of monetary policy to the European Central Bank. Interest rates will be determined by the needs of the European, not the Irish, economy. While all members of EMU will be in the same position in this respect, the Irish economy has been weakly synchronised with average EU economic conditions in the past. Hence, the argument goes, conflict is likely to arise often in future. When we need high interest rates, we are likely to get lower rates, and vice versa.

Introducing the euro will be costly. On this, opponents and advocates of EMU are agreed. By the year 2002, prices will have to be quoted in euros. Automatic teller machines and accounting systems will have to be adjusted to transactions in euros. The cost will have to be borne by private business and ultimately, one suspects, by consumers. Brussels has made clear that it will not foot the bill. The transition process will create opportunities for confusion, fraud and unwarranted price increases, as uneven and awkward figures are rounded up. Economists tend to see these costs as similar to the up-front costs of launching a new product, which should be capitalised and written off against a future stream of benefits lasting for many generations. Viewed in this way, they come out as being fairly small.

Thus, going into EMU has potential downsides. Opponents of EMU, however, tended to underplay the serious downsides of staying out. First, there was the risk that foreign investors would perceive it as evidence of a weakening commitment to Europe. There are intangible benefits to being close to the centre of decision-taking in European monetary policy. The IDA claimed that failure to participate in EMU would have a serious adverse affect on inward investment. Second, abstention from EMU might have weakened the government's commitment to fiscal control and a lower debt/GDP ratio. Such an eventuality would have been truly calamitous. Without the disciplining effect of the Maastricht criteria on Irish fiscal policy, the nineties boom would never have happened. Ireland's economic prosperity and competitive exchange rate up to 1998 were the consequence of the Government's commitment to participate in EMU. They were connected phenomena. This was a basic flaw in the 'if it ain't broke, don't fix it' argument for staying out of EMU.

Third, the picture promoted by critics of EMU of a high-octane Irish Central Bank, fine tuning the economy from year to year and providing soft landings or quick recoveries à la carte, is not entirely plausible. This strand in the anti-EMU case relied on an exaggerated faith in the effectiveness of counter-cyclical monetary policy. The Federal Reserve Bank in the United States, of course, operates such a system quite successfully. But for a small open country it is a different matter. Adjusting interest rates according to the cyclical pattern of the economy can generate large, and often uncontrollable, swings in the exchange rate. Studies of the economics of introducing a flexible exchange rate regime in Ireland have repeatedly concluded that the exchange rate uncertainty of such a regime would impose excessive costs on our trade and foreign investment. Business generally dislikes exchange rate uncertainty, which explains why it tended to favour the EMU project (in Britain and Sweden as well as in the euro area).

A curious aspect of the EMU debate in Ireland was that while opponents warned that EMU would be bad for Irish business, Irish business itself tended to be strongly supportive of the Government's position. Ireland's main political parties, business representatives and trade unions remained firmly pro-EMU right through the debate.[17] Likewise the Irish voter. The Maastricht referendum in 1992 recorded a 'yes' vote of just under 70% of all votes cast. Some opponents of EMU brush this result aside on the basis that the Irish people did not know what they were voting for. But a referendum vote cannot be dismissed so lightly.

A further consideration is that Structural Funds received during the 1990s were designed to assist Ireland in its professed objective of building up its economic strength and participating fully in EMU. Having received, and spent, this assistance, and subsequently prospered and passed the Maastricht criteria with flying colours, could an Irish government credibly declare that it had changed its mind and decided not to join until the UK joined too? After all, the sterling factor and the 'asymmetric shocks' problem have not hit us out of the blue. More important, would such a policy reversal not go against the whole thrust of Irish political economy over the past 30 years, which has been to lessen our economic dependence on Britain and establish an independent role on a broader international stage? Also account should be taken of the likelihood that Ireland's economic relations with continental Europe will strengthen further as a result of EMU.[18]

The ineffectiveness of the anti-EMU case can be traced to three main defects. One relates to timing – the anti-arguments have come too late in the decision-making process. Another defect relates to content. The arguments are substantive, but not compelling. A final problem concerns perspective. A decision to go into or stay out of EMU should not be dictated by short-term considerations, whether they be the specific sterling exchange rate in any month, or the existence or absence of a housing boom in Dublin. A decision to stay out of EMU would have required the articulation of an alternative strategy for Ireland's long-run development, not just a simple 'no'.

Hence, Ireland was ineluctably drawn towards early participation in the single currency. Over the long run, EMU could result in a fusion of the benefits of the fiscal consolidation, low inflation and fast growth experienced in recent years. But we are speaking of probabilities, not certainties. Much will depend on how the levers of domestic policy still left to us are deployed – incomes policy, education and infrastructure policy, tax policy, for instance. If the UK stays out of EMU and sterling behaves with as much volatility as in the past, the Irish economy can expect lots of turbulence. In such circumstances, things often have a habit of going wrong on a broad front. Loss of competitiveness vis-à-vis the UK could be accompanied by stagnant demand in export markets, an excessive rise in Irish costs, deterioration of the budget position and unpleasant encounters with the Stability and Growth fiscal limits. In short, adapting to the new disciplines and opportunities of EMU will be a serious challenge.

ADVERSE EFFECTS OF MEMBERSHIP

Can integration ever actually harm a weaker Member State? At various stages since 1973 concern has been expressed about the danger of cumulative decline. Many arguments drew on the core-periphery school for sustenance. As we have seen, the highly influential report of the National Economic and Social Council drafted by Rory O'Donnell (NESC, 1989) wove these arguments into a powerful case for Structural Funds. The case was made that the free market outcome could be one of increasing divergence between core and periphery; in order to ensure that convergence occurred, market failure would have to be corrected by government intervention. Interestingly the same viewpoint was taken in response to the 1970 Werner Report on EMU. According to Maher:

> The Werner Report and the Commission's proposals were subjected to close scrutiny in the Department of Finance and the Central Bank. Both were concerned with the implications which economic and monetary union could have for Ireland. A working group representative of the Department of Finance and the Central Bank undertook a detailed examination of those implications. That examination showed the need for the adoption of a Community regional policy to deal with the problem of regional disparities which would otherwise be exacerbated. (Maher, 1986, p. 287-288)

Some years later Chris O'Malley, MEP warned that, following the implementation of the Single Market, the poorer regions of Europe could face collapse in the near future without continuous large-scale transfers of funds from strong regions to weak (O'Malley, 1988, p. 10).

Why should economic divergence occur as a result of European integration? One reason advanced was that economies of scale would favour the big firms in the large Member States. Greater market size would drive down their unit costs enabling them to take over, or drive out of business, smaller Irish firms. Thus, access to the European market would prove an empty promise to poorer regions. Job losses in import-substitution industries would not be compensated for by new jobs in export industries. The benefits of trade would accrue largely to the richer countries. That such an outcome might be considered possible was not just a reflection of Celtic pessimism. Core-periphery models continue to be developed by trade theorists to this day.

Another potential cause of divergence arose because of the liberalisation of EC trade with third-world countries. Imports from these countries, it was feared, would lead to a deterioration in pay for unskilled workers in Ireland, and a rise in unemployment. Poorer regions, with relatively more unskilled workers, were likely to be disproportionately affected (Wood, 1998, p. 1463).

European labour-market policies have also been a source of concern. These have been something of a disaster area for the Community, as evidenced in the poor record of employment growth and the prevalence of high unemployment.

Lack of flexibility in pay and terms of work, excessively protective employment legislation and high replacement rates have contributed to this. To the extent that such standards were imposed on a country such as Ireland, the unemployment problem would worsen. Such considerations prompted Britain to opt out of the Social Charter. But Ireland signed up. The long-run impact of this decision has yet to be worked out. By the end of the 1990s, however, it seemed that the effects on labour costs were fairly minimal.[19]

The above arguments have been vigorously debated over the past 25 years. With hindsight, convergence, not divergence, has been the outcome of integration. Specialisation has led more to higher incomes than to greater vulnerability. True, the wage gap between white-collar and blue-collar employees has increased (from 43% to 47% between 1979 and 1995) but the relationship between this and Ireland's imports from developing countries seems to have been statistically insignificant (Figini and Georg, 1998).

IRISH INFLUENCE ON EC ECONOMIC POLICY

The Irish approach has been to ask what Brussels has done for the Irish economy rather than the corollary. Policy has been dominated by the desire to maximise receipts from Brussels, while minimising the amount of interference in domestic policy (in the application of funds, competition policy and other areas) and seeking derogation on difficult points.

What has Ireland done for Brussels in terms of economic policy? Scott (1994) is one of the few to address this question in an elegant monograph. His volume is revealingly slim. He distinguished between Ireland's policy contribution and its human contribution to EU policy.

Ireland's human contributions are certainly impressive. Garret FitzGerald on Lomé and regional policy, Peter Sutherland on competition policy, Ray MacSharry on CAP reform, Jim Dooge on institutional reform and Maurice Doyle on regional policy and the EMU, all made an outstanding impact. The contribution of Irish public servants to the work of the Community institutions, and of MEPs of European class such as Pat Cox, also deserves mention.

In terms of policy contributions, however, the pickings are decidedly thin. Ireland appears to have made little original contribution to strategic policy formulation in Europe. Our forte has been in the management and adaptation of policy. One major thrust among Irish efforts was the development of the Community's regional policy. This may have been to some extent self-serving, but other regions benefited in the process.

Ireland's social consensus model also may have contributed to the wider Community debate about the appropriate economic model for Europe. And the success of the Celtic Tiger has perhaps provided support to several themes in Brussels' economic thinking. It showed that fiscal restraint is perfectly compatible with fast growth, and that the adoption of the Maastricht fiscal criteria can help economic progress. Likewise, the productive use of the Structural Funds has impressed many European economists, by showing how financial assistance can spur economic performance.

CONCLUSIONS

This chapter asks what difference did the EU make? My focus has been primarily retrospective. In assessing the consequences of membership, one must beware of over-attribution. Some benefits of integration would no doubt have been negotiated for the manufacturing sector (though not for the agriculture sector) had we not become members. Also, a disadvantage of the type of historical and associative analysis utilised in this contribution is that one's judgement can easily be over-influenced by recent economic performance. As we have seen, the dramatic convergence of Irish to EU living standards is a relatively recent phenomenon. Prior to 1994, Ireland's self-image as an EU Member State was that of 'a small, poor, peripheral country' (Scott, 1994, p.6). All has changed over the last five years.

The success of the Irish economy has called into question the relevance of theories about the inevitability of decline in peripheral regions that were a staple of the core-periphery literature. However, if the Irish economy were ever to under-perform again, those ideas could make a comeback. The Irish economy of the late 1990s is more vulnerable to the danger of hubris than of a demoralised dependency-syndrome.

Thus, we conclude that membership of the EU was good for Ireland, but not in the way expected. There were many 'surprises'. Foreign investment played a more vital role than anticipated; and most of it came from the United States, not from the affluent countries of Europe. Another unexpected turn was that bad domestic policy went near to wrecking the Irish economy's capacity to utilise the advantages of market access. The fiscal situation was retrieved just in time. Another surprise was how well the Irish economy responded to the opportunities of the Single Market programme. This initiative proved important in generating foreign investment and improving efficiency in the services sector. Participation in Europe and early commitment to EMU made a major contribution to the restoration of fiscal balance in the economy. The Maastricht criteria acted as a lodestar, and provided an objective that was acceptable to both left and right of the political spectrum, and around which our politicians could rally popular support for otherwise unpalatable measures.

As has been said many times, for Ireland, the days of wine and roses from Brussels are approaching an end. CAP price supports are being phased out, the Structural Funds are being gradually reduced, and Ireland could soon become a net contributor to the European budget. Integration with the global economy is proceeding alongside integration in an enlarging European Union. How the economy responds to these challenges will no doubt be the subject of another chapter – perhaps 25 years from now!

NOTES

1. Kennedy (1991) for instance shows that national disposable income per person rose much more slowly relative to the EU than GDP or GNP up to 1990. His paper gives an interesting insight into how European integration was viewed up to 1991.
2. One reason for this might be that economists writing about these matters tend to exhibit above-average geographical mobility in their personal lives. Since they may also be above average in ability, they are more likely to be beneficiaries than victims of the integration process.
3. For convenience, I employ here the vocabulary of trade negotiation, not economics.
4. The importance of this effect would become evident in Eastern Europe where the absence of external competition resulted in capital equipment and production techniques being a generation out of date.
5. Evidence that IIT caused lower adjustment costs than inter-industry trade is presented in Brulhart et al. (1998). See Brulhart and McAleese (1995), Brulhart and Elliot (1998) and Brulhart et al. (1999) for further details.
6. In or out of the EU, Ireland would probably still have enjoyed free access to the European market. Yet, the Industrial Development Authority argued that EC entry was essential because investors would not have regarded the two situations as equivalent. Membership of the Community carried with it a security of access

which no trade agreement could replicate. The prospective harmonisation of EU economic and social policies was seen as an additional attraction to the foreign investor. (McAleese, 1975 pp 158-159)

7. Alan Matthews "Income Support for farmers must be turned on its head" *Sunday Business Post*, 1 November 1998; Department of Agriculture and Food, *Annual Review and Outlook*, 1997

8. "Share out of CAP payments described as social scandal" *The Irish Times*, Tuesday November 17, 1998. The same source reports the European Court of Auditors finding that 40% of CAP payments have gone to only 4% of Irish farmers.

9. "In the very long run, the CAP will have to be modified and the European system of agricultural protection gradually rationalised. Before that time comes, however, Ireland will, it is hoped, have availed of the breathing space afforded by the CAP's protection to build up the cattle herd and to establish a strong selling position in the enlarged Community's market for agricultural produce." McAleese (1975, p. 159)

10. It would be an interesting thesis to review these reports and compare predictions against subsequent performance.

11. "When particular manufacturers have been so far extended as to employ a great multitude of hands, humanity may require that the freedom of trade should be restored only by slow gradations and with a good deal of reserve and circumspection." Adam Smith, *Wealth of Nations*, Book IV, ch II p. 491 Cannan edition 1776.

12. One reason for this is that existing foreign owned companies, in insurance for example, are not geared for and often are discouraged by head office from breaking into export markets, as this would be seen as "poaching" their parent's markets. In this respect they were similar to British manufacturing subsidiaries set up in Ireland under protection. A point of contrast, however, is that there appears to be a higher proportion of new foreign service industries of European origin than there were in the manufacturing sector.

13. Sections 4 and 5 of the Competition Act for example are almost identical with Articles 85 and 86 of the Rome Treaty. Recent actions by the re-invigorated Competition Authority in the case of taxis and pubs may presage a gradual change in such attitudes.

14. Structural Funds include the European Regional Development Fund (ERDF), European Social Fund (ESF) and the Guidance Section of the Agricultural Fund (FEOGA). I also include Cohesion Funds.

15. The finding of only a slight macro-impact is consistent with the

economic aid literature (World Bank, 1998).
16. The case against Ireland joining EMU is made in Thom (1997), Thom and Neary (1997), Neary (1997).
17. Ireland's main business and employer organisation, IBEC, has been a proactive and unequivocal supporter of participation in EMU in the first round. Small business organisations have, perhaps not surprisingly, been more tentative.
18. But it would be unwise to press this argument since the share of Ireland's trade transacted with the euro area has declined in recent years.
19. There was a fourth argument to the effect that the Community's aid programmes would foster a dependent, rent-seeking mentality in Ireland, thereby reinforcing our relative disadvantage. The Culliton Report (1992), for example, expressed concern that structural funds might have underwritten a level of public expenditure in Ireland that would not otherwise have been possible. McCarthy (1992) expressed concern that, "whereas the Marshall Plan helped post-war markets in Europe to work better sooner, the Structural Funds may be enabling Ireland to avoid market realities longer." (p. 152)

REFERENCES

Baker T., FitzGerald J. and Honohan P. (1996) *Economic Implications for Ireland of EMU,* Dublin: Economic and Social Research Institute
Barrett Sean D. (1997) "The Implications of the Ireland-UK airline deregulation for an EU Internal Market" *Journal of Air Transport Management*
Barrett Sean D. (1998) "Rent, Competition and Airports" Dublin Economics Workshop Conference, Kenmare
Bradley J., FitzGerald J. and Kearney I. (1992) *The Role of the Structural Funds: Analysis of the Consequences for Ireland in the context of 1992,* Dublin: Economic and Social Research Institute
Brülhart Marius and McAleese Dermot (1995) "Intra-Industry Trade and Industrial Adjustment: The Irish Experience" *Economic and Social Review,* January
Brülhart M. and Elliot R. (1998) "Adjustment to the European Single Market: Inferences from Intra-Industry Trade Patterns" *Journal of Economic Studies* 25
Brülhart, Marius and F. Trionfetti (1998) "Industrial Specialisation and Public Procurement: Theory and Empirical Evidence" mimeo
Brülhart M., Murphy A. and Strobl E. (1998) "Intra-Industry Trade and Job Turnover" paper to IESG Annual Conference, "Globalisation and Regionalisation" St Anthony's College, Oxford 18-20 September
Brülhart M., McAleese Dermot and O'Donnell Mary (1999) "Country Case

Study – Ireland' in M. Brülhart and R.C. Hine (eds) *Intra-Industry Trade and Adjustment: the European Experience,* London: Macmillan

Coe D. and Helpman E. (1995) "International R&D Spillovers" *European Economic Review*

Coombes David ed. (1983) *Ireland and the European Communities: Ten years of Membership,* Dublin: Gill and Macmillan

Corden W. M. (1998) Review in *Economic Journal* July pp 1217-9

De Buitleir Donal and Thornhill D. J. (1993) *EMU and Irish Fiscal Policy,* Dublin: Institute of European Affairs

Doyle M. F. (1989) "Regional Policy and European economic integration" in *Report on economic and monetary union in the European Community* (the Delors Report), Brussels

Drudy P. J. and Dermot McAleese (eds) (1984) *Ireland and the European Community,* Cambridge: Cambridge University Press

Figini P. and Görg H. (1998) "Multinational Companies and Wage Inequality in the Host Country: The Case of Ireland" *Trinity Economic Papers* no 16 July

Gray Alan (1998), "Challenges for Ireland in the Integrated European Union" in F. O Muircheartaigh (ed) *Ireland in the Changing Times: Essays to celebrate T. K. Whitaker's 80 Years,* Dublin: Institute of Public Administration

Honohan P. et al. (1997), *Evaluation of Structural Funds,* Dublin: ESRI

International Monetary Fund (1993), "Trade as an Engine of Growth" *World Economic Outlook* May

Johnson David (1997) Review of John O'Hagan (ed) "The Economy of Ireland" *Journal of Economic Literature* March 1997

Kennedy Kieran A. (1992) "Real Convergence: The European Community and Ireland" *Journal of the Statistical and Social Inquiry Society of Ireland* 1991/1992

Lane P. R. (1998a) "International Diversification and the Irish Economy" *Trinity Economic Papers,* Technical Paper no 98/11

Lane P. R. (1998b) "Disinflation, Switching Nominal Anchors and Twin Crises: the Irish Experience" paper to Banco de la Republica/ World Bank conference "Why is it important to reduce inflation and how to do it: the international experience and lessons for Colombia" Bogota May 4-5

Maher D. J. (1986) *The Tortuous Path: the course of Ireland's entry into the EEC 1948-73* Dublin: Institute of Public Administration

Matthews Alan (1988) "Common Agricultural Policy Reform and National Compensation Strategies" *Journal of the Statistical and Social Inquiry Society of Ireland* 1988/89

McAleese Dermot and John Martin (1972) "Ireland's Manufactured Exports to the EEC and the Common External Tariff" *Economic and Social Review,* pp 615-631

McAleese Dermot (1975) "Ireland in the Enlarged EEC: Economic Consequences and Prospects", in John Vaizey (ed.), *Economic Sovereignty and Regional Policy,* Dublin: Gill and Macmillan, pp 133-160

McAleese Dermot (1986) "Ireland in the World Economy" in Kieran A Kennedy *Ireland in Transition,* Dublin: Mercier Press

McAleese Dermot (1987) "European Integration and the Irish Economy" *Administration* Winter

McAleese Dermot (1997) *Economics for Business* London: Prentice Hall

McAleese Dermot and F. Hayes (1995), "European Integration the Balance of Payments and Inflation" in John O'Hagan *The Economy of Ireland* London: Macmillan

McGettigan D. and Kenny G. (1996) "Inflation in Ireland: Theory and Evidence" *Journal of the Statistical and Social Inquiry Society of Ireland* 1996/97

Neary J. P. and D. R. Thom (1997) "Punts, pounds and euros: In search of an optimum currency area" *IBAR – Journal of Irish Business Administration and Research*

Neary J. P. (1997) "The EU Stability Pact and the Case for European Monetary Union" Centre for Economic Research University College Dublin Working Paper 97/28

National Economic and Social Council (1989) *Ireland in the European Community: Performance, Prospects and Strategy* Dublin, August

National Economic and Social Council (1991) *The Economic and Social Implications of Emigration,* Dublin.

O'Donnell Mary and McAleese Dermot (1998) "A Comparative Analysis of Export Promotion Strategies and Growth in Selected Asian and European Economies" , paper presented to Phare Workshop "Export Promotion and Institutional Change in Transitional Economies: Lessons of Experience", Budapest, March 1998 (to be published)

O'Donnell Rory (1992) "Policy requirements for regional balance in economic and monetary union" in A. Hannequart (ed) *Economic and Social Cohesion in Europe: a new objective for integration* London: Routledge

O'Malley, Chris (1988) *Over in Europe; the issues facing Ireland in the European Community,* Dublin: The Orchard Press

O'Malley Eoin (1990) "Ireland" in "The Impact of the Internal Market by Industrial Sector: The Challenge for Member States" *European Economy/Social Europe*

O'Rourke, Kevin (1994) "Industrial Policy, Employment Policy and the Non-Traded Sector, *Journal of Statistical and Social Inquiry Society of Ireland* 1994-95

Ruane, F. and H. Görg (1996) "Aspects of Foreign Direct Investment in Irish Manufacturing since 1973: Policy and Performance" *Journal of Statistical and Social Inquiry Society of Ireland* 1996/97

Ruane, F. and H. Görg (1997) "The Impact of Foreign Direct Investment on Sectoral Adjustment in the Irish Economy" *National Institute Economic Review* April

Scott, Dermot (1994) *Ireland's contribution to the European Union* Dublin: Institute of European Affairs

Sheehy, S. J. (1994) "The Common Agricultural Policy and Ireland" in P. J. Drudy and Dermot McAleese *Ireland and the European Community* Cambridge: Cambridge University Press

Tansey Paul (1998) *Ireland at Work: Economic Growth and the Labour Market 1987-1997* Dublin: Oak Tree Press

Thom, D. R. (1997) "Economic and Monetary Union" Centre for Economic Research, University College Dublin Working Paper 97/3 January

Wood, Adrian (1998) "Globalisation and the Rise in Labour Market Inequalities" *Economic Journal* September

World Bank (1998) *Assessing Aid: What Works, What Doesn't and Why* Oxford University Press

CHAPTER 9

Diluting Lobbies and Unleashing Growth

Dr Garret FitzGerald

INTRODUCTION

I propose at the outset to say something about the rationale of Ireland's accession and of the preparations that were made for EU membership. Then, after commenting on the peripherality issue, I shall discuss briefly the effects of membership upon the three main sectors of the economy – agriculture, industries and services. Finally, I want to dwell on the extent to which the long-term dynamic impact of EU membership on the Irish economy has derived principally from what was initially seen here principally in negative terms – the freeing of industrial trade – rather than from the CAP and Structural Funds, the EU and its policies.

PREPARATIONS FOR EU MEMBERSHIP 1959-72

The changing of the guard in Fianna Fáil 37 years after the establishment of our state, with Lemass succeeding de Valera as Taoiseach, took place just six months after General de Gaulle's termination of the negotiations for a Free Trade Area that would have comprised the Community and most of its European neighbours – including Ireland. In the discussions about this Free Trade Area we had sought a twenty-year derogation period for the ending of industrial protection. It was this pessimistic assessment of the capacity of Irish industry to face free trade in anything but the very long term that lulled many into assuming that full membership for Ireland was ruled out for the foreseeable future: thus the decision in July 1961 to make just such an application came as a great surprise to most people, including the Opposition parties in the Dáil.

Lemass had moved almost at once to prepare the way for Irish association with, or membership of, the EU in parallel with what he believed would be eventual British entry: he proposed to the Federation of Irish Industries that it initiate a review of the likely impact of free trade on our protected industries.

Together with Gerry Quinn I was asked to start this process, a task for which I had begun to prepare myself two years earlier when I

111

resigned from a management post in Aer Lingus and as a Research Assistant in TCD initiated a study of the industrial sector which would bring me into direct contact with 250 manufacturing firms.

The pilot study of one industry which we were asked to undertake demonstrated that the task was of a magnitude that could not be undertaken within any reasonable time-scale without the participation of the public service, and our recommendation to this effect was accepted in July 1961 when the Committee on Industrial Organisation was established.

Dermot McAleese suggests, in his chapter, that it might be worthwhile to look back at the several dozen reports prepared by this Committee with a view to seeing how accurate was their assessment of the impact of free trade on our protected industrial sector. In the absence of such a retrospective review of the work of the Committee I would be slow to rely on my memory to answer that question, beyond saying that I believe the Committee, whose review of Irish manufacturing was remarkably detailed and comprehensive, judged correctly which sectors were most at risk.

What is certain, anyway, is that this exercise had a very important educational effect on our indigenous industries, the losses in which would have been far worse if this exercise had not been undertaken, for it alerted both managements and unions – and it should be said that the unions joined in this exercise in a very constructive manner – to the scale of the readjustments that would need to be made if much of protected industry was to survive under conditions of free trade.

Lemass's second move to incite industry to face up to free trade was the imposition of several unilateral ten per cent tariff cuts, but the resistance this evoked, and the very slight impact on trade of these cuts – in what were very high tariff levels indeed – then led him to take a most radical step – negotiating with Britain in 1965 a Free Trade Area Agreement that would give industry in that country free access to the Irish market within a period of a decade.

Because most Irish industrial products already had free access to the UK, this Agreement was estimated to gave Britain benefits three times greater than Ireland would receive in return[1], but this was sufficient of a fig-leaf to cover Lemass's objective: to force Irish industry to face the reality of free trade – a reality that because of the postponement of EU accession had begun to fade in the minds of many of its leaders.

This was of course a gamble: had Britain – and Ireland – been indefinitely excluded from the Community, we should have found ourselves more dependent than ever upon what by that time was clearly Europe's slowest-growing economy. But the gamble paid off handsomely: the freeing of trade with the EU coincided and overlapped with the closing stages of the freeing of trade with Britain. In effect this gave us an overall eleven-year transitional period, from January 1966 to January 1977.

The fact that Britain was then the slowest-growing market in Europe (and had been so since before the end of the 19th century) was undoubtedly a factor in our decision to seek access to the more dynamic markets of the Continent. Dermot McAleese remarks in Chapter 8 that, from 1977 onwards, the British market ceased to fall behind that of the rest of the Continent. But, while this may be true in general terms, it is the Continent rather than Britain that, then and since, has proved the more dynamic market for our products and especially for the goods produced by the new high-tech industries locating here.

Thus, between 1977 and 1997, the value of Irish exports to Continental EU countries increased almost twenty-fold, whereas exports to Britain rose by a factor of less than six. In 1995, less than 30% of our exports to the EU of products of externally-owned high-tech industries were shipped to Britain and over 70% to Continental EU countries, whereas Britain takes a much larger share of our more traditional exports to EU countries, the growth of which is, of course, much slower.

Incidentally in that year the EU, including the UK, took two-thirds of all our high-tech exports (92% in the case of software), the US 10%, and East Asia a slightly smaller proportion. (Time has not permitted me to update my somewhat laborious 1995 analysis of these exports but I doubt these proportions have changed much in the past couple of years.)

One further point relating to our accession to the Community may, perhaps, be worth making. During the 1960s and early 1970s it was universally believed that we could not afford to join the Community until and unless Britain also became a member. Dermot MacAleese clearly shares this view, which may well be correct.

However, it is interesting to note that when in 1974 the new British Labour government sought a renegotiation of the UK's entry terms, and it seemed for a moment possible that a failure of this process might lead to Britain withdrawing from membership, an equally overwhelming 'conventional wisdom' emerged in Ireland to the effect that if that happened we should remain in the Community. And this view was, if I recall correctly, confirmed by a study which, however, became available only after the matter had been settled at the Dublin European Council of 1975.

At the time I could not help wondering how, in the short space of fifteen months, the balance of advantage in relation to EEC membership without Britain could have changed so decisively and whether the earlier negative view about our joining without Britain might not, perhaps, have been over-cautious?

PERIPHERALITY

Dermot McAleese points out that another view very widely held at the time – that peripherality would make it impossible for a country such as Ireland to maintain a growth rate comparable with the growth rates of more centrally-located states – has since taken a severe knock. In the Irish case, he says, convergence, not divergence, has been the outcome of integration.

But it is not just Ireland which has demonstrated that peripherality is compatible with faster growth: this has been the experience also of Spain and Portugal. Since they joined in 1985 their GDP has risen by 49% and 55% respectively, as against a 35% increase in the 'core' Member States. Greece has had more difficulty with accommodating itself to the EU and benefiting from membership, but even in the short period of five years since Finland joined and started to recover from the sharp down-turn of the 1990-93 period, it has had a growth rate double that of the rest of the Union.

AGRICULTURE

I cannot disagree with Professor McAleese's verdict on the agricultural sector. The loss by Britain – virtually the only market open to our farmers – of its capacity to pursue a 'cheap food policy', a loss which was, of course, accompanied by the opening of Continental EU markets, gave Irish agriculture an enormous boost in the mid-1970s, and offered relief to the Irish exchequer on a scale no one had thought possible.

We had calculated this relief at £30m in the first year, i.e. over £200m in today's money terms. Indeed the February 1973 Election was largely fought – and perhaps won by the National Coalition – on the issue of how this money should be spent. In the event, this figure was exceeded by one-quarter in that year – and within five years these payments from the Guarantee Fund had risen to £365m, which represents over £1.2bn in today's money.

During that period agricultural prices had risen more than three-fold, which, even allowing for the general inflation of that period, involved a real price increase of almost one-third, and this was accompanied by a small increase in the volume of farm output. In conjunction with a continuing fall in the number of farmers, this increased the purchasing power of the average farmer's income by well over two-fifths.

Of course this development was not sustained thereafter – indeed farm income fell back in 1979 and by the end of the decade many farmers who had been misled by this boom into over-spending, especially on housing, found themselves in financial difficulties.

Then and since there has been a notable lack of forward-thinking in agriculture. I would add to Dermot McAleese's strictures on this subject a further criticism. Instead of being satisfied with the huge accession price increases secured by Irish farmers, Ministers for Agriculture succumbed to short-sighted farmers' pressure for increases in the EU price level itself. This not alone sent a wrong signal to the farming community – encouraging the euphoria that was leading to reckless spending. It also helped to keep in business marginal high-cost farmers in other EU countries, thus preventing this country from cashing in on our natural advantage as a low-cost producer of milk and beef. My own attempts as part of the overall EU policy co-ordination process to argue this case fell on deaf ears. As so often happens in politics, short-termism prevented any serious discussion of long-term strategy.

The sectoral orientation of parts of the public administration have all too often inhibited not just the service of the general interest of society but also the long-term interests of the sector in question. It will be clear from what Dermot McAleese has said that this has been a problem with agriculture throughout the period of our membership of the European Union.

INDUSTRY

But something similar happened also in the industrial sector during the 1960s, when, despite the strong commitment to this policy of their former Minister, Sean Lemass, who had become Taoiseach, the Department of Industry and Commerce, as it then was, failed to adjust to the prospect of free trade. As a result, the burden of preparing Ireland for industrial free trade had to be carried disproportionately by the Department of Finance, well supported by the Federation of Irish Industries (FII) and the Irish Congress of Trade Unions (ICTU).

Inevitably, these efforts were only partially successful. A significant proportion of protected industry disappeared. Several years ago, examining the data at the maximum level of disaggregation permitted by our industrial statistics, I found that by 1994 about one-fifth of the jobs that had existed in the food-processing sector in 1961 had disappeared, while in the rest of the manufacturing sector three-eighths of the 1961 jobs had gone – a job loss of 50,000 in all. However, half of these lost jobs in each of these sectors had been replaced in other parts of the traditional sector, and by 1994 this net loss of 25,000 jobs in the traditional sector had been much more than offset by almost 70,000 new jobs in the externally-owned high-tech sector. And since 1994 almost 50,000 more jobs have been created in manufacturing, bringing the scale of manufacturing employment to a level that is now almost 100,000 higher than in 1961 – an outcome inconceivable back in the 1960s.

SERVICES

But what is perhaps not generally realised is that this industrial growth has generated a quite remarkable expansion of employment in business services – which includes such sectors as banks, insurance companies, other financial institutions, and the business-oriented professions, such as accountancy, law, engineering, architecture, advertising, and auctioneering. Since 1961 the number of such jobs has more than trebled, rising by almost 100,000, from less than 40,000, to about 135,000.

COMPETITION

Dermot McAleese comments on the wasted efforts that were all too often put into negotiating safeguards and temporary derogations for import-substituting industries which had no long-term survival prospects. He has also remarked on our

> tendency to side with the more protectionist stance of the Mediterranean states rather than with the liberalism of the UK and the Low Countries …Irish policy-makers were not inclined to rock the boat in protected public utilities where producers' priorities, mainly the trade union and management, ruled supreme …Liberalisation tended to be labelled Thatcherite and automatically condemned.

I have to agree that all that is largely true, but two points are worth making in this connection.

First of all, the need for competition among those supplying electricity and gas, as well as in areas such as insurance, banking, and building, was in fact recognised as long ago as 1967. For in that year the National Industrial Economic Council published a report on how we should tackle the task of securing full employment. The Council suggested that there should be procedures for referring lack of competition in such areas to the Fair Trade Commission.[2]

The fact that nothing was done about these problems during the following quarter of a century was thus not because the need for action had not been publicly identified by industrialists, trade unionists and the civil service. As in so many other cases our considerable ability to identify problems and to point to how they might be resolved was simply not matched by an equivalent willingness to take possibly unpopular action to resolve them.

However, while Dermot McAleese may well be right in saying that competition was eventually introduced only reluctantly into telecommunications, banks and insurance, I must assert that this was not the case, as he has suggested, with air transport. The decision in 1986 to license Ryanair as a competitor with Aer Lingus was taken by Jim Mitchell on its own merits, putting Ireland, with Britain and the Netherlands, in the forefront of the move towards competition in air transport. And more recently Mary O'Rourke liberalised an important element of telecommunications a year ahead of the EU deadline.

Such good deeds, however few in number, deserve to be recognised!

Dermot McAleese is right, however, in giving the EU credit for the belated restraint of Irish government interventions in seeking to save lame ducks – interventions of the kind also occasionally undertaken, it must be said, by Thatcherite governments, such as that led by Margaret Thatcher herself!

The truth is that democratic national governments tend to be subject to such strong pressure from vested interests within their own territories that many of their decisions operate against the interests of society as a whole. The sharing of sovereignty at EU level, where ultimate legislative decisions are made by the Council of Ministers but only on the basis of proposals made by the independent Commission, using its exclusive power of initiative, has greatly improved the capacity of European politicians to govern in the public interest.

I recognise that this may not be a popular view, for many people are reluctant to recognise the vulnerability of parliamentary democracy to pressures from interest groups. These pressures may take the form either of mobilisation of a block of single-issue voters in support of their own narrow self-interest or, even more undesirably, of financial support for a political party or parties. At

European level such pressures are greatly diluted and much less dangerous.

That is not to dismiss the reality of a democratic deficit at the European level – or to dispute the desirability of filling this deficit, for example by empowering the Parliament both to determine the composition of the Executive – the European Commission – and to change that composition as the membership of the Parliament itself shifts in response to movements in public opinion. But, as and when such a democratic constitutional reform is carried through, the European system emerging from this reform will still remain better-equipped than our national systems to withstand pressure from interest groups in favour of policy decisions that would support the private interests of specific groups as against the general public interest.

EMU

Dermot McAleese's analysis of the debate on EMU is particularly useful in setting out the often overlooked arguments against staying out of EMU. I have to say that I have never understood why so many Irish economists have been so strongly opposed to Irish participation in EMU. The argument about the dangers of adverse consequences flowing from future EMU/Sterling fluctuations have always seemed to me to have been exaggerated and over-influenced by the experience of 1992, which was clearly quite exceptional.

The likelihood of a repetition of those events in post-EMU conditions has always seemed too small to be allowed to determine our whole future. And the suggestion that we should pass up the long-term benefits of much lower interest rates just because in our case the timing of the reduction is less than ideal, smacks equally of a short-termism that is uncharacteristic of the economists' profession. Moreover, the failure to give adequate weight to the downside of staying out has also been hard to understand.

ECONOMIC GAINS FROM MEMBERSHIP – ACCESS TO THE EU MARKET

In Ireland's case the most important single benefit of membership has been the most obvious: access to the huge EU market.

It has to be said that the advantage we would gain from such access for non-agricultural products was grossly underestimated during the run-up to membership. Throughout the 1960s our tax incentives and industrial grants had, of course, been attracting industry to Ireland, helping to sustain a growth rate 50 per cent higher than that of Britain and only slightly lower than that of the six-member EEC of that period. But most of the firms investing here at that time had come from other parts of Europe, mainly Britain and Germany but also the Netherlands and France – and there was then insufficient realisation of our potential as an English-speaking EC Member State to attract firms outside the Community, e.g. from countries such as the United States and Japan.

The educational revolution that has since quadrupled numbers in secondary and higher education had begun only in 1968, and at the time we joined the Community had yet to produce results in the form of a greatly expanded flow of well-educated labour. No one foresaw the scale of investment we would eventually draw, from the United States in particular, as an English-speaking member of the EU with a well-educated work-force, a ten per cent Corporation tax rate, and, latterly, a pattern of moderate pay increases and fiscal conservatism.

Before we acceded to the EEC, domestic industry was so strongly oriented towards the home market – and in the case of a minority of firms the British market – that its potential for exports to Continental EEC countries was grossly underestimated. In 1965, as Consultant to the Federation of Irish Industries, I carried out a survey of domestic industry's expectations in the context of EEC membership. Grossing up the responses I found that domestic Irish industry expected to be able, under free trade conditions, to increase its exports of goods to Continental EEC countries by only £6m – the equivalent of about £50m in today's money terms!

But in 1996 Irish-owned firms actually exported about £1,350m-worth of goods to Continental EU countries, – that is, 27 times the figure forecast three decades earlier. Two years ago these exports were giving employment to about 12,500 Irish workers.

Naturally, the gross underestimation of the industrial potential that was eventually unleashed by accession was paralleled by a similar underestimation of the multiplier effect of this export-led industrial growth upon other sectors of the economy, through sub-contracting, purchases of materials and services, factory construction and, of course, the enormously increased spending by workers of their wages and salaries.

Moreover, as Dermot McAleese points out, the fact that our growth has been export-led has ensured that even when, as during the past five years, consumer demand has been strongly boosted by increased employment, our external payments have remained in surplus.

Of course, if the growth of our labour supply had remained at the

EU level of about one per cent per annum, we would have been quite unable to satisfy the demand for Irish labour in Ireland that has been created by the opening of the Continental EU market to goods made here: even with the high productivity increases deriving from the inflow of high-tech firms, our growth rate in recent years could not have exceeded 4.5% to 5%. It is the fact that, for quite unrelated reasons, the growth of our labour supply in the mid-1990s has been running at four times the average EU rate that has made it possible to achieve – for a brief period – an 8% growth rate in the mid-1990s.

Four distinct factors have contributed to this demographic phenomenon, which has no parallel in the industrialised world. Two of these are unintended and unforeseen consequences of the conservative Roman Catholic ethos of earlier decades.

First, fidelity to Church teaching postponed until the second half of the 1960s the introduction of contraception to Ireland on any significant scale, with the result that our birth rate peaked in 1980, much later than elsewhere in Europe, giving us today 50 per cent more education leavers per capita of our population than in the rest of the Community. And, second, until around the same period, few married women worked outside the home, with the result that even today the flow of married women into the labour force from what is still a large pool of women engaged in 'home duties' is on a much larger scale than elsewhere.

These two sources of additional entrants to the job market are, moreover, currently being supplemented by a big movement into employment from the exceptionally large pool of unemployed that had accumulated between the late 1970s and 1993, as well as by a large flow of immigrants, both returning Irish emigrants and others with special skills that we lack, including foreign languages.

The first and third of these sources of additional labour flows into the employment market (from education and unemployment), are essentially quite temporary in character, with no more than a couple of years to run, while the second and fourth (women and immigration) are unlikely to continue indefinitely at their present rate. Thus, even if there were no world recession, reducing the scale of demand for Irish labour in Ireland, labour supply constraints will soon start to affect our exceptional growth rate. And these constraints will create dangerous inflationary pressures unless we have the wisdom to do what has hitherto been unthinkable, viz. take steps to reduce what will soon become an excessive and unfulfillable demand for Irish labour in Ireland.

NEGATIVE FACTORS – CHANGES IN THE CAP
AND STRUCTURAL FUNDS

The economic benefits of membership that loomed so large at the outset – the CAP and Structural Funds – will from now on be of diminishing importance, and will indeed in both cases face us with problems of readjustment.

So far as the Structural Funds are concerned, the difficult part of the adjustment will be psychological – weaning the electorate from the milch-cow state of mind that has been such a depressing feature of Irish attitudes in the early decades of membership of the Community. Even making full allowance for a reduction in our present exceptional rate of economic growth, replacing these phasing-out funds from our own domestic resources should pose no insuperable economic problem – although it will call for long-term planning of a kind for which our public administration and our political system have hitherto demonstrated a depressing lack of enthusiasm.

The readjustment of Irish agriculture to the regime of global free trade towards which we seem to be moving will be a much more difficult task – in economic and political terms as well as psychologically. There will be a strong political temptation to succumb to populist pressures to resist inevitable changes, instead of seeking intelligently to channel these changes along constructive lines that will secure the survival of a viable Irish rural economy in conjunction with a radically transformed agricultural sector.

Such a transformed farm sector will have to be capable of selling its products at market prices in a global economy within which these prices, while higher than world market prices today, will, because of the removal of the present distortions of competition, certainly be much lower than those to which European farmers have hitherto become accustomed.

CONCLUSION

Thus, we face a challenging future. But we should do so with some confidence. After all, we have an administrative and political system which – with one, admittedly very serious, exception twenty years ago – has over three decades been successful in combining ten changes of government within the space of 30 years with a consistency of key economic policies, the outcome of which is the envy of the rest of our Continent.

Contending with the problems of success in an admittedly rapidly changing European context should not be beyond the capacity of such a system.

1. FitzGerald, *The Irish Times*, 29.12.1965 – 41/1966.
2. National Industrial Economic Council Report No. 18, March 1967, p. 77.

PUBLIC
ADMINISTRATION

CHAPTER 10

Rapid Adaptation and Light Co-ordination

Brigid Laffan

INTRODUCTION

Membership of the European Union in 1973 represented the continuation of an Irish foreign policy tradition favouring multilateralism dating from the foundation of the state. Participation in the Commonwealth, the League of Nations, the Organisation for European Economic Co-operation (OEEC), the United Nations (UN) and the Council of Europe signalled a preference for multilateral institutions. However, the EU represented a radically new environment for the state and its civil service because Ireland had not been party to the economic groupings which emerged at the end of the 1950s in Europe. The impact of the EU on the domestic polity, economy and society was likely to be profound. The aim of this chapter is to explore the impact of EU membership on Ireland's system of public administration.

Since the first of January 1973, Irish civil servants operate in a dual framework, the national and the European. While remaining formally the servants of the Irish state, they are also servants of the EU collective system, committed to engage in shared governance with their partners in the other Member States. Civil servants were among the first to face the tension and the challenge of operating in a highly complex and multilevel system of policy-making. This tension emerges clearly in Bobby McDonagh's account of the negotiation of the Amsterdam Treaty in which he emphasises that policy-making in the Union is engaged in by people who continue to think largely in national terms and that 'the pursuit of national interests remains at the heart of the European Union'. McDonagh acknowledges, however, the possibility that the national interest of the Member States 'can be transformed slowly so that it is seen increasingly as embracing the wider European interest'. (McDonagh, 1998, p.15). National interests and preferences continue to have a privileged position in the Union but are framed in an entirely new political and institutional context. The very fact that all of the Member States, in their self-interest, constructed and developed the EU as a co-operative arena, limits the extent to which states can pursue their self-interest at the expense of their partners and the system as a whole. By joining the EU, states submit to a mutual vulnerability and shape their preferences and interests within an extended political space. The national and the European become entangled in the iterative process of EU policy-making. Ireland's position as a small state in the system carries with it the need to build coalitions with one's partners and with EU institutions. Standing alone or being an outlier is neither wise nor comfortable in the coalition politics that dominate the EU.

CHARACTERISTICS OF THE EU

In order to reflect on the impact of the EU on the Irish civil service, it is useful to sketch the most important characteristics of the Union which have reshaped the civil service environment. These are:
- the unsettled and evolving nature of the Union in terms of its constitutional framework, institutional balance, decision rules, geographical boundaries and range of policies. The unsettled nature of the Union poses a constant challenge to the national systems because they have to manage a dynamic and fluid environment. The pace of change has accelerated since the mid-1980s with big projects such as the internal market, the single currency, the Delors I and II packages, and developments in justice and home affairs.
- the EU's institutional system has become much more dense during the period of Ireland's membership. There are now many more Council compositions, working parties, comitology committees and Commission advisory committees, in addition to European agencies, observatories and a continuous stream of conferences. The system has become more demanding of national governments and administrations, with more and more national groups drawn into the Brussels web. (See Table 1.)
- Growing institutionalisation has been accompanied by a widening policy scope over the last 25 years. There are now few areas of domestic public policy without a European dimension. It is not just that the range of EU policies has widened but that more significant areas of domestic policy are now the subject of deliberation in the EU system, notably, money, taxation, justice and home affairs. As the tentacles of the Union have spread, more sensitive issues have been drawn within its ambit.
- The EU process works to its own time-frames with Presidency cycles, a rhythm of Councils and European Councils, medium-term policy decisions with built-in reviews and sectoral programmes. The EU calendar imposes constraints on the

TABLE 1:
The Growing Density of the Union as a System of Governance

	1960	1975	1990	1994
Council Decisions	10	575	618	468
Council Compositions	7*	12	22	21
Council Working Groups	10	91	224	263
Council Sessions	44	67	138	98
Coreper+ WG Sessions	602	2,215	2,218	2,789
Comitology Committees	–	93	297	409

* 1967 figures.
Source: Forward Studies Unit, Tables for Integration Indicators, August 1996.

amount of time that can be spent discussing and debating national strategy and preferences.
- The stuff of policy-making in the EU tends to be highly technical which places a premium on expert specialist knowledge. In the EU the 'devil is in the detail' as it is the nitty-gritty of legislation that matters during the implementation phase.
- The EU establishes an additional legal framework within which the government and its civil servants must operate. EC laws must be implemented within specified time-frames and if not, proceedings can be issued against the Irish state.
- The EU is an arena of continuous negotiations characterised by a shared commitment to collective outcomes. EU negotiations demand not just preparing assessments of national preferences and promoting them in Council, they also demand a commitment to serious negotiations with the other Member States with a view to finding common solutions. This implies knowledge of and a sympathy towards the interests and preferences of the other Member States. It also implies a willingness and an ability to assess when a particular dossier is ripe for decision and what concessions must be made. Given the extraordinary range of EU business and the intensity of EU negotiations, these kinds of judgements are being made on a continuous basis by Irish civil servants in working parties, COREPER and in advice to Ministers in Council.

The EU has fundamentally and radically altered the environment of Irish civil servants by adding an EU layer to government and politics in Ireland. Government may begin at home but it no longer ends there. Managing the interface between the national and the European is central to the core tasks of government and administration in contemporary Ireland. Implementing the EU's policy outcomes is part and parcel of the warp and weave of public administration. A cursory look at how departments list their functions on their web sites highlights the pervasive impact of EU membership on public policy-making in Ireland. How then has Ireland's system of public administration adapted to the demands and opportunities of EU membership?

THE FIRST PRESIDENCY:
AN EARLY APPRENTICESHIP

In the pre-accession period, attention was focused on negotiating the Accession Treaty and on the pre-membership referendum. Very little thought or attention was given to managing membership. The key consideration was the first of January 1973, not how the system could be lived with once Ireland was part of it. The Irish public administration had just two years to learn the rules of the EU game before it had to take responsibility for Ireland's first Presidency in 1975, and the first European Council in December of that year. One year after accession, the Minister for Foreign Affairs, Dr Garret FitzGerald, highlighted the resource problem when he concluded:

> The first ten months of Community membership have placed enormous strains on this country's human resources in the public service and in the many vocational bodies whose interests are affected by membership. We were simply not prepared for all that membership entails. In my own department the number of staff hitherto available for EEC work has fallen short by one-third of the absolute minimum to undertake this task in a manner that will safeguard Irish vital interests. (FitzGerald, 1973, p.2)

The resource shortage was ameliorated by the recruitment of additional staff to the Department of Foreign Affairs and in the home departments with a large EU responsibility. It is estimated that in the period 1973-80, between ten and twenty per cent of the posts created in the civil service arose as a result of EU membership (Scott, 1983). The 1975 Presidency served as the final apprenticeship in the nuts and bolts of the EU system because the Presidency is an EU office that carries responsibilities for the running of the system as a whole. The 1975 Presidency demonstrated that Ireland went beyond a narrow definition of its interests to embrace the wider European system. Dr FitzGerald in speeches at the time spoke also of the psychological benefits of membership in the following terms:

> For those of us who have in one way or another the task of representing Ireland's interests in the Community, there is, of course, the exhilaration of finding ourselves, at last, participating fully and on an equal footing with our partners in efforts to organise, run and develop the Economic Community itself. (FitzGerald, 1974)

Twenty-five years of membership perhaps may have dimmed that early exhilaration which was copper-fastened by the successful 1975 Presidency.

ORGANISING FOR BRUSSELS

By and large, EU business was grafted onto the pre-existing pattern of public policy-making in Ireland through a process of what might be called 'internalisation'. Because of the political consensus in Ireland on Europe and the high level of support for membership in the first referendum, Irish civil servants did not face the challenge of participating in EU policy-making in a hostile political or parliamentary environment. They did not have to control, disguise or attempt to contain the impact of EU policy at national level. Rather, successive governments and the senior civil service were largely free to chart Ireland's course in the EU. The political consensus and the weaknesses of the parliamentary committee system in Ireland led, however, to weak parliamentary oversight of EU business.

Irish administrative adaptation is based on the primacy of the 'lead department' in so far as the individual departments are responsible for those areas of EU policy that fall within their functional competence. The impact of the EU is thus uneven across the system with some departments entrenched in the Union's policy processes and others with an uneven and more intermittent interest. A distinction needs to be made between the overarching, multi-sectoral and sectoral departments. The Departments of Foreign Affairs, Finance and the Taoiseach are the main overarching departments. The Department of Finance had the longest tradition of involvement in EU business dating from the early 1960s, whereas the Department of Foreign Affairs was transformed by membership. The role of the Taoiseach's department was accentuated by the development and growing importance of the European Council. From the beginning, the Department of Agriculture was the main sectoral department affected by membership, but is now one of many embedded in the EU's policy process. What is now called the Department of Enterprise, Trade and Employment has major EU responsibilities across a range of EU policies. (See Table 2.) With the exception of the Department of Defence, all departments of state have been gradually brought within the ambit of the Union's policy processes.

The primacy of the 'lead department' reflects Irish administrative culture that accords considerable latitude to the sectoral ministries, notwithstanding the doctrine of collective responsibility and the role of the Cabinet in co-ordinating public policy. Segmentation at national level is exacerbated by the fragmented nature of the Council system. The principle of 'lead department' breaks down when an issue has implications for a number of government departments or has no obvious home in the domestic administration. For example, environmental taxes clearly involve Environment, Finance, and Enterprise and Employment, and views are likely to differ across these departments on the merits of such taxes. Hence processes are needed to deal with issues that cross sectoral or interdepartmental

TABLE 2:
Ministerial Involvement in the Council of Ministers

Council	Irish Minister/Department	Council Meetings in 1994
Foreign Affairs	Foreign Affairs	16
Agriculture	Agriculture	11
ECOFIN	Finance	11
Budget	Finance	2
Internal Market	Trade and Tourism	3
Environment	Environment	4
Research	Enterprise and Employment	4
Industry	Enterprise and Employment	4
Transport	Transport, Energy	4
Development	Foreign Affairs	2
Social Affairs	Enterprise and Employment Social Welfare	4
Fisheries	The Marine	5
Energy	Transport, Energy and Communication	2
Consumer Affairs	Enterprise and Employment	2
Health	Health	3
Culture	Arts, Culture and the Gaeltacht	2
Justice and Home Affairs	Justice	4

Source: Ireland (1996), p. 343 and Hayes-Renshaw F. and Wallace H., 1996, *The Council of Ministers,* London: Macmillan, p. 30.

boundaries. Co-ordination is necessary to ensure coherence in national policy in relation to the 'history-making decisions' or the 'grand bargains' which are made in the system from time to time. Over the past decade the 'history-making decisions' have included the internal market, the Single European Act (SEA), Delors I, the Treaty on European Union (TEU), Delors II and, more recently, the Agenda 2000 negotiations.

Co-ordination is achieved at the apex of the Irish system by the Cabinet which is responsible for the broad thrust of public policy. It deals with European issues much as it manages domestic issues with memoranda from individual ministers tabled for consideration. The Irish Cabinet system seems not to be buttressed by an extensive committee system. At an administrative level, day-to-day co-ordination is the responsibility of the Economics Division of the Department of Foreign Affairs, which has a watching brief over all EU policies. The division is responsible for co-ordinating briefs for the General Affairs Council (GAC), the main co-ordinating council in the EU system and 'A points' on other Council agendas. An interdepartmental committee chaired by the Department of Finance co-ordinated the early applications for membership. The only change after accession was that the Department of Foreign Affairs assumed responsibility for chairing and providing administrative back-up to the European Communities Committee. This shift from Finance to Foreign Affairs was based on a decision in Cabinet that did not go uncontested by Finance.

The Committee was chaired by the Assistant Secretary responsible for the Economics Division in Foreign Affairs. It was inactive for a number of years in the mid-1980s (1983-85) and was ultimately replaced by a successor committee (March 1987) chaired by the Minister of State for European Affairs, Máire Geoghegan-Quinn attached to the Taoiseach's Department. The committee was essentially a committee of senior civil servants with a political chair, which met monthly and was responsible for the co-ordination of Ireland's approach to the strategic aspects of Community business at that time. In 1989, this committee became a planning committee, responsible for organisational and logistical functions in the run-up to the 1990 Irish Presidency. Its policy co-ordination functions were superseded by a Ministerial Group for the Presidency established by the then Taoiseach, Charles Haughey. Mr Haughey also established a Ministers and Secretaries Group (MSG) to co-ordinate the preparation of the National Plan for Delors I and to negotiate the Community Support Framework. This committee represented an institutional innovation by bringing together key cabinet ministers and senior officials. Once the Presidency was over, there was no standing mechanism for co-ordination at either Ministerial or senior official level, other than ad hoc co-ordination groups working on the IGCs and related dossier. In 1992, the Taoiseach Albert Reynolds re-established the Committee, this time under the chairmanship of Minister of State, Tom Kitt, hence the so-called Kitt Committee. This format has since been superseded by the Ministers and Secretaries Group (MSG) which took over responsibility for the preparations of the Irish Presidency in 1994-95. The MSG is currently (1999) the central co-ordinating mechanism and is serviced by a Group of Senior Officials (GSO) who prepare its work. The Committee meets on average once a month but has no pre-ordained cycle of meetings. There are also a number of inter-departmental groups dealing with such issues as Agenda 2000 and comitology, among others. The Irish system of inter-departmental co-ordination differs from those in the other Member States in being less institutionalised and less stable. The consequences of this for Ireland's policy style are discussed below.

A central feature of organising for Brussels is the role of the Permanent Representation Centre. The Representation is the control centre for Ireland's formal dealings with the Union's policy process. The Irish Centre consists of civil servants drawn from the Department of Foreign Affairs and all of the home departments that deal with Brussels. As the tentacles of EU policy spread, so too did the staffing of the Representation. The Permanent Representative and his Deputy are career diplomats who, in addition to managing the internal running of the Representation, are Ireland's representatives on COREPER 1 and 2. Since 1973, Ireland has had five Permanent Representatives in Brussels and a number of those have served also as deputies in the Representation. At present Foreign Affairs has twelve staff in Brussels, Finance (3), Enterprise, Trade and Employment (5), Transport, Energy and Communications (3), Agriculture (2), the Revenue Commissioners (2), Health (1), Social Welfare (1), the Environment (1), Marine (1) and Justice (1). In 1999, there were 32 administrators in contrast to 22 in 1978. Apart from Luxembourg, Ireland has the smallest Representation.

Although formally, the pathway for information and instructions from Dublin to Brussels should pass through the Department of Foreign Affairs, the domestic civil servants in Brussels tend to deal directly with their home departments, while keeping Foreign Affairs informed. Civil servants at the Representation exercise a Janus-like role between the EU and the domestic. They are primarily responsible for ensuring that Irish interests and preferences are put forward in the policy process but they are also a critical source of intelligence on the attitudes of the other Member States and on the flow of negotiations. They are well placed to advise Dublin on when a deal looks like coming to fruition and when concessions must be made. The Representation is also the 'early-warning' nucleus of the system. Officials in the Representation Centre must establish good working relations with the Irish Cabinet, Commission services, other representations and the Council Secretariat because such relations are the key to successful outcomes in the negotiations.

IRELAND'S POLICY STYLE IN EUROPE

Ireland's policy style in Europe is influenced by its size, political and administrative resources, state tradition and culture. By and large, Ireland has adapted to the political and administrative demands of the Union, although the character of its involvement has been influenced by the small size of the Irish bureaucracy and personnel shortages over the last ten years. European public policy-making is managed much like domestic policy-making within the same standard procedures, norms and rules of the game. The style is consensual, collegial and pragmatic, with a marked emphasis on those areas of Union policy that are regarded as vital to Ireland — agriculture, the budget, Structural Funds, taxation and EU regulations that might affect Ireland's competitive position. The resources of the civil service have been heavily focused on the key policy areas. Ireland's style owes much to the intimacy of the senior echelons of the Irish civil service and the ease of personal contact. Interests can be identified and aggregated with relative ease. How then does Ireland position itself in the EU's policy process? There are three key features of Ireland's approach.

The Commission as 'best friend'?

Protection and promotion of the role of the Commission is a key feature of Ireland's approach to the EU. This is not to suggest that relations are always smooth and cosy between Ireland and the Commission, rather that the overall approach is one of support for the Commission. This stems from a realisation that the Commission is influential at the early phase of the policy process and that it is more likely than any Member State or group of states to adopt a policy approach that meets the concerns of all states. Persuading the Commission about the merits of one's argument and ensuring that it is knowledgeable about domestic circumstances, are central to obtaining outcomes that can be lived with. The establishment of good working relations with key Commission officials in the cabinets and in the Directorates-General is part of the management of EU business. Hence the emphasis in Irish policy of maintaining a member in the College of Commissioners. A former Secretary General of the Commission, M. Emile Noel recounted that the Irish approach to the Commission dates from the accession period when he claimed that 'The Irish delegation knew the important overall advantages that would result from accession, and had realised the role the Commission might play, particularly in relation to the Community's small and medium-sized countries, as an impartial interlocutor, willing to take their problems and difficulties into account. It was accordingly along with the Commission that the transition periods and special clauses in favour of Ireland were detailed, and the Commission applied its efforts to getting them accepted by the six.' (Noel, 1993) This pre-accession approach survived in the post-membership environment.

Notwithstanding the identification of the Commission as 'best friend', there have been periods of considerable conflict and tension with the Commission. The 'eight-billion saga' in 1992-93 is one such episode. The then Taoiseach, Albert Reynolds, interpreted the Edinburgh deal as amounting to a doubling of the flow of Structural Funds to Ireland for the duration of the planning period, eight billion pounds or 13.5 per cent of the funds. This claim became embroiled in the domestic negotiations about government formation and in the implementation of the agreement for government. DG 16 and Commissioner Millan made it clear that on objective socio-economic grounds, Ireland could not anticipate a figure of eight billion pounds and the Taoiseach would not accept a penny less. The Taoiseach's stance was based on the fact that he had the support and agreement of the Commission President, Jacques Delors. Ireland threatened agreement on the entire package unless it got what it considered to be a fair deal from the EU. Fergus Finlay, programme manager to the Minister for Foreign Affairs, Dick Spring, gave a graphic account of the negotiations in Brussels on 20 July 1993 over the share-out of the funds. The long night involved brinkmanship by the Foreign Minister, Dick Spring, mediation by the Irish Commissioner and a telephone call to the Taoiseach to ensure that he could live with the deal. Ireland was offered what was called a *furchette*, an upper and lower limit with a maximum of IEP 7.85 billion (Finlay, 1998, p. 177).

The transaction, although concluded by a hand-shake between Dick Spring and Jacques Delors, was not written in stone. In the event, Ireland got 6.5 billion, the level considered equitable by DG16 using objective socio-economic criteria. During this episode, Ireland's relations with the Commission, particularly DG 16, were strained and a considerable amount of political and administrative capital was deployed to little effect. The Irish had failed to track the changing balance of power within the Commission and the degree to which DG16 was reducing the margin of political manoeuvre on the distribution of aid by using a set of standard indicators.

Getting the Tactics Right

The Irish system is largely reactive and agenda driven. The focus is on influencing Commission proposals at the preparatory stage and as they wind their way through the Council hierarchy. This involves entering reservations to those aspects of the proposal that are not viewed with favour, seeking alliances with like-minded states, ensuring derogations where possible, and changing the wording of a proposal to suit Irish circumstances. If a drafting solution will suffice, then this is the favoured strategy, followed by derogations and so on. Irish negotiators seek to get the tactics of negotiations right by talking to the Commission and like-minded states rather than devoting energy to position papers which would attempt to fundamentally alter the Commission's original proposal. Garret FitzGerald's memoirs provide an illustrative example of how one gets the tactics of EU negotiations right. A Foreign Affairs Council was addressing the issue of better access for Iberian products under the EU's Mediterranean policy, an area of little interest to Ireland. The only Irish interest was the early onion crop from Castlegregory, Co. Kerry, which needed an extra fortnight of protection each year beyond what was proposed by the Commission, to dispose of its crop before competing onions would be allowed in from Spain. Dr FitzGerald, then Foreign Minister, describes how:

> Throughout the long and tedious debate I remained silent on this issue, calculating that my best chance of securing the extra fortnight was to wait until the final package was ready and then to whisper in the ear of the President ... a last minute request. He would, I felt, be so grateful to me for having refrained from adding to his troubles over two difficult days that he would be prepared to slip our onion fortnight into the package at the last moment, without anyone even noticing. My manoeuvre succeeded. Castlegregory was saved without a word being spoken by me at the Council meeting. (FitzGerald, 1992, p.143)

The pattern of voting in the Council suggests that Irish policy-makers tend to steer a middle course in negotiations, not wanting to find themselves as outliers when negotiations edge towards agreement in any one area. This strategy is based on the understanding that if you vote against a proposal you get no concessions, whereas if you are part of the winning coalition, you will get something from the negotiations. An analysis by the European Institute of Public Affairs (EIPA) in Maastricht seems to bear this out. One of its reviews suggests that Ireland 'has an almost legendary status as a country which consistently succeeds in winning favourable outcomes from EU programmes' (Kelly, 1995, p.5). The explanation for this is that in negotiations it 'is almost always clear what the Irish demands are, and what scope exists for negotiation' (ibid.). Furthermore, 'the Irish negotiating position is almost always clearly established in advance, and that Irish delegations are confident in accepting or rejecting compromises' (ibid.). Because of Ireland's economic benefits from the EU, successive governments have felt the need to contribute to the business of the Union where possible, notably by running good Presidencies of the Council. And by being reasonably *communautaire* on most agenda issues, the Irish are then prepared to 'go it alone' on issues that are deemed vital, such as the milk superlevy negotiations in 1983.

Relatively Light Co-ordination

Cabinet and interdepartmental co-ordination is less institutionalised, more informal and less paper-driven than systems in the other Member States. In most administrations there is a 'Bible of European Procedures' which sets out the formal system for the management of EU business. In Ireland, there are a number of administrative circulars and a series of decisions by Government which are not codified. The system of Cabinet and interdepartmental co-ordination is largely reactive and agenda driven with ad hoc groups established when the agenda requires. The Ministers and Secretaries Group (MSG) and its preparatory group of senior officials represents an attempt to upgrade co-ordination given the big history-making decisions in the making. The MSG meets at most once a month whereas such committees in most other Member States meet weekly and are buttressed by an array of standing inter-ministerial committees. The practice in Ireland is to establish ad hoc Cabinet and inter-departmental committees to manage discrete negotiations or the Presidency when the need arises. Administrative departments are left to manage areas that fall within their jurisdiction, unless a particular issue has cross-departmental implications or a major package deal is being negotiated. The 'lead department' in Ireland is more influential than its equivalent in other Member States where there are stronger countervailing pressures and processes.

THE IMPACT OF THE EU ON GOVERNMENT IN IRELAND

The Working Environment

Membership of the EU altered the working environment of Irish diplomats and civil servants by breaking down the barrier between the internal and external, between the domestic and the international. The EU created a political and administrative milieu which is neither domestic nor international but an admixture of both. A former Secretary of the Department of Agriculture, Donal Creedon, said that 'The European dimension brought extraordinary excitement to administration and to the civil service' (McNamara, 1990, p.71). Visits to the Commission, servicing comitology committees and Council working parties became internalised in the day-to-day, week-to-week lives of Irish civil servants. The train from Gare Centrale to Zaventam is now part and parcel of their weekly routines. A piece by Olivia O'Leary in *The Irish Times* in 1979 describes the process: 'you take the evening plane to Brussels after work. Prepare for the next day's meeting in your hotel-room (Brussels can be a dull place to visit unless you overeat a little like the Belgians, or overdrink a little, like the Irish). Hope they reach your item on the agenda next day. Otherwise, you'll be back again next week, or next month.' (*The Irish Times*, 31 September 1979) The novelty of Brussels soon wore off, it simply became part of the weekly or monthly routine.

The EU had an impact on the rigid hierarchy which characterised Irish bureaucracy and on the processing of files. There was a time when each file made its way slowly up the hierarchy, with checks at each level, until it reached the Secretary who was the only channel of communication to the Minister. The demands of EU policy-making, both in terms of time and paper work, meant that there had to be greater delegation of responsibility downwards and less checking at each level of the hierarchy. Irish civil servants had to go beyond committing their thoughts to paper and had to develop the skills necessary to represent Ireland's position at meetings in Brussels. Furthermore, civil servants in a widening range of policy fields have had to become familiar with the policies, practices and interests of their EU partners. They have had to become open to policy approaches and institutional procedures emanating from the EU and the Member States. It required going beyond Whitehall as a source of policy inspiration. The EU arena became a major source of policy initiative and policy ideas in many areas of public policy.

Participation in the Union altered the career environment of civil servants by opening up the possibility of working in the Commission or Parliament, Commission cabinets, the Permanent Representation and in EU-related divisions in the home departments. There are considerable numbers of civil servants on special leave to the Commission Services or working as national experts. In addition, service in the Permanent Representation provides an additional career opportunity for home civil servants. European expertise emerged as a distinctive and prized area of specialisation within the civil service. It is not uncommon to find civil servants who have been in Brussels managing a key area of EU policy back in Dublin. For example, one of the main officials managing the Agenda 2000 negotiations in the Department of Finance served in the Representation from 1992 to 1996. Given the nature of the EU process, which places a premium on insider knowledge and technical expertise, such specialisation is necessary if Ireland is to manage the demands of the EU system. The Centre for Management and Organisation Development (CMOD) regularly runs induction courses on the EU, with specialised courses to prepare officials for the Presidency. For the civil servants, who are drawn into the Brussels web, the impact goes far beyond career paths: they work and live in a multilingual and multicultural environment mixing socially with their counterparts from the other Member States. The most effective officials are clearly those who are at home in such a multicultural transnational environment.

Impact on Processes of Public Policy-making

Although the EU dimension has been in large measure grafted onto the processes and procedures of domestic policy-making, it has been a source of change and experimentation. The operation of the structural funds and the Community Support Framework (CSF) have had a significant and beneficial impact on policy-making in a number of different respects. When the Delors 1 plan was launched in 1988, public investment in Ireland had been sharply reduced in an effort to bring the public finances under control. The availability of CSF monies provided a window of opportunity for the development of long-term projects, although there were undoubted tensions between the Structural Fund Division in the Department of Finance and the Public Expenditure Division, which was more concerned with debt control than spending. The process of programming which was central to the reform of the funds in 1988 has strengthened the strategic dimension of public policy-making by forcing government and the administration to prioritise across key elements of economic planning and infrastructural provision. The operation of the CSF required an elaborate system of monitoring committees at national level and for each sector. This brought the Commission and many of the interested groups into a monitoring relationship with central government. The first CSF enhanced the multi-annual dimension of the Irish public finances and allowed for medium-term plans, rather than an over-reliance on the annual budgetary process. This was a major contributor to the development of a medium-term budgetary perspective. According to the report of the Assistant Secretaries who examined civil service reform in Australia and New Zealand:

> A multi-year budget helps to give greater coherence and certainty to programmes, allowing implementing agencies to take a more strategic approach. It also allows government to look at the broad trust of future policies and priorities away from the set-piece battles of the annual estimates' process. (Byrne et al., 1995, p. 111)

Pressure from the Commission led to the development of evaluation units in a number of government departments with major CSF budgets. These were followed by an overall evaluation unit for the CSF attached to the Department of Finance. The focus on evaluation stemmed from a desire to ensure that best practice would permeate the system.

The EU has had an ambiguous impact on territorial politics in Ireland. The Commission's support for partnership as a principle of government began to loosen the highly centralised nature of Irish public policy-making and add a territorial and not just sectoral element to the operation of the Structural Funds. The original regional structures established in 1988 were largely an administrative expedient that added a weak regional layer to the implementation of the CSF, and thereby satisfied the Commission. However, the resurgence of community groups in Ireland and the need to tackle the development blackspots led to a renewed focus on the local in the second national plan. Community initiatives such as Leader, the area-based partnerships, and the county enterprise boards all reinforced the territorial dimension of development but were not in themselves capable of giving Ireland sustainable local and regional government. The organisation of sub-national government in Ireland has been the subject of more consultative papers than any other aspect of government but one that has never been tackled with political energy and capacity. The current debate on regionalisation displays an underlying attitude of expediency towards the institutional fabric required for good government below the level of central government. The management of the Structural Funds which was contained within the narrow confines of central government and the large state-sponsored bodies has evolved to include diffuse interests including local authorities, community groups, environmental groups, and the social partners, all in search of a slice of the Brussels pie. EU monies created a new kind of politics which encouraged people to look both below and beyond the state. Access to EU monies gave community groups additional authority and leverage vis-à-vis central government. On the other hand, the availability of EU largesse reinforced clientelism, a central feature of the Irish political culture (O'Toole, 1998). The experimental nature of the EU had an important impact on the willingness of the Irish public service to engage in experimentation and micro-social interventions.

The secular increase in regulations emanating from the EU had a major impact on the shaping of regulations in many areas of public policy, such as state aids, company law, telecommunications, environmental law and health and safety. In response to EU developments and the modernisation of the regulatory framework in Ireland, there was considerable institution-building with the establishment of the Employment Equality Agency, the Health and Safety Authority and the Environmental Protection Agency, for example. These agencies would have evolved without EU membership as Ireland was transformed from being an agricultural economy to an industrial and services one, but EU membership provided the regulatory context for these agencies and shaped their development. All of these agencies have extensive contact with the Commission and their counterparts in other Member States.

A BALANCE SHEET?

A cohesive and professional administrative culture, added to the ease of personal relations, meant that Irish officials and politicians adapted to the day-to-day interface with Brussels with relative ease. EU policy-making was a liberation from an over-concentration on Whitehall and Whitehall policy models. The EU provided opportunities for talented officials who became adept at operating in a multileveled and multicultural negotiating arena. It allowed them to operate beyond the confines of a small state and to contribute to a wider stage. Irish participants in the Brussels process have a reputation as good networkers, a useful skill in a highly fragmented and complex policy process. Ireland has been served by distinguished diplomats and civil servants who contributed not only to representing Ireland's interests, but who helped build the EU as an arena of public policy-making. By and large, the balance sheet of 25 years of membership is extremely positive for public administration in Ireland. If, however, this review was taking place ten years ago, it might not be so positive. In the early 1980s, there was considerable debate about Ireland's performance and a pervasive sense of Ireland's failure. Professor Joe Lee, in a number of different pieces, gave a robust account of Ireland's failure and he accorded some of the responsibility for this to the public service arguing that an 'exceptionally wide gap exists in Ireland between the potential and the performance of our public services'. (Lee, 1985, p.3) Tom Garvin in a piece on Irish democracy spoke of short-term opportunism at the expense of long-term thinking, of a tendency to discount the future because the 'environment and the future are left to God rather than man's ability to manipulate them'. (Garvin, 1989, p. 47)

In 1984, Professor Lee analysed the performance of the civil service in the Brussels arena and drew a distinction between the negotiating skills of Irish officials and the calibre of their conceptualisation. He concluded that 'The agile negotiator will appear the more effective performer. And the "political" skills of Irish representatives in negotiating situations are widely acknowledged. But there seems to be no comparable criterion for assessing the calibre of conceptualisation of the Irish case before negotiations begin at all. The Irish fight their ground well. Whether they choose the right ground on which to fight remains more conjectural.' (Lee, 1984, p.5) Lee went on to offer a critique of the Irish civil service and the intellectual infrastructure for dealing with Europe. He identified what he called the dead-weight of seniority, a lack of mobility, a weakness of language competence and to what he called the fair supply of 'negative personalities' in the Irish civil service (Lee, 1984, p.6-7). He lamented the over-reliance on Whitehall models and the absence of any thinking about continental administrative models, such as a cabinet system. He was scornful of the beggar-bowl mentality, Ireland's weakness in strategic thinking and the absence of a distinctive Irish contribution to the development of the EU.

Both Lee and Garvin were writing at a time when Ireland was experiencing political turbulence, with three elections in eighteen months, strife within the major political party, a public finance crisis, a deteriorating situation in Northern Ireland and, even, moving statues. The circumstances of the time coloured views of Ireland's performance but also highlighted the need for Ireland to find cultural and institutional solutions to the acute crisis of the early 1980s.

Irish society and the body polity had the resources to search for and find devices to address the failure of this period. Those involved were motivated by the high costs of failure. Many different strands contributed to the transformation but a key role must be accorded to the development of the system of social partnership between the state and societal interests. This enabled successive governments to move beyond the short-termism and clientalism of the early 1980s, and to embed public policy in a consensual strategic environment. Finance Ministers of whatever political hue were converted to the ideology of sound public finances and stable money.

The National Economic and Social Council (NESC) provided the critical analysis of external and internal economic and social developments. The Tallaght strategy pursued by Alan Dukes in opposition ended a period of damaging adversarial politics.

During this period, Ireland developed a highly distinctive form of partnership with real strength which could now be mobilised as an Irish contribution to the European debate on competitiveness. Senior Irish civil servants played a critical and innovative role in the development of the partnership model and a quiet 'mandarin revolution' was set in train which would begin to tackle the criticisms of the system of public administration.

The EU and Reform of Irish Public Administration

Reform of Irish public administration is an intermittent issue on the Irish political agenda. The Devlin Report of 1969 coincided with Ireland's last push for EU membership but paid little attention to the demands of internationalisation. Devlin resulted in piecemeal and partial changes in the Irish system but its main proposals were never implemented. In the 1980s there was another attempt to modernise the Irish system with the publication of 'Serving the Country Better' in 1985.

This was the product of a Government decision developed by a Minister for the Public Service with a remit to promote reform. The report again resulted in little macro-reform because it was attempted at a time of severe cut-backs in the public finances which stymied innovation and clear sight.The change in Government in 1987 was a further blow to the process of reform. However, a number of changes were put in place that contributed to a process of cultural change in the bureaucracy.

From 1984 onwards, the secretaries of government departments began to hold an annual conference, which contributed to the development of an esprit de corps at this level. This was accompanied by the Top Level Appointments Committee which increased the level of interdepartmental mobility in the system and superseded the previous system which was based on seniority.

The practice of ministers having programme managers in the 1993-97 governments, furthermore, introduced external blood to departments and provided a useful preparatory forum for Cabinet discussions. The media debate on the programme managers with its undue focus on cost meant that the system was never assessed with a cold eye to see if its merits outweighed its undoubted costs.

The cultural changes in the 1980s, in addition to the deficiencies highlighted by the tribunals of enquiry and reports such as that of the Industrial Policy Review Group in 1991, placed reform back on the agenda. The 1994 Strategic Management Initiative (SMI) launched another process of reform in public administration. Responsibility for driving the SMI rests with the Departments of the Taoiseach and Finance, in addition to a Co-ordinating Group of Secretaries.

The most significant outcome of the reform process to date was the passage of the Public Service Management Act in 1997. All government departments have agreed strategy statements and are in the process of relating these statements to the establishment of priorities and to the allocation of staff resources internally. There are inevitable tensions between processes of fundamental review and the day-to-day work of administration. Given the overloaded nature of the policy process, arising partly from the EU, embedding the SMI in the Irish system is a difficult challenge. The SMI initiative is, however, necessary if Ireland is to manage the interface with Brussels in the long term.

The theme of this chapter so far is that Ireland adjusted with relative ease to the demands of participation in the 1970s but that it took it much longer to develop internal policies that would enable it to live with and benefit from involvement in the highly competitive market environment. This required cultural and institutional changes which inevitably took time.

The processes are still working themselves out in the Irish polity and the wider society. From the perspective of public administration, there are still gaps in the system of managing EU affairs.

Thinly Spread Human Resources

Managing major negotiations in the EU fall on the shoulders of very few people both in Foreign Affairs and in the home departments. The negotiating teams are thinly spread which means that those involved are overworked and confronted with very tight deadlines. Small numbers of people are responsible for working out global strategy and the approach for each discrete set of negotiations, while at the same time getting the government to focus and prioritise the key issues involved. The attitudes and approaches of the other Member States and the Commission must be constantly monitored and assessed in the dynamic of negotiations. This requires deep knowledge of the major issues involved, on the one hand, and command of the nitty-gritty, on the other. The outcome of the negotiations will depend in large measure on the quality of the political and official home work conducted in the domestic system.

Fiscal deficits forced cut-backs in the number of civil servants for many years in the 1980s, with the result that all departments and individual units came under considerable pressure and had to stretch existing resources still further. All of the smaller EU Member States – Belgium, Denmark, Finland, Greece, Portugal and Sweden – have twice the number of overseas missions and twice as many diplomats as Ireland. Yet this small service has had to adapt to a significant expansion in the work of the Union since the mid-1980s while its resources remained static. Equally, the number of civil servants working on European matters in the domestic ministries remains limited. This has meant that Irish civil servants service a wider range of committees than their counterparts in other Member States and, in turn, are responsible for the implementation of legislation once it is passed.

Because the Irish system is weakly institutionalised, enormous responsibility falls on small teams of people responsible for navigating the major dossier through the Council system. Thus, the calibre of individual officials matters more than it would in a better resourced and more elaborate system of administration.

Resource shortages affect implementation and not just policy-making. The enormous expansion in EU regulation that followed the Single Act put considerable strain on the Irish system. At the beginning of the 1990s, Ireland's implementation record, which was relatively good up to then, began to deteriorate. It took a number of years to improve the transposition of EU legislation into national law. Implementation difficulties were caused by staff shortages in the Attorney General's office and the sheer number of EC directives.

Late implementation can cost the government money if Irish nationals use the courts to seek judicial redress. For example, late implementation of a gender equality directive in social security in the 1980s led to successful legal challenges by a number of Irish women through the Irish and European legal systems.

The Co-ordination Conundrum

As already stated, the Irish system of co-ordination is less institutionalised and committee driven than any other state in the EU, apart from Luxembourg. This is both a strength and a weakness. On the positive side, the informal and personal nature of Irish administration and the wider culture, makes the Irish system less bureaucratic and inert than the systems in other countries. The predominant mode is to allow those responsible get on with the job without embedding them in an elaborate system of committees and tortured discussions. This system is probably well adapted to the shifting sands of EU negotiations and provides the flexibility that is always necessary in negotiations. Having a capacity to tack to the wind in negotiations is clearly an advantage. There are, however, a number of less positive dimensions to the Irish system. It is a system that may not always have a sufficiently proactive capacity to pick up on critical issues at an early stage in their development, within the Commission, for example. The thinness of the resources may lead to a focus on a small number of critical issues to the detriment of what might appear to be less important ones, in the short term. The lack of institutionalisation places a premium on good working relations between the key players involved. If these break down, the Irish system is not sufficiently institutionalised to neutralise the inevitable personal tensions that can arise within and between organisations. And there are always dangers in a system that allows a high degree of departmental autonomy. Policies and approaches can become fixed and rigid within an individual department and may not be in the overall national interest and public good. Countervailing pressures in the Irish system to the dominance of departmental autonomy are not sufficiently developed.

Public v Private Interests

The most damaging gaps in the Irish system of public management were exposed by the beef tribunal. The Common Agricultural Policy with its myriad of rules and regulations was an easy target for abuse and fraud. In addition, there was a perceived need among successive

Irish governments to bolster the capacity of Irish beef processors so that they could compete internationally. In the process, corrupt and very damaging relationships developed between a number of Irish politicians and private beef processors. In the process, what were private interests became defined and promoted as public interests, although as is clear from the beef tribunal these interests were breaking the laws of the land and of the EU, at a high cost to the Irish taxpayer. While the focus of the beef tribunal gave us an opportunity to witness the dark side of government/industry relations, it also exposed weaknesses in the management of the EU intervention system, and in the co-ordination and exchange of information between departments. The Department of Agriculture had a deeply ambivalent relationship with the Irish beef processing industry. In was aware, for a considerable length of time, that there were significant abuses of the intervention scheme in the meat factories but did not begin to stamp out these abuses until the issue was politicised. In relation to import licences under the GATT, when the regime changed in 1989, the department 'twice deliberately misled the EC Commission and broke both Irish and EC law' (O'Toole, 1995).

Re-positioning Ireland?

As this is one of the later contributions to this volume that was compiled to reflect on Ireland's experiences over the last 25 years, it is also appropriate to muse about the next phase of membership. Ireland is at present at a critical juncture in its relations with the EU because Ireland is changing and so too is the nature of the EU. The easy fit between Irish preferences and the broad balance of EU policies may not continue into the future. In fact, there is every sign that they will not. While responsibility for managing the process of change rests with the government and the wider political class, the civil service has a critical role to play in advising the government and in positioning Ireland in sub-Council negotiations. There are a number of distinct but interconnected strands to the changes taking place in the system. First, Ireland has caught up with EU average income levels in the 1990s and is no longer perceived as a poor peripheral state. For the foreseeable future, there will be many more poorer states demanding their share of EU solidarity. Second, the 'net contributors club' to the EU budget is now larger and more vocal than it has been in the past. Third, Ireland is a very successful competitor for job creation, with unemployment levels in Ireland falling below EU levels for the first time since membership.

This draws attention to Ireland's system of corporate tax which is seen as far too low in relation to continental corporate tax levels. The fact that, with the agreement of the Commission, corporate tax will be reduced in Ireland over the next four years is likely to cause further tension with Ireland's partners in Europe. The impact of the reduction on the domestic debate on taxation could well be to make it more difficult to maintain a social partnership approach to industrial relations. Fourth, Ireland unlike the other EU neutrals, will only belatedly join the Partnership for Peace, which has made it an outlier on European defence and security questions. For all of these reasons, Ireland has to chart its future in the EU in a new and less favourable context.

REFERENCES

Fitzgerald, F., text of address to European Movement Seminar, Dublin, 27 October 1973

FitzGerald, G., Text of address to Galway Chamber of Commerce, 11 January 1974

Garvin, Tom, (1989) 'Democracy in Ireland: Collective Somnambulance and Public Policy', *Administration*

Kelly M., 'The Irish Performance in the EU', *Seirbhís Phoiblí,* 15:1, 1995, pp.5-14

Lee J. (1984), *Reflections on Ireland in the EEC,* Dublin: ICEM

Lee J. (1985), 'A Third Division Team?', *Seirbhís Phoiblí,* 6:1, pp.3-8

McDonagh B., (1998) *Original Sin in a Brave New World,* Dublin, IEA

Noel E., (1993), 'Some thoughts on Ireland's Membership of the European Community', unpublished paper, 1 February

O'Leary O., (1979), 'The Road to Brussels', *The Irish Times,* 30-31 September

O'Toole F., (1995) *Meanwhile Back at the Ranch,* London:Vintage

CHAPTER 11

Serving in New Spheres

Sean Cromien

In the years after the Second World War, the Irish public administration began to reach out cautiously towards involvement in international organisations. Immediately at the end of the war, Ireland joined the organisation which was the vehicle for Marshall Aid, namely the OEEC (the Organisation for European Economic Co-operation), which later became the OECD (the Organisation for Economic Co-operation and Development). We joined the United Nations in 1955 and the IMF and World Bank in 1957. And then, in 1973, in the most dramatic step of all, we were admitted as a member of the European Economic Communities. This paper is an attempt to discuss the effects of this step on Irish public administration over the past 25 years.

Perhaps initially, Irish public officials, as I remember from my early years in the civil service, had something of an inferiority complex, or at least a sense of unease, in operating in an international milieu. This was not true, of course, of the officials of the Department of External Affairs (as it was at the time) but international affairs were, after all, their métier and they were expected to spend much of their working lives abroad, working closely with foreign officials. This was not so for other civil servants, who had infrequent contact, if any, with foreign administrations, had little experience of travel abroad and little knowledge of foreign languages.

How this has changed was brought home to me when I accompanied my Minister, Bertie Ahern, to a meeting of the ECO/FIN Council just before I retired in June 1994. In preparing for the meeting, I sat with the Minister and my colleagues at the corner of a table in a room in that overheated and uncomfortable office of the Permanent Representation on rue Galilée. As I did so, I glanced around and was struck to note that the Secretary of the Department of Agriculture and a group of his officials were briefing their Minister in another corner of the room; in a nearby room was the Secretary of the Department of the Marine doing the same for his

Minister, while the Minister for Foreign Affairs, with visiting officials from Dublin, breezed in for a General Affairs Council. This pattern is, of course, a daily event in the mission. The centre of administration for many Irish senior civil servants has moved for at least part of each month nowadays to Brussels or Luxembourg. How specifically has membership of the European Community and Union affected the public service in Ireland? I propose to examine this under three headings – the effect on policy choices, on the structure of Government departments and on civil servants as individuals.

EFFECT ON POLICY CHOICES

Perhaps the most dramatic effect on Irish public administration, as far as senior civil servants are concerned, has been the narrowing of policy choices available to them when they make recommendations to Ministers and the Government. In a Department such as Agriculture, it is obvious that most of the policies affecting Irish agriculture are now determined by the Irish Minister for Agriculture only in collaboration with his fellow EU Ministers in Brussels. The same is true, although in lesser degree, for many other Government departments while most, as Professor Laffan shows in her paper, are affected at least in some way – with, as she points out, the Department of Defence as the only exception.

Perhaps surprisingly, the Minister for Finance has found his policy options as progressively limited as other Ministers. I say 'surprisingly' because the power to tax is one that in every administration is very closely guarded as an assertion of a country's sovereignty, and taxation is, of course, an area where unanimity is required for Council decisions. These sensitivities were very obvious at discussions of Ministers for Finance at ECOFIN in the early 1990s, when proposals to harmonise taxes as part of the introduction of the Single Market were under discussion. Nevertheless, Member States have, over the years, accepted considerable limitations even in this area of decision-making and are discussing others. I need only mention the successful agreement to harmonise indirect tax rates in the Single Market; the current debate about company taxation and aids to industry; the debate on taxation of savings and so on. A further dimension will be added for Ministers for Finance when Ireland becomes a full member of the EMU on 1 January 2000 and shares a common currency with other Member States, with all that implies for surrendering control over interest rate changes, monetary policy and related matters.

The effect of all this is that, compared with civil servants in, say, the 1950s and 1960s, modern senior officials have all the time to accept that their policy options are now more restricted than heretofore. They have to be conscious of Community legislation and proposals, and aware that their recommendations, if accepted as Government policy, will be scrutinised by Commission officials to see if they are compatible with the intention of such legislation. I particularly remember in the late 1980s an agonising debate on how – within the ambit of Community legislation – the problem of people shopping in Northern Ireland could be handled. You will recall how something not unlike the great migrations of the Dark Ages took place at that time, when, because of differences of tax rates north and south, large numbers of shoppers travelled by bus every weekend from every corner of the country to Belfast and other Northern cities to take advantage of lower prices.

In mentioning this limitation of policy options, I am not to be understood as in any way to be regretting the change. There have been so many benefits of membership, as Professor McAleese's paper shows, that the price we have paid for pooling our sovereignty with other Member States has been a small one.

The truth, in any case, is that our apparent freedom to take independent action in the period before entry was illusory in many respects. A small country is always hampered in taking action independent of trends elsewhere. Before entry we were closely linked to the British economy through our currency and banking system, and actions we would have liked to take at certain times were restricted by this link. For instance, if the British authorities raised interest rates to combat inflationary pressures, we had to suffer the same high rates, even if they were not necessary in Ireland, because otherwise, investors would have moved their funds to Britain to take advantage of the differential.

Nowadays, indeed, with free movement of capital around the world and 24-hour banking in the global village, even the larger countries are quickly affected by international pressures. So far as EMU is concerned, we will at least have a voice, albeit a small one (although not an inconsiderable one if joined with that of other equally affected Member States), in influencing decisions of the Union which will have repercussions for us – which was not the case in our relationship with the UK in the 1950s and 1960s.

Dr Garret FitzGerald, in responding to Professor McAleese's paper, makes a provocative point about policy. He says:

The truth is that democratic national Governments tend to be subject to such strong pressure from vested interests within their own territories that many of their decisions operate against the interests of society as a whole. The sharing of sovereignty at EU level, where ultimate legislative decisions are made by the Council of Ministers but where the shape of the legislation upon which they vote is determined by the independent Commission, using its exclusive power of initiative, has greatly improved the capacity of European politicians to govern in the public interest.

While I have some hesitation in accepting this approach as a general proposition – Dr FitzGerald admits that his view may not be popular – I do agree that the introduction of the Maastricht guidelines, for example, was an enormous help to Finance officials, such as myself, in persuading Irish Governments to accept disciplines on public expenditure and borrowing which might otherwise have been too unpalatable for them to support. As in other areas of EU business, the reason why discipline was acceptable in this case was because there was something in it for Ireland: by keeping to the guidelines we became eligible for membership of the final stage of EMU.

While our political and administrative systems have been very successful in handling European matters, there has been one obvious deficiency. This is that it has proved very difficult to establish a way of appraising all the Community initiatives which are under consideration at any one time and deciding on an integrated national strategy for them, setting bargaining tactics and priorities, based on what is considered to be best for the country. Professor Laffan emphasises the fragmented nature of the Council system itself and says that this exacerbates segmentation at national level. It certainly has the disadvantage that each negotiation at ministerial level tends to be carried out at a separate Council. I am not sure that, even at Cabinet level, there has been a common vision of policy which would allow us, for example, to be less intransigent in negotiations at the Agriculture Council – if one could visualise such a thing being possible – in order to gain more support from other Member States or the Commission in bargaining for Structural Funds. The system does not seem to work that way.

EFFECT ON THE STRUCTURE OF GOVERNMENT DEPARTMENTS

The biggest effect on the structure of public administration has probably been the sheer volume of work that membership of the Community and Union has generated. As I have said above, every

Government department has been affected in one way or another, some fundamentally. The exact organisation of departments to take account of the new burden of work has evolved over the years, perhaps a little haphazardly. Initially, a small section dealing with EC matters was all that was needed, but eventually in all the bigger departments it became obvious that there were many areas of work which had themselves developed a European dimension. Each of these had to be kept aware of the effect of EC legislation on their work while increasing emphasis had to be placed on co-ordinating their efforts within the department.

While a lot of new duties arose out of our obligations under EC and EU legislation, there have been other areas of administration where, under the same pressure, we were required to stop doing certain things. A case in point has been the changes in the Revenue Commissioners which resulted from the implementation of the Single Market, when considerable numbers of customs staff became redundant and were redeployed elsewhere. Something similar happened in the structure of the Department of Industry and Commerce when protection was phased out in the early years of our membership of the Community.

Has membership had an effect on Irish civil servants themselves?

Membership has impinged on Irish civil servants in many ways. The first way has been through the amount of foreign travel officials in many departments have had to undertake. The sheer physical effect of this on many civil servants' lives has been dramatic. It is enormously time-consuming and tiring. It was amusing to note that, after the first flush of enthusiasm for European membership passed, the work to be done in routine Community committees was quickly delegated from senior officials to their colleagues at middle management or lower. Senior civil servants then tended, as they still do, to restrict themselves to attending Council meetings and such with the Minister. This is reasonable enough and has happened in other administrations also. The physical strain is anyway, I suppose, better borne by younger men and women, a practical application of the old Latin tag *Juniores ad labores*!

Has membership changed the type of civil servant needed?

When I first joined the civil service in 1949, it was very different from what it is now. Officials were much more desk-bound. In many departments, there was only limited contact with the general public and then largely by written communication. In fact there was a great reliance on writing everything down, a survival from earlier British times. There were amusing stories told of persons in the same room communicating with each other by way of written memos, with a higher executive officer on one side of a desk writing a carefully-dated instruction to his subordinate executive officer on the other side ('Mr Murphy. Please open a file on this matter.' 'Mr O'Brien. Done. File now attached.'). Conditions have changed greatly since that time. The modern type of civil servant needs different skills. Much of his or her work is now concerned with public appearances before Dáil Committees, attending meetings with the social partners and individual interest groups, addressing conferences, even appearing on radio or television to elucidate some aspect of government policy. He or she must now be good at oral communication and, more than ever, must be able to persuade and influence people. Many of the skills displayed nowadays by civil servants have been honed at wearying meetings in Brussels or Luxembourg, often going on until late hours, as they have negotiated with colleagues from other Member States and with Commission officials. The changes in the civil service would have happened anyway but they have been accelerated by our membership of the Community.

The negotiations in Europe which I have mentioned call for particular skills. Officials must be able to bargain, to cajole, to do deals, to judge a situation and make the most of it from a national point of view. I need not labour the point how successful Irish officials have been in this way in Europe. They have at times been the envy of other Member States, particularly in the negotiations for Structural Funds. They have been thoroughly professional.

This is not to under-emphasise or decry in any way the enormous importance of ministerial actions. It has, of course, been the political input by Ministers which has been paramount in obtaining support from our fellow members, and gaining sympathy and goodwill from influential members of the Commission. But it was the civil service which delivered on this support and goodwill.

The culmination of the Irish administration's work on EU matters has always been the six months of the Presidency. It has been acknowledged – and not just by ourselves – to have been very successful on each occasion we have held this burdensome but exciting task. Bobby McDonagh in his interesting book on the Amsterdam Treaty,[1] recently published by the Institute of European Affairs, has well described the feelings of those of us who have taken part in this great national event when he says:

The sensation on assuming a Presidency is like walking into a sudden pool of light – the spotlight on a stage or the searchlight in a prison yard, depending on whether the giddy excitement or the cold fear predominates.

Secondment to the Permanent Representation

The experienced officials of the Department of Foreign Affairs stationed in the Permanent Representation in Brussels have been in the front line in negotiations such as those I have described. Through a useful arrangement, their efforts have been assisted by persons seconded from a number of other Government departments, including the Department of Finance, for a period of years at a time. As I have said earlier, it is the métier of Foreign Affairs officials to engage in this work but it is in some ways an unusual task for these seconded persons, in that the type of work is largely of a representational nature. They attend meetings with foreign officials, sometimes held in French without translation facilities; take notes and alert departments at home to what is going on; keep closely in touch with Commission officials and members of other delegations; and brief visiting Ministers and home officials. This arrangement has, I think, been in general valuable for both the Department of Foreign Affairs and the home department involved.

At times during the period when I was in senior management in Finance there were, strangely enough, problems in recruiting people to go for a period of years to Brussels. This was mainly, I suspect, because of the family circumstances of officials at the level at which people were recruited for this work. They were often persons with children of school-going age and it was difficult for them to pull up their roots for a number of years and go abroad. Also, despite the substantial perks associated with the work, some officials undoubtedly preferred to make their career without breaking their service in their own department. Perhaps in some departments there was a perception of some ambiguity among senior management about a spell in Brussels, a feeling that the heat and burden of the day were borne most by those who soldiered on in the department at home.

Recruitment to the Community institutions

Another interesting question that arises in this area relates to persons who have been recruited to the Commission and other Community institutions. When Ireland acceded to the European Economic

Communities, the then Irish government were keen that Irish persons should be encouraged to go to the Community institutions. Arrangements therefore were made to ensure that vacancies were drawn to the attention of serving staff and that secondment was available. This resulted in some very effective persons going there and making a good career for themselves. Others inevitably were not so effective. I have never been certain whether there was an absolutely clear-cut policy about Irish membership in the Commission. Perhaps not enough attention was given to this in the hurly-burly of other more obviously urgent matters. It may be slightly tactless in these enlightened times to refer to the idea of targeting certain posts but, if this was an objective, it is not clear that it was particularly successful.

The difficulty may be that action here fell between three or four different stools, being handled by the Department of Foreign Affairs, the Departments of Finance and the Public Service (later merged in 1987) and the Department of the Taoiseach, all of which were involved to a greater or lesser degree. Initially, Finance and Foreign Affairs were the main players but, with the development of the new concept of holding European Council meetings, the Department of the Taoiseach also became involved. An interesting point is that it has been very unusual for persons who have worked in the Commission in jobs other than ones of short duration ever to return to the Irish civil service, although many of them have enjoyed long periods of secondment. The reasons for this would be interesting to explore.

Irish nationals who become members of the Commission staff take on a new allegiance and work for Europe. Nevertheless, they are still Irish. In Christopher Tugendhat's book on his years as a member of the European Commission[2], he discusses the Commissioner's role and refers to the Brussels euphemism that a Commissioner will be particularly concerned with 'the country he knows best'. Commissioners and Commission officials have obviously different roles. There is nevertheless no doubt that, while all officials are *communautaire*, they will each be interested in 'the country they know best'. Perhaps closer contacts with the home administration in the case of Irish officials would be beneficial to both the Commission and the home country.

Learning foreign languages

One of the immediate priorities which arose on joining the EEC was to encourage the learning of foreign languages, and especially French. Irish people for various reasons have not been good at learning

continental languages and most of those who were senior in the civil
service at the time knew no French or were rusty in speaking it. The
Department of the Public Service therefore organised classes in the
then Civil Service Training Centre in Lansdowne Road. These classes
had the benefit of excellent teachers, headed by a very dedicated lady,
Adele McAvock, who became legendary for her work. They were
held in a prefab in the garden of the Training Centre and I regret to
say that, despite Mrs McAvock's good humour and enthusiasm, they
became known as 'The Agony in the Garden'.

Younger civil servants nowadays are better at foreign languages. It
is a pity that the older generation of Ministers, like the older
generation of civil servants, have not been fluent in French at least.
Lack of a foreign language has been a limitation for them, I think. In
my experience, they were restricted to some extent in informal
discussion to chatting to English-speaking Ministers, such as those of
the Netherlands or Scandinavia. (Curiously, they tended to have less
contact with the Ministers of the UK than one would imagine, usually
because of different approaches to EU matters, especially when
Margaret Thatcher was the British Prime Minister.)

This raises another matter. There has been, so far as I can judge,
little transference of administrative experience from continental
Europe to us. I wonder how many examples there have been of a
Minister saying to an official 'I was talking to the Dutch Minister and
he said they were trying an interesting experiment in the
Netherlands...'. I suspect there have not been all that many. Perhaps
the systems of administration here and on the continent are so
dissimilar that changes do not transfer easily from one to the other.
One of the few examples I can think of immediately has been the
introduction of the Programme Manager system. This was
introduced on the initiative of Ministers who had seen the cabinet
system of the Commission in operation, itself based, I understand, on
a French model. To what extent its introduction here has been
successful is a matter of controversy. At best it can be said to sit
uneasily with the traditional non-political nature of the Irish civil
service.

Having made this point about the limited extent of transference
here of administrative experience abroad, I would have to qualify it
by saying that I am aware that heads of public service departments in
the Union meet once a year and exchange knowledge of new
developments. There is also the important role which the European
Institute of Public Affairs in Maastricht – an Institute which,
incidentally, is the other reason why the name of Maastricht is famous
in European circles – plays in disseminating similar knowledge. I am

glad to say that we were one of the first members to support the setting up of this Institute and have played a big part in its development.

I should also acknowledge the role played by another Institute, the Louvain Institute for Ireland in Europe, which has provided a valuable focus for knowledge and contacts on EU matters between the Northern Ireland civil service and the Irish civil service, both of which support this Institute.

Commission system of administration

Another aspect of this matter is the different systems of administration in the Commission and here. There has been some influence by the Commission on administrative structures here through their requirement, for example, to evaluate arrangements for Structural Funds in place, as Professor Laffan says. The same applies for monitoring of FEOGA payments. The use of the measure of the General Government Deficit as a supplement to the Exchequer Borrowing Requirement has been another example. Outside examples such as these, the Irish and the Commission systems of administration do not appear to have drawn much closer to each other, despite 25 years' contact.

I have never had the experience of working in the Commission but I am aware that Irish civil servants who go to work there find it very different to the system they are used to. The hierarchical arrangements which are normal in devolving work in the Irish civil service are not characteristic of the Commission; the system of keeping records is different; one works with persons of different nationalities, who have different approaches to the work. Commission officials also have considerable freedom in comparison with Irish civil servants. They can give their views in public speeches; they can talk to the press. I used to be surprised to read in the newspapers that 'the Commission will oppose such and such an approach from Ireland'. I learnt from experience to discount these statements as often being the views of some unrepresentative official, at best at middle-management level, who had access to an Irish journalist.

Then there is the relationship of officials of the Commission to Commissioners, which is so different from that between Irish civil servants and Ministers. The Commission, as an institution of the Community, has of course an independent existence in a way that the Irish civil service has not, even under the new Public Service Management Act. Also, as Tugendhat points out in the book which I mentioned above, the members of the Commission come from different backgrounds and different political parties. When they leave Brussels they go off in different directions. They do not have the cohesiveness of an Irish Government, made up of politicians who, even if they lose office at a particular time, continue to make their career in Irish politics, and may return to administer Government departments again at some time.

THE FUTURE

I do not propose to speculate on how the Irish public administration will change over the years ahead. Will there be more cross-fertilisation of ideas between Brussels and Dublin in administrative matters? Will our ever-closer links with the Commission and other Member States bring changes in our own civil service practice? Will the aim be to integrate the administrative systems of Member States ever more closely, or will this be looked on as a question for subsidiarity? An interesting question will be whether Irish civil servants will think it a vital part of their career to spend a few years in the Commission. It seems inevitable that, with the advent of Economic and Monetary Union and the accompanying closer integration of Ireland and other members into the Union, questions such as these will arise. We will, however, probably have to wait for the Institute of European Affairs' celebration of the 40th anniversary of membership in 2013 before we will know the full answers.

1. Bobby McDonagh, *Original Sin in a Brave New World*, Dublin: Institute of European Affairs, 1998.
2. Christopher Tugendhat *Making Sense of Europe*, London: Viking Books, 1986

OVERVIEW

CHAPTER 12

The New Ireland in the New Europe

Rory O'Donnell

The profound change is being made possible essentially by the new method of common action which is the core of the European Community. To establish this new method of common action, we adapted to our situation the methods which have allowed individuals to live together in society: common rules which each member is committed to respect, and common institutions to watch over the application of these rules. Nations have applied this method within their frontiers for centuries, but they have never yet been applied between them. After a period of trial and error, this method has become a permanent dialogue between a single European body, responsible for expressing the view of the general interest of the Community, and the national governments expressing the national view. In the European Communities, common rules applied by joint institutions give each a responsibility for the effective working of the Community as a whole. This leads the nations, within the disciplines of the Community, to seek a solution to the problems themselves, instead of trading temporary advantages.

Jean Monnet, *A Ferment of Change,* 1962

INTRODUCTION

In this overview, I synthesise the political, economic, social and administrative dimensions of Ireland's participation in European integration. The Community Ireland joined in 1973 has changed dramatically since the mid-1980s. The Single Act, the internal market and the transition to EMU have greatly increased the salience of the EU. The process of embedding the national in the European and the European in the national accelerated in the mid-1980s. A series of enlargements has altered the Union. This chapter takes particular account of this deepening of European integration, by presenting an interpretation of the effects and meaning of membership.

Rather than address the political, economic, social and administrative dimensions separately, I adopt a broadly narrative approach, dividing the first 25 years into two periods, 1973 to 1987, and 1987 to 1999. I believe a narrative approach brings out the main arguments.

- European integration and governance have been centrally important in the economic transformation of the past decade.
- The alignment of state strategy with the action of economic and social interests is the critical determinant of success or failure in the new Europe, despite the central role of the state in the formulation and implementation of EU policy and law.
- The question of accession or membership is dwarfed by the changes in the nature of the EU since Ireland joined.
- The state of the Union – and a correct understanding of its nature – are of critical importance to Ireland.
- In managing membership there is a complex relationship between strategy and action, between strategic thinking and pragmatism.
- There is little sense in a discussion of whether we are 'real Europeans' or in counter-posing Ireland's relationship with America and Europe.
- There are some important, if subtle, surprises in our experience in Europe.

The next section reviews Ireland's motivation, preparation and expectations concerning membership of the EC. I then describe and analyse Ireland's first period of membership, from 1973 to 1987. This reveals a movement from confident adjustment to crisis and despair. The next part outlines the dramatic advance of European integration since the late 1980s and its impact on Ireland. An overall interpretation of the role of Europe in Ireland's development is then offered. The implication of this interpretation for Ireland's future orientation with regard to European integration is considered. A concluding evaluation is then presented.

MOTIVATION, PREPARATION AND EXPECTATIONS

Background

The background to Ireland's membership of the EC was the switch in strategic orientation made in the late 1950s and early 1960s. The switch to an outward-orientated strategy was prompted by the severe balance of payments difficulties, recession and emigration of the 1950s. Ireland's decision to switch from protectionism to outward orientation was a highly conscious one. It was intended to achieve an exporting economy by modernising and reorienting the indigenous economy and attracting inward investment. Meticulous studies were undertaken and new public organisations and policies were created to address the perceived weaknesses. In Chapter 9, Garret FitzGerald argues that these studies had a very important educational effect on indigenous industries. They alerted both management and unions to the scale of the adjustment that would need to be made in order to survive under conditions of free trade. In the context of these pessimistic studies, Lemass's 1961 decision to apply for membership was a 'great surprise'. It was motivated, in part, by the emergence of economic growth, and in part by the difficulty of creeping unilateral tariff reductions. FitzGerald's account suggests that Lemass's action – negotiating the Anglo-Irish Free Trade Area Agreement in 1965 and pushing for early membership of the EC – had the same bold pragmatism as that shown by the founding fathers of the European Community. In addition, Miriam Hederman O'Brien points out that Irish membership of the UN and its consequent role in the Congo 'had a significantly positive effect on public opinion as far as Irish involvement in international affairs was concerned'.

Motivation

In some respects, Ireland's motivation in seeking EC membership is relatively obvious. Membership offered the prospect of access to a large, high-priced, heavily subsidised market for the country's food surplus. In addition, as FitzGerald points out, the fact that Britain was the slowest-growing industrial market in Europe, was undoubtedly a factor in the decision to seek access to the more dynamic markets of the Continent. Yet an account which is confined to these material motives is unsatisfactory. The papers in this volume bring out two other factors: Ireland's desire to find a more satisfactory set of external relationships, and the drive to overcome the limits of closure and isolation. The point here is not to counter-pose these to the material concerns, but to see how the material and other motivations were interwoven.

In seeking an accurate view of how these were combined, it is important to recognise that the motivation for EU membership differs in each Member State. In Chapter 4, Garvin identifies the diverse security, cultural and political reasons which motivated France, Germany, the Benelux countries, Spain, Portugal and Greece to participate in integration. It follows that the effects of membership, and ultimately the meaning of membership, varies from country to country and, indeed, within countries. This point is frequently missed by the critics of European integration, who correctly see the difference between countries, but see 'Europe' as an entity (or putative super-power), rather than Europe as a set of relationships. The difference between countries is real. But it cannot be assumed that nationality is a primordial reality which sets limits to European integration. It might as easily result in diverse motives for integration, and diverse experiences of integration. Indeed, part of the genius of the project has been its ability to place European integration within the vocation of each Member State, even within each modern European nationalism. As Garvin emphasises, the diverse motivations for participation are not purely economic. Yet integration can only meet countries' diverse cultural and political needs, if it meets the members' shared need for economic prosperity and security.

As Garvin says 'All joined Europe in what they each see as their own interest, not because of some vision of an ideal, united Europe'. Some think this implies that a focus on the over-arching constitutional framework of the Union – and the creation of institutions to express and protect the European interest (such as the Commission and the Court) – only cloaks the underlying reality of selfish diplomacy. But that is precisely the wrong reading. The constitutional and institutional architecture are the very condition in which it is possible for diverse states and societies to see that their interest is advanced by integration. Note that although Garvin provides a graphic account of the diverse motivations for integration, he opens his chapter with a clear rejection of the journalistic view that EU membership consists mainly of a new version of pork-barrel politics (see below, for a further discussion of this view).

Garvin argues that Ireland's involvement in European integration should be understood in terms of her long-term relation with Anglo-Saxon and Protestant civilisation, represented in the past two centuries by Britain and America. Ireland faced the cultural predicament of marrying 'together cultural systems which many looked upon as antithetical: Tridentine authoritarian Catholicism of an isolated and besieged type and Anglo-American liberal democracy'. He argues that there is an extraordinary cultural continuity, since the time of O'Connell, in Irish attempts to create what might be described as a foreign policy. Irish leaders have, over a very long period, attempted to achieve a link with foreign powers which might alleviate or counter-balance the overwhelming cultural and socioeconomic embrace of Britain. As Brendan Halligan shows in Chapter 3, even in 1972 Ireland 'was a politically independent region of the British economy'. Garvin suggests that the true prehistory of the modern Irish engagement with Europe is 'a half-remembered but very deep longing for an alliance, a friendship, that was non-imperial and psychologically satisfying, combined with a culturally determined wish to be self-sufficient and to be true to no one but one's collective self'.

An important part of this argument derives from the limits of nationalism, independence and, particularly, isolationism, as means of escape or self-realisation. What Garvin describes as the 'alliance of Priests and Patriots' had, by the mid-20th century, achieved a kind of independence and a cultural defence against the English-speaking outside world of disbelief, scepticism, anti-Catholicism and greed. But the result was not only economic failure and continued emigration, but a stifling political and civic culture dominated by an authoritarian Catholic church. A striking feature of the contributions to this volume is their uniformity in describing Ireland before EC membership as having an under-educated population, 'a rural ethos and a monolithic culture based on Catholicism', 'a hatred of independent thinking', 'a fear of authority', as being a 'cosy, insular, world', 'male dominated, authoritarian, unequal and much given to public expressions of piety not always reflected in private life', 'less than a totally free country'. Garvin's central argument is that 'What Europe has done is offer everyone a way out of the historical trap in which Ireland was caught'. This captures well the Irish understanding of what involvement in Europe means. Ryan emphasises that among the motives for membership was a desire 'to transcend the bounds of geographical insularity, post-war isolation and the confines of protectionism'. He notes that 'There was an acute awareness that a nation that was left behind economically would most likely be left behind socially and culturally also'. Indeed, Halligan cites Jack Lynch's 1967 statement as providing the best insight into the motivation within political and official circles for membership: 'Our future lies in participation in a wider economic grouping. Failure to achieve this objective would result in economic and political stagnation.' It is this instinctive rejection of political and economic stagnation which has driven Irish support. It has over-ridden technical arguments, orthodox economic doctine and the ideology of national sovereignty.

Garvin's argument has a number of implications which might be noted. One, which he highlights himself, is that given the long historical emergence of a form of democratic Catholicism, 'the republican versus home rule division was by comparison superficial'. A second implication is that the period of closure, from the 1930s to the 1960s, and the characteristics and values it incubated, can now be

seen as exceptional, rather than definitional, in the long development
of Irish society and politics. When we fully apprehend this fact, we
will have redefined what it is to be Irish and re-invented Ireland. A
third important aspect of his argument is the adoption of what might
be called an 'agent view' of Ireland's external relations. The
dominance of the imperial relation with Britain can lead us to see
Ireland as passive, acted-upon but not acting – a habit that some
continue in studying Ireland's experience in Europe.

Preparation

Ireland's preparation for EC membership poses a difficult issue of
interpretation. It is widely agreed that Ireland's overall preparation
was thorough. Irish officials, especially in the Department of Foreign
Affairs, developed a sophisticated understanding of the EEC, created
a network of contacts with the institutions and Member States and
arrived at detailed conclusions about the national interest. While
Halligan suggests that they were 'unrepresentative of the body politic
and were left free from vulgar interference', he notes that 'the
capacity of the Irish political system to respond to new challenges
was greater than had been believed'. Indeed, he suggests that by 1972
the Government's 'internalisation of the European project' was such
that the accession White Paper summarised the two fundamental
considerations underlying its policy in seeking EEC membership as,
'firstly, European unity and, secondly, the national interest'. This
important aspect of Ireland's approach to the Community, before
accession and since, is well captured in Halligan's description of
Ireland as 'a psychological insider within the integration process'.

    At a formal level, this thorough political and psychological
preparation was mirrored in economic policy. Indeed, the delay
between the initial application in 1961 and accession in 1973 gave the
country time for significant modernisation of the economy. Yet, as
discussed in Chapter 8 and my next section, the first fifteen years of
membership saw the decimation of indigenous manufacturing
industry. Does this mean that Irish preparation was inadequate,
particularly that government failed in its preparation? The argument
developed below suggests that, if policy failure is to be cited, it was
primarily policy after accession which was at fault, rather than the
preparation – although FitzGerald does argue that the Department of
Industry and Commerce 'failed to adjust to the prospect of free
trade'.

Debate and Decision

The most important aspect of the debate on accession was the opposition to membership advanced by the Labour Party and the trade union movement. Their fear of job losses in manufacturing industry was not sufficient to counterbalance other arguments, but was to prove well-founded. Both Hederman O'Brien and Garvin note that the Labour movement was the element of Irish society most influenced by British ideas and practices. It should not be forgotten that in the 1960s and much of the 1970s, Britain stood for things that seemed progressive. It is shown below that the emergence of a positive and sophisticated view of Europe among Irish trade unions in the late-1980s was one of the most important developments in the first 25 years.

There is some difference of interpretation concerning Irish attitudes and understanding during the accession debate and in the early years of membership. In Chapter 3, Halligan presents what is probably the dominant view, that the accession White Paper, and hence the debate, displayed an awareness and acceptance of the political and security dimensions of the European project. By contrast, in Chapter 2, Hederman O'Brien argues that some Irish people accepted British political and media assumptions about the scope and remit of the European Communities. Although she acknowledges that the majority of Irish people took a more positive view regarding membership, she considers that 'there was no great appetite in either country for exploring fully the political implications'. She argues that the Irish Council of the European Movement was almost alone in pointing out that the Community was a unique political structure, designed to achieve peace and social and economic security in Europe, 'which carried political obligations'. Instead, it was the inclusion of agriculture which created most favourable reaction in Ireland.

These viewpoints can be synthesised, if we note the nature of the EC and reject an excessive distinction between material, political, social and cultural motivations. While the CAP offered the prospect of direct transfers, the wider economic motivation should not be cast as rent-seeking. Indeed, Hederman O'Brien makes the important point that 'The limitations of national sovereignty in matters of trade, commerce and the financial markets were well known to the Irish sectors which were thus involved' – adding that this 'understanding was also found throughout the general population, particularly among those whose children had been forced to emigrate through lack of opportunities in Ireland'. Given this healthy scepticism concerning national autonomy, most of the Irish population were, and remain, part of the Europe-wide 'permissive consensus' which has allowed European integration to proceed so far in the past 40 years. Those who needed to explored the wider political implications. The sophistication and wisdom of that pragmatic position should not be underestimated. If people sensed that membership created open-ended political and security implications, they also sensed that it would be slightly ridiculous to try to visualise the context in which these obligations would become concrete and to agonise over them. Furthermore, we should not imagine that this was a purely Irish phenomenon, marking us off as more material, and 'less European', than other Member States. The CAP – often cited as clinching proof of the EC as being about material interest pursued through inter-state bargaining – was not, after all, an Irish invention. More importantly, it is of the very nature of the EC that it advanced by creating an initial over-arching agreement, making implementation of many principles and policies the subject of subsequent negotiation.

In Chapter 3, Halligan uncovers a contrast which is of current interest. He reminds us that the strong argument for membership was based on the expectation of modest enough Community financial transfers, certainly no firm anticipation of significant Structural Funds, and an expectation that membership would result in an end to neutrality. With apparent irony, he says it is 'intriguing that such admissions did not deter the electorate from voting 'yes' '. This raises two interesting questions. First, how did it come about that Irish membership could be summarised – as it is in much of the media – as support for Structural Funds (or other financial transfers) but reservations on security? Is it true that Irish support for European integration would evaporate if financial transfers ceased and European security policy developed? These questions are addressed below.

FROM ADJUSTMENT TO CRISIS, 1972 TO 1987

The background to the success of the past decade is the more painful adjustment to EC membership experienced between 1973 and 1987, particularly in the 1980s. Despite the slowdown in the world economy and initial adjustment to EC membership, the Irish economy performed relatively well throughout most of the 1970s. However, this apparently strong performance masked fundamental problems in the country's economic, social and political adjustment to European integration and internationalisation. In this Section, I summarise the impact of EC membership on the economy, society, politics and administration in the years from 1973 to 1987 and offer an interpretation of the profound economic, political, social and cultural crisis of the 1980s.

Economy

The first fifteen years of EC membership saw dramatic change in the Irish economy. As noted below, much of that change, in both agriculture and industry, was positive and much of it was directly related to Ireland's place in the EC. Yet by the mid-1980s the overall economic position had deteriorated. This raises important questions about the impact of membership, which are addressed throughout this chapter.

By and large, the expected benefits to Irish farmers materialised (as outlined by McAleese in Chapter 8). Between 1970 and 1978, agricultural product prices rose 35 per cent in real terms and real incomes per capita in agriculture more than doubled. The qualification to this positive experience was some increase in the volatility in farm incomes. McAleese explains how the benefits from the CAP consist of both 'budget transfers' and 'trade transfers', and suggests that over the period 1979 to 1986 the combined gain amounted to around 6.5 per cent of GNP.

Indeed, McAleese argues that 'the scale and duration of the CAP transfers vastly exceeded expectations'. Consequently, the CAP provided a long breathing space in which adjustment in agriculture could take place. As he says, from an historical point of view 'the question is how well this breathing space has been used'. While livestock and dairy output have undoubtedly increased, 'whether Irish food has also established the hoped-for brand image and selling position in the European market is a matter of some debate'. He cites the NESC's observation that, while the CAP had much to recommend it, it had one unfortunate consequence:

> It could conceal the need for a range of long-term national policies concerning the role of agriculture in the overall development of the economy, and the need for national policies to achieve agricultural objectives which were not, and probably could not be, addressed by the CAP.[1]

Indeed, in Chapter 9, FitzGerald argues that in the early years, and since, there has been a notable lack of forward thinking in agriculture. Instead of being satisfied with the huge accession price increases,

Ministers for Agriculture succumbed to the short-sighted pressure for increases in the EU price itself. He reports that his own attempts to argue this case, as part of the overall EU policy-co-ordination process, fell on deaf ears. 'As so often happens in politics, short-termism prevented any serious discussion of long-term strategy.' A fundamental and enduring feature of Irish policy since accession was the judgement that, given the exportable surplus of food, Ireland's national interest lay in maximising CAP prices and agricultural supports. For a variety of reasons, this goal was seen as over-riding, or not fundamentally at odds with, possible countervailing concerns: the input prices facing Irish food-processing, the long-term development of the agricultural and food sectors or the prices to be paid by Irish consumers. This has attracted some criticism, as discussed later in this chapter.

In discussing the experience of industry in the first fifteen years of membership we must distinguish between foreign-owned and indigenous firms. As FitzGerald notes, the potential growth of manufactured exports to Continental Europe 'was grossly under-estimated during the run-up to membership'. There was an unexpected increase in foreign direct investment by American companies, which sustained high growth of both exports and employment in chemicals, pharmaceuticals and engineering.

The experience of indigenous industry was more difficult. While manufactured exports to Continental Europe increased faster than expected, many sectors suffered import penetration. While there was a high rate of investment and new job creation, there were significant closures and job losses. The net outcome was positive in the 1970s, but it turned sharply negative in the 1980s, when international recession was reinforced by Irish fiscal correction. As McAleese explains in Chapter 8, 'Few indigenous firms (or foreign subsidiaries established under the protectionist regime) succeeded in making the necessary adjustment'. The collapse of indigenous industry, and the prolonged recession in the Irish economy in the 1980s, drove unemployment to unprecedented levels and created a new wave of emigration.

This radical adjustment in the structure of the Irish economy was interpreted as the response of firms to European integration.[2] The removal of inefficient practices (the cold-shower effect) and an element of product specialisation (intra-industry specialisation) offered some breathing space to indigenous manufacturers. But it did not, as in other countries, complete the process of adjustment. Because Irish firms' basic scale was too small relative to their new competitors, and because they suffered a range of other competitive disadvantages, that breathing space was only temporary. Competitive pressure for further adjustment built up, forcing contractions of output and employment. In industries where economies of scale exist, contraction of employment and output tends to raise costs rather than lower them. Consequently, such 'adjustments', rather than re-establishing Irish competitiveness on a new basis, were the start of the process of long-run decline, inherent in specialisation between industries. The experience of Irish manufacturing between 1973 and 1987 can be seen to be consistent with a modern and realistic understanding of how trade and integration work where there are initial differences in levels of development, technology and scale of production.

The appalling experience of the 1980s, and its analysis as a failure to handle economic integration, had a significant influence on the approach of policy-makers and social partners to the dramatic deepening of European integration initiated by Commission President Delors in the mid-1980s. However, as shown below, it did not prompt a retreat from European integration or internationalisation.

Society

The period of adjustment to European integration, from 1972 to 1987, was one of profound change in Irish society and Irish identity. Ryan observes in Chapter 6, that 'Irish society has changed more over the past 25 years than at any time in its history'. Furthermore, 'what took over 100 years in Britain and much of western Europe has all happened in Ireland in the space of a generation'. As in the economy, politics and public administration, there was a complex combination of positive change and modernisation, on the one hand, and severe crisis and disorientation, on the other.

While the emergence of population growth in the 1960s – after a century of population decline – halted the erosion of national self-confidence, problems of dependency soon emerged. Economic dependency, the number of dependants per hundred workers, reached exceptionally high levels in the mid-80s. This rapid demographic transformation from population decline to population growth was an important source of the economic, social and political difficulties experienced in the first fifteen years of EC membership. It exacerbated the historical shortage of jobs, and called for greatly increased public spending in health, education, housing and welfare. Despite the emerging crisis in public finance, participation in second- and third-level education rose steadily, reflecting a strong Irish policy commitment.

Ryan shows that the social impact of EC membership has come from five main sources: legislation, funding, the EU administrative system, EU language and terminology, and the smaller programmes aimed at poverty, disability and gender equality. In the first period of EC membership, the most significant of these was legislation.

EC directives, combined with a new level of consciousness and organisation among Irish women, led to significant legislative changes on gender equality. When an attempt was made to postpone implementation of the Equal Pay Directive in 1975, Irish feminists appealed to the Social Affairs Commissioner, Patrick Hillery. His decision, that the directive must be implemented, provided an early demonstration of the significance of membership. Not only was a new political arena emerging, but its legal and political force was sufficient to transform participants, both Commissioner Hillery and Irish feminists and trade unionists, from national actors into players in a wider European political forum.

It can be argued that the good social effects of Europe, such as the legislation on women's rights, were 'double-edged'. O'Toole observes that, instead of working through profound changes in our collective attitudes, we were presented often with a *fait accompli*. The directives happened to us, we didn't make them happen. 'This is why so many of the changes in Irish values seem to have such shallow roots.'[3] This may underestimate the role of Irish feminists and trade unionists in the emergence of gender equality legislation, and their role in seeking to have the law enforced. It may also underestimate the speed with which values can change, and the fact that institutions and laws can re-shape values.

I want to focus in a little more detail on one social change which is directly related to the EC and which is, in my view, critical to an understanding of modern Ireland. In an important paper, Damian Hannan and Patrick Commins have analysed the significance of small-scale landholders in Ireland's socio-economic transformation.[4] They show that small-scale landholders, undoubtedly a disadvantaged group at the time Ireland joined the EC, devised a remarkably successful set of survival strategies in the subsequent decades. While the numbers in Irish farming fell steadily, the number of landholders has been stable. A range of EC and national policy measures and economic opportunities encouraged them to retain their land. They adapted their farm production, took off-farm employment, diversified their sources of family income and availed assiduously of the increasing educational opportunities. The result was that total disposable income increased faster than that on larger farms. More importantly, the educational participation and attainment of children from small farm backgrounds surpassed those of children from unskilled manual backgrounds. This is critical, given the role of education in determining access to occupational position in the new economy.

Hannan and Commins point out that these findings raise doubts about the image of cultural and socio-psychological 'demoralisation' which has dominated Irish rural anthropology, and indeed, political discourse. If we add to this the experience of those larger Irish farmers who received much greater support from the prices and markets elements of the CAP, then we reach important additional conclusions about Ireland's experience. For all its faults, an important effect of the CAP (and the other policies which favoured rural Ireland relative to the cities of the east and south of the country) was that the project of Irish modernisation and European integration did not become divisive along urban-rural lines. Rural Ireland was, and remains, an enthusiastic participant in the integration project.

Hannan and Commins's analysis, combined with this wider observation, has, in my view, important implications for the interpretation of Ireland's experience in the EC. In particular, it knocks a major hole in the interpretation, developed by John Waters and Desmond Fennell, which identifies, indeed advocates, a conflict between urban and rural Ireland, 'blues' and 'greens', 'natives' and 'native settlers'.[5] It is doubtful that dividing Irish society in these ways makes sense. But, even if it did, the interpretation involves a gross misreading of the evidence of who has won and who has lost.

To the social and economic changes in the first period of EC membership – inward investment, industrial closures, mass unemployment, widened consumer choice, a new wave of emigration, increased rural prosperity, changing gender roles and rights, increased dependency, a fall in fertility – must be added a profound cultural and political crisis. The most striking example of this was the phenomenon of moving statues. To this can be added the Kerry babies case, the tragedy at Granard and the debate on the 1983 referendum on abortion. A nation which prided itself on its political tradition – whose citizens had for over a century survived, and often prospered, in the most advanced counties, whose political elite had skilfully negotiated a place in the world's most benign international regime – seemed happier to tear itself apart over abstractions, rather than look its problems in the face and act to solve them.[6]

Politics and Administration

Ireland was scarcely in the Community when it had to assume the Presidency. The 1975 Presidency produced an accelerated learning process in the procedures and principles of the EC, and effectively transformed the Department of Foreign Affairs. The main elements of Ireland's administrative and political style in Europe, described and analysed by Brigid Laffan in Chapter 10, were established in the early years.

The high level of support among the Irish public for membership and the absence of splits in the political parties on Europe facilitated an easy fit between Ireland and the Union. As Halligan says, 'Ireland slid effortlessly into the new role that awaited it in the EEC'. Ireland's policy style in Europe is agenda-driven, reactive and informal. European policy is managed much like domestic policy. The style is pragmatic, with a marked emphasis on those areas of Union policy that are regarded as vital to Ireland – agriculture, the EU budget, Structural Funds and EU regulations that might affect Ireland's competitive position. Like other small states, Ireland places a high value on the right to the Presidency and would strongly reject any idea that small states are less effective in that role. Irish participants in the Brussels process have a reputation as good networkers, a useful skill in a highly fragmented and complex policy process.

Ireland's administrative and policy adaptation to membership was shaped by the evolution of the Union itself. The elaboration of the Council of Ministers, following the Luxembourg compromise, both enhanced the role of civil servants and technical experts in the overall EU system and burdened them with heavy workloads. The emergence of the European Council increased the role of the Department of the Taoiseach in the management of EU business.

In addition to the relatively smooth adaptation of the political and administrative system to EC membership, some historically important decisions regarding Ireland's place in Europe were made in the first 15 years. One was the decision of the Fianna Fáil government that Ireland would participate in the European Monetary System (EMS) and, particularly, the Exchange Rate Mechanism (ERM), on their establishment in 1979. While the creation of the EMS was a significant step for Europe, for Ireland it was a radical departure, economically, politically and psychologically. It involved renunciation of our 150-year-old link with sterling, and therefore a redefinition of Ireland's economic and monetary relationship with Britain. As well as having immediate and on-going effects on the functioning of the Irish economy, it expressed the different approaches which Britain and Ireland would take to Europe in the following twenty years.

A second critical decision was that of Taoiseach FitzGerald, leader of the Fine Gael/Labour coalition, at the Milan European Council in 1985. Ireland supported the vote to convene an Intergovernmental Conference on the internal market and institutional reform. The use of the vote itself was historic and the outcome was historic, the Single European Act. Through that decision, and the subsequent Irish chairmanship of the Dooge Committee, Ireland placed itself firmly on the side of the re-launch of the Community led by President Delors, discussed further below.

Interpreting the First Fifteen Years of Membership

Ireland's new economic and political strategy had four significant successes between 1960 and 1987.[7] First, after a century-and-a-half of virtual stagnation, the country achieved relatively strong economic and demographic growth. Second, the country had achieved membership, on good terms, of the European Communities and become, as mentioned above, what Halligan calls a 'psychological insider' in the European project. Third, there was a dramatic structural adjustment of the economy. In 1960, agriculture, forestry and fishing accounted for almost 37 per cent of all employment. By 1987, this had fallen to 14 per cent, reflecting rapid productivity growth. Fourth, these achievements were accompanied by a distinct modernisation. The period after 1960 saw a strong increase in living standards and expectations. Incomes, wages and welfare provisions converged with those of the UK and the quantity, quality and range of consumer goods increased strongly.

However, these successes were qualified in important ways. The development of viable, employment-generating businesses outside of agriculture was in doubt. The adjustment of indigenous enterprises to international competition failed more often than it succeeded. By default, Ireland's economic strategy came to rely heavily on inward investment. While Ireland proved itself to be an attractive location, it was not clear that this was a basis for development. This raised questions about the adequacy of the industrial policy and prompted arguments in favour of a greater focus on building strong indigenous enterprises and sectors.

Ireland's late baby-boom yielded an increase in social needs and the labour force at a time of acute international and domestic difficulty. Growth and international comparison created increased aspirations, distributional conflict, new social needs and intensified political competition. Despite strong economic growth, inconsistent claims on Irish output were allowed to develop and were resolved in ways which created major economic problems. Ireland's strong recovery from the recession of 1974-75 was largely driven by increased public spending and borrowing. Buoyant domestic growth in the 1960s and 1970s postponed the day of reckoning for much indigenous manufacturing industry and cloaked the problems of Ireland's political economy. However, in the 1980s the underlying weaknesses were cruelly exposed.

At a national level, the severity of the experience of the 1980s altered perceptions of the Irish economy and society. The failure, once again, of indigenous development, and the emergence, once again, of emigration as the best option for the young, gave rise to a number of major studies of Ireland's 'economic failure', in which Ireland's position within the EC figured prominently. Crotty argued that Ireland should be compared with third-world countries, in which the social and political structures established under colonialism are used by the state in ways which favour entrenched elites.[8] O'Hearn traced Ireland's long-run failure to its outward-looking free market strategy, which made Ireland a 'classic case of 'dependent' relations: slow growth and inequality caused by foreign penetration'.[9]

From the current vantage point, it is possible to interpret the experience from 1960 to 1987. Despite the enthusiasm for EC membership, the approaches adopted reflected insufficient awareness of international competition. Inevitable adversities were allowed to become divisive and produced delayed and insufficient responses. The inconsistent claims on Irish output were resolved by inflation and public borrowing. Although Ireland handled certain aspects of EC membership relatively successfully, particularly the CAP and Structural Funds, and although it was instinctively supportive of new European initiatives, such as the EMS and the 1995 Intergovernmental Conference, these were allowed to occlude the wider policy and behavioural requirements of internationalisation. The common factor in each of these failures would seem to be insufficient appreciation and acceptance of interdependence in the economy and society: between the indigenous economy and the international economy, between the public and the private sectors, and between the economic and the political. Organisational and institutional arrangements capable of identifying and mediating these mechanisms and pressures were not in place, and seemed beyond the capability of Ireland's political, administrative and interest-group system. By the mid-1980s – with the national debt rising towards 120 per cent of GDP, unemployment at 17 per cent of the labour force and emigration returning towards the levels of the 1950s – Ireland's economic, social and political strategy was in ruins, and its hope of prospering in the international economy was in considerable doubt.

EUROPE RELAUNCHED AND IRELAND TRANSFORMED

The turnaround achieved in Ireland in the late 1980s involved both intense reflection on the experience of European integration and a relaunch of the integration process at European level. From within the traumatic experience of the 1980s there emerged a new perspective on Ireland's position in European integration and a globalising economy. This Section summarises the main developments in the period from 1987. It begins by noting the major innovation – the social partnership approach to economic and social management – and by discussing the role of Europe in its emergence. Attention then turns to the remarkable advances in European policy – the internal market programme, the doubling and reform of the Structural Funds and the transition from EMS to EMU – and an assessment of their impact on Ireland.

Social Partnership

A major development during the period of transformation after 1987 was social partnership. In a context of deep despair in Irish society in the mid-1980s, the social partners, working through the National Economic and Social Council (NESC), hammered out an agreed strategy to escape from the vicious circle of real stagnation, rising taxes and exploding debt. The NESC's 1986 *Strategy Report* formed the basis upon which a new government and the social partners quickly negotiated the 'Programme for National Recovery' to run from 1987 to 1990. This was the first of four agreements which brought Ireland through more than a decade of negotiated economic and social governance.[10]

The partnership programmes enlisted trade union support for a radical correction of the public finances. In return, the government accepted that the value of social welfare payments would be maintained. Each programme outlined agreement on wage levels in both the private and public sectors for a three-year period. In addition, they established agreement on a wide range of economic and social policies – including tax reform, the evolution of welfare payments, trends in health spending, public-sector reform, measures to combat social exclusion, enterprise-level partnership, exchange-rate policy and the Maastricht criteria. New institutional mechanisms were created to monitor implementation and ensure ongoing dialogue between government and the social partners on economic and social policy. An important feature of the recent Irish approach is the attempt to widen partnership beyond the traditional social partners (unions, business and agricultural interests) to include the community and voluntary sector, women's groups, the unemployed and the disabled.[11]

Social partnership can be seen as related to Ireland's deepened involvement in Europe. There were a number of definite, if indirect, European influences on the development of partnership after 1987. The intensification of international competition, Ireland's disastrous competitive performance in the 1980s, and a new shared understanding that competitiveness was the precondition for achievement of all other economic and social goals, formed the central motivation for the partnership experiment. The need to adhere to the disciplines of the EMS – in both wage-bargaining and public finance – was both a motivation and concrete goal of the partnership programmes. This way of achieving low inflation – a hard currency peg (or independent monetary policy) combined with co-ordinated wage-setting – was typical of the most successful continental European countries, and contrasted with that of the UK. Social partnership shifted Irish economic policy, and particularly Ireland's political economy, from a British towards a European model.

More directly, involvement in Europe had exposed Irish trade union and business leaders to the models of consensus-based 'social partnership' in many European countries. Fintan O'Toole exaggerates only slightly when he says 'The language of consensus and partnership, derived directly from the EU, became the new political vernacular'.[12] This is certainly true in the area of industrial relations. Ireland had inherited the adversarial British approach, and had followed Britain in moving towards industrial conflict in the 1960s and 1970s. This contrasted with the institutions and methods used in the more successful European countries during the post-war period. Irish unions gradually became aware of alternative approaches, and by the late 1980s several union leaders cited the German 'social market economy' as a desirable model, and a reassurance that the new emphasis on fiscal correction and market conformity was not the same as the low-road, neo-liberal model emerging in Britain.

While the emergence of Ireland's social partnership is undoubtedly part of its Europeanisation, this should not be seen in reductionist terms as an Irish adoption of a superior, 'European' approach. The integration process seldom works like that. There is no single European model of 'social partnership'. For many years, the most conspicuously neo-corporatist countries – Sweden, Norway and Austria – were not participating in European integration. The Irish version of social partnership has turned out to differ significantly from other European models, particularly that of Germany. As Ireland moved towards social partnership, many European countries seemed to be moving away from it. Nevertheless, it remains true, as Peter Cassells emphasises in Chapter 7, that in a critical period important Irish actors saw partnership as validated in continental Europe and necessary for success in the emerging European economic and monetary union. Indeed, the 1990s have seen a re-emergence of tripartite, consensus-based, public policy-making in many Member States. The social pacts emerging across the Union are similar to the partnership programmes in place in Ireland since 1987. A European process is undoubtedly underway in the area of social concertation, although it remains to be adequately analysed and characterised. Study of the wider integration process warns us not to expect simple convergence towards a single, pre-existing, European model.

A New Perspective on European Integration and Internationalisation

It is notable that those studies, which saw Ireland's engagement in European integration and the international economy as the source of ongoing economic failure, were never seen as offering a guide to practical action. Indeed, the significant development in ideas and policy in the late-1980s involved a new recognition of the link between domestic policy (and action by non-state actors) and international developments. Far from accepting the analysis of Crotty or O'Hearn, there emerged a view that internationalisation, and European governance, while they had exposed critical weaknesses in Ireland, were no longer the *cause* of those weaknesses. Indeed, even deeper European integration and internationalisation, when properly understood and managed, came to be seen as a route to success.

This widely shared new perspective was reflected in Irish approaches to the key dimensions of integration. While membership allowed the country to achieve one of its agricultural policy aims – access to a large, high-priced market – attention turned to problems in agriculture which remained despite, or because of, the CAP. The loss of so many indigenous businesses was traced to failure of industrial policy and the uneven growth of domestic demand. A considerable advance was made in the understanding of economic and monetary union and there was greater recognition of the constraints which interdependence, particularly the EMS, places on domestic monetary and fiscal policy. It was noted that the effects of integration can take considerable time to work themselves out, adjustments to membership of the EC being experienced in the 1980s as well as in the 1970s. Indeed, it came to be recognised that internationalisation is an ongoing process which throws ever-greater sections of the economy and society into international competition.

While Ireland's approach to the Community continued to focus, to a considerable extent, on the cohesion question and the Structural Funds, an attempt was made to put cohesion in the correct perspective. The continuing importance of domestic policy was emphasised, and a perspective sustained on how the cohesion question relates to the wider set of EU goals and policies.

The political dimension of European integration was more deeply and, importantly, more widely, understood in the late 1980s. This was reinforced by the Single European Act (SEA), the analysis and implementation of which undermined the element of opposition to European integration which had developed within Fianna Fáil during the early 1980s. Economic actors came to recognise what Irish officials had long understood: that small states generally benefit from the formal, legal, supranational elements of integration, whereas larger and more powerful states can work intergovernmental negotiations to much greater effect.

NESC summarised its detailed study of Ireland's experience in the EC with the general lesson that 'membership of the Community does not reduce the need for clear Irish policy aims and methods. In particular, membership of the Community does not diminish the need for a national ability to identify solutions to national problems – even where those solutions require Community policies and action.'[13]

The European Internal Market Programme

Perhaps the most significant aspect of Ireland's first 25 years in the EC has been the completion of the internal market. At EC level, there was a growing recognition in the mid-1980s that the common market in industrial goods remained incomplete and the common market in services, capital and labour was scarcely begun. This was because cross-border business activity was hampered by a range of non-tariff barriers, such as state aids to business, national technical standards, nationalistic government procurement, national professional qualifications and national regulatory regimes in sectors such as banking, insurance, telecommunications, transport, energy and postal services. As explained by McAleese in Chapter 8, Commission President Delors used an ambitious programme to remove these non-tariff barriers as the flagship for his relaunch of the Community. The internal market programme consisted of 300 legislative measures to deepen the internal market in goods, establish an internal market in services, make real the free movement of workers, and enforce Community principles in public procurement, state aids and competition. In many sectors, such as transport, energy and telecommunications, the creation of an internal market required the formulation of a sectoral policy by the Community.

Given the decimation of indigenous Irish industry in the earlier phase of integration, it would not have been surprising if Irish leaders had resisted the internal market programme. Attention did focus on the possible effects of deeper economic integration on the regional pattern of economic activity in Europe. This suggested that while there was no determinate trend, there was a risk of greater concentration of economic activity in the core of Europe. Irish and Spanish articulation of this possibility, and the Commission's desire to balance market deepening with greater economic cohesion, were important factors in the doubling and reform of the Structural Funds which accompanied the internal market programme.

Industry-specific analysis suggested that, in many areas of manufacturing, the fragmentation of the European market was of more advantage to the large Member States than to the small. While the creation of international competition in services, such as banking, insurance, telecommunications, energy, and transport, created some risks for Irish firms, many of these sectors had consolidated and achieved scale. In any case, the long-term competitiveness of Ireland's overall economy required more competitive service sectors.

From intense study and deliberation, there emerged a recognition that the '1992' program must be seen in the context of other changes in the general economic environment affecting business, many of which are independently encouraging internationalisation. Overall, it was judged that the prospects for a small peripheral Member State were better in a deeply integrated economic, monetary, social and political union, than in a free trade area which left more decisions to the play of diplomatic power.

For example, the Irish Congress of Trade Unions (ICTU), which had opposed not only accession in 1972, but also the SEA in the referendum of 1987, was, by 1989, promoting integration in a campaign entitled 'Make Europe Work for Us'.

As it transpired, the completion of the European internal market was a most important factor in the recovery and reorientation of the Irish economy. It also had a profound effect on the relation between the state and the market. It is now clear that Ireland's overall approach to market and social regulation has been significantly reshaped by membership of the EU.

First, the internal market was a cause of the increase in US and Japanese investment in Europe in the late 1980s and early 1990s, as companies sought to get inside the large, new, single European market. Ireland's membership of the EC, and clear intention to participate in the deepening of integration, was a major element in our attractiveness to the new wave of companies investing in Europe.

Second, for Irish companies which had survived the shake-out of the early 1980s, and for new firms, the internal market provided both new market opportunities and a focus for their business strategy. Each sector and company was invited to analyse its readiness for intensified competition and wider market opportunities. Issues of peripherality and market access were widely discussed, and all sorts of solutions found. One of the striking changes in Irish business in the past decade is precisely in the field of logistics.

Third, this energising effect of the internal market was particularly important in services – such as banking, insurance, finance, aviation and road haulage – which had operated in a relatively protected environment. Irish citizens and companies benefited significantly from the lower prices and better quality induced by more competition. Irish companies have responded to increased competition by adopting aggressive strategies at an international level. McAleese points out that there was very significant inward investment in services, particularly in the International Financial Services Centre. Much of the increase in Irish employment in the 1990s has occurred in the market services sector.

An important element of the European internal market was free movement of capital. This was promoted by abolition of exchange controls throughout the Community and creation of a regulatory framework for a 'European financial area'. This has benefited Irish individuals and companies, allowing them to access capital abroad, diversify their portfolios and maximise their return on capital. It has assisted fiscal correction by imposing an element of market discipline on government. However, increased capital mobility has made tax evasion and avoidance easier. As McAleese notes, governments in high-tax jurisdictions are under pressure to reduce tax rates so as to minimise incentives to transfer capital to lower-tax jurisdictions. In the years to come, taxation will undoubtedly become a matter of international co-ordination, with the EU playing a key role.

Fourth, during the 1990s, Irish competition policy was aligned with European law and the role of the Competition Authority strengthened. This has benefited Irish consumers and enterprises. A deeper long-term effect may be the emergence of a competition culture in Ireland.

Fifth, a critical aspect of the internal market programme was increased EC monitoring and control of state aids which distort competition between firms in different Member States. In Chapter 8, McAleese observes that 'an Irish government untrammelled by Brussels would have found difficulty in turning off the flow of subsidies to several economically weak but politically sensitive companies (Irish Steel, Aer Lingus and the beef processing industry for instance)'. The internal market strengthened the hand of government by limiting its freedom to provide state aid. It did not entirely undermine the state's developmental role, as the EU has allowed more leeway for state aids in Objective 1 regions. While the restriction of state aids to the large state-owned firms forced them to review and improve their commercial performance, there remains a fear that the clientelist tendency in Irish politics has been diverted to new sectors and new types of support.

Sixth, the internal market was, and will be, the cause of radical change in public utilities – telecommunications, electricity, gas and postal services – which have traditionally been high-priced, inefficient, and tend to be run more for the benefit of providers than as a service to the public.

Overall, the combination of social partnership and the European internal market programme is a particularly interesting aspect of the Irish story. Social partnership has all sorts of advantages. But one possible limit of consensus is the difficulty of undertaking radical action which disrupts entrenched interests, such as those in Telecom Eireann, the ESB, Bord Gáis, An Post or protected sectors such as banking and insurance. As McAleese says, Irish policy-makers were not inclined to rock the boat in protected public utilities and services. (Although, in my view, we were even less likely to achieve change in these sectors without social partnership, given the power of lobbies over Irish political parties.) In any event, while social partnership stabilised the Irish economy, European integration produced a steady pressure to make public utilities and services more efficient, consumer-oriented and independent of overt or covert state subsidy or protection. Thus Ireland benefited from an unusual, but benign, combination of institutionalised co-ordination of the key economic actors and pressure for market conformity.

As the century ends, it is clear that Ireland's approach to market regulation, and the relationship between market, state and society, has been significantly reshaped by membership of the EU. One way to see this is to list the independent regulatory agencies established since accession, particularly those created since the internal market programme in the late 1980s. The process began with the creation of the Employment Equality Agency in 1977 and the Director of Consumer Affairs in 1978, both the direct result of EC policy. As the internal market programme took hold, we saw the creation of the Health and Safety Authority in 1989, and the Pensions Board in 1990. There followed a torrent of institution-building with the establishment of the Competition Authority, the Environmental Protection Agency and the Radiological Protection Institute in 1992, the Irish Aviation Authority and the National Milk Agency in 1994, the Food Safety Authority in 1995, the telecommunications regulator in 1997, with a new energy regulator to be in place by 2000.

These new regulatory agencies have three important characteristics. First, they are independent of government and politics. The independence from government contrasts with the traditional Irish approach, which involved public ownership of most public utilities – such as electricity, gas, postal services, telecommunications and many other companies – and direct state responsibility for the setting and enforcing of rules in highly regulated sectors, such as financial services. Second, they separate supply of a product (or provision of a service) from regulation. Previously, state agencies, such as An Bord Bia (the Food Board) or An Bord Bainne (the Milk Board), had responsibility for both the commercial development of these sectors and for standards within them. The creation of the Food Safety Authority and National Milk Agency assigns the regulatory function to a separate agency. Third, most of these new agencies are a part of a network of European regulatory agencies. For example, the Environmental Protection Agency works in a network with the European Environmental Agency and the agencies in other Member States. Research at EU level suggests that involvement in these European networks enhances both the technical expertise and professional standard of independent regulatory agencies.

This reconfiguration of market regulation is a major change in Irish public administration and policy. While it moved certain functions from government departments to independent agencies, the internal market programme nevertheless intensified the interaction between the Irish administration and Europe. It increased the EU workload in those Departments which had existing relations with the Union, and brought European policy issues, directives and regulations to the work of new Departments, such as those regulating services and public utilities. This increased workload occurred without the recruitment or secondment of additional staff because of severe financial constraints. As Laffan shows in Chapter 10, this accentuated an existing feature of Ireland's administrative approach. Irish civil servants service a wider range of committees than their counterparts in other Member States, and are responsible for the implementation of laws once passed.

Indeed, the enormous expansion in EU regulation which followed the Single Act did lead to problems of implementation. At the beginning of the 1990s, Ireland's implementation record, which had been relatively good, began to deteriorate. It took a number of years to improve the transposition of EU directives into national legislation. Late implementation of a gender equality Directive in social security in the 1980s led to successful legal challenges by a number of Irish women through the Irish and European legal systems.

Structural Funds and Policy Innovation

Assessments of Ireland's membership of the EU often emphasise the receipt of Structural Funds in the late 1980s and 1990s. It is important to note that the internal market programme, and the Treaty of Maastricht, provided the context in which the Structural and Cohesion Funds were increased and reformed in what are known as the Delors I and Delors II packages. Indeed, as is shown below, the true impact of the funds cannot be ascertained outside of that context. There is no doubt that the Structural Funds have had a significant impact on the Irish economy, administration and public policy.

During the decade from 1989 to 1999 Ireland's receipts from the Structural Funds amounted to about 2.6 per cent of GNP (McAleese, Chapter 8). This scale of assistance can be compared with World Bank estimates of aid flows to middle-income developing countries of 1 per cent of GNP. If receipts under the guarantee and guidance sections of the CAP are included, Ireland's net receipts from the EU averaged over 5 per cent of GNP throughout the 1990s, peaking at 7.6 per cent in 1991.

The impact of the Structural Funds on the Irish economy and society is hard to quantify. Most statistical estimates calculate the impact on economic growth assuming a certain rate of return on investment in infrastructure, training etc. As McAleese says, most people are rather surprised by the modest effects thrown up by these economic impact studies. They suggest that the Structural Funds received under the Delors I and Delors II packages have increased the level of GNP by 2 percentage points. McAleese suggests that the econometric models may underestimate the impact because they necessarily exclude certain important non-quantifiable effects. Among these is the impact on public policy. Irish policy had a strong developmental bias since the late 1950s. The severe fiscal crisis of the 1980s meant that expenditure control became an absolute priority. While this was necessary, it did have the effect of crowding-out developmental considerations. The doubling of the Structural Funds in the late 1980s, and the significant reform in their principles and procedures, had an important effect in re-introducing developmental thinking and procedures to the Irish public service.

In addition, the emphasis on programming, monitoring and evaluation in the reformed Structural Funds had a significant impact on the procedures of Irish public administration. For a variety of reasons, the Irish system did not have a strong tradition of monitoring and evaluation. The Structural Funds prompted the creation of new Evaluation Units, whose work has made an important contribution to the revision and improvement of Irish policy. The increased Structural Funds produced a step-increase in the administrative engagement with the Union. The civil service had to rely on the semi-state sector for technical support and analysis.

Membership of the EU has had significant implications for the auditing of public expenditure. While Irish public administration has a long tradition of political independence and a high level of propriety, financial transactions between the Union and national level have introduced a new layer of auditing.

Through the Structural Funds, EU membership has begun to have some effect on the regional dimension of Irish policy. In the 1970s, the Structural Funds reinforced the centralisation of Irish policy. However, the reform of the Funds in the late 1980s introduced the principle of 'partnership'. The Community was anxious that the development programmes supported by the Funds be designed and implemented by a partnership between national government, regional interests and, in some contexts, the social partners. In order to comply with this, the Irish government established a set of regional consultative committees and eventually a set of Regional Authorities. While opinions differ on the significance of regional consultation and monitoring, there is no doubt that the politics of development has evolved to include diffuse interests including local authorities, community groups, environmental groups, and the social partners. There was also a European dimension to several of the innovative and experimental policy approaches adopted by Irish government and public agencies in the past decade. One example is the partnership approach to local development, involving the social partners, the community and voluntary sector and state agencies. This approach was prompted both by earlier Community Initiatives on poverty and rural development, and a recognition, in the 1990 national partnership programme, of the limits of mainstream, centralised, government policy in solving problems of long-term unemployment and local degeneration. After a pilot programme, this approach was included in Ireland's National Development Plan in 1993 and supported under the Structural Funds. Indeed, the Irish government made local development one of the themes of its 1996 Presidency, and found great interest in other Member States. Ireland's approach to local development was the subject of an OECD study, which judged it to be an experiment in economic regeneration and participative democracy which was, potentially, of international significance.[14] There is much evidence that the Union, through the Commission, is a stimulus to policy innovation and experimentation. The Irish experience supports this view.

From EMS to EMU

Britain's unsuccessful post-war combination of macroeconomic policy and income determination, characterised by confrontational industrial relations and a political business-cycle, weakened Ireland's competitiveness and imparted an inflationary and conflictual bias to our wage-bargaining. As Halligan says in Chapter 3, Ireland's membership of monetary union with Britain meant that neither exchange nor interest rates could be used to stimulate economic growth. He notes that 'this restriction on the exercise of economic independence excited little political comment, and none at all from the class of academic economists which has been so critical of EMU in recent years on precisely these grounds'.

Ireland joined the European Monetary System on its establishment in 1979, thereby abandoning its 150-year-old link with sterling. With sterling volatile and outside the system, the EMS was naturally a difficult regime for Ireland. The painful experience of the early 1980s showed the need for greater discipline in both public finance and wage-bargaining. Ireland used the realignments in the ERM to pragmatically steer a middle course between sterling and the DM. Consequently, the regime was associated with very high and volatile interest rates and a fairly volatile exchange rate against all our trading partners. 'Nevertheless,' says Honohan, 'it has to be acknowledged that the fiscal crisis was not allowed to spill over into monetary excess and accelerating inflation, such as has been experienced in many other countries in fiscal crisis.'[15]

A policy approach consistent with low inflation and economic growth was achieved through a combination of the EMS and social partnership programmes, which were in place from 1987. These produced wage growth consistent with competitiveness and embodied a negotiated consensus on a range of economic and social policies, including the Maastricht criteria for entry to EMU.

With the completion of the internal market, the issue of full monetary union was reopened at Community level. The internal market deepened economic union, undermined the ERM and led directly to the Maastricht Treaty. It became widely accepted that only through EMU could Europe avoid damaging exchange-rate volatility. In the longer term, there was a strong sense that the US could not have developed as it had, or have remained the world's leading economy, if its states or regions had retained separate currencies. The length and depth of Europe's quest for exchange-rate stability is not recognised or understood by those Irish economists who see monetary union as a purely political project.

Given its difficult experience in the EMS, Ireland was supportive of the move to EMU. This was reinforced by a new perspective on the regional effects of integration. In the 1960s, it was believed that it is the monetary stage of integration that presents weaker or peripheral regions with the greatest problems. By the late 1980s, there was more focus on the economic forces unleashed by free trade and mobility of labour and capital, and less belief that devaluation could offer protection from competition. This new perspective – which is borne out by our history – took Irish concern away from monetary integration and focused it on the real factors which determine international competitiveness. For at least a decade from 1988, it was the working assumption of Irish leaders that we would join EMU. This was seen not so much as a surrender of sovereignty, as a focus on areas of effective sovereignty – supply-side measures, social cohesion and co-operation – where Ireland could still influence its own prosperity.

It is significant that social partnership and European integration were the subject of consensus, across both the social partners and the party political spectrum. Adopting this approach, Ireland has made major advances in economic management and performance. This consensus took the exchange rate, and therefore inflation, outside day-to-day party political competition and industrial relations conflict. It freed government, management and unions to focus on the real economy. EMU was seen as offering Ireland the opportunity to copper-fasten that approach.

Although the Maastricht Treaty was ratified by referendum in 1992, there was a mini-debate on EMU in the late 1990s. Given UK non-participation, it was not hard to show that EMU might occasionally yield an exchange rate with sterling that was not ideal. This was the main basis for argument against EMU advanced by certain economists in the late 1990s. EMU was criticised on the assumption that the 'correct' exchange rate could be costlessly identified and achieved. But the real alternative was different, and had three negative aspects.

First, the comparison should have been between an imperfect EMU and a regime of currencies undershooting and overshooting. Second, the alternative to EMU would have brought the exchange rate back into the political arena. Ireland had eight changes of government and seven elections after joining EMS in 1979 – a high number by European standards. If even one significant political party had been persuaded by the opponents of EMU, then it is hard to imagine that we could have had the consistent economic policy of the past thirteen years. The non-EMU framework would have enmeshed policy in inconclusive doctrinal and technical debates. Third, the alternative was one that would have abandoned or undermined the social-partnership approach. It is no coincidence that the opponents of EMU are also the most vehement critics of social partnership. They have argued that social partnership is undemocratic, increases trade union power, maintains high unemployment, reduces flexibility and prevents adjustment to movements in sterling. These arguments employ a doctrinal notion of wage flexibility, missing the substantive flexibility, and incentives to co-operation, in the more pragmatic partnership approach.

McAleese summarises well when he says that the failure of the anti-EMU case can be traced to three main defects:

> One relates to *timing* – the anti-arguments have come too late in the decision-making process. Another defect relates to *content*. The arguments are substantive, but not compelling. The final problem concerns *perspective*. A decision to go into or stay out of EMU should not be dictated by short-term considerations, whether they be the specific sterling exchange rate in any month or the existence or absence of a housing boom in Dublin. A decision to stay out of EMU would have required the

articulation of an alternative strategy for Ireland's long-run development, not just a simple 'no'.

To be fair to the opponents of economic and monetary union, they might be considered to have offered an alternative strategy. For, as noted above, the case against the deepening of European integration was closely linked to the case against social partnership; and with the case for decentralised, de-politicised, wage bargaining and the retention of currency sovereignty as an instrument of activist macroeconomic management. But that alternative economic and political strategy – with its textbook separation of market and state, objection to the linking of economics and politics, and insistence on the sovereignty of government both internationally and domestically – had limited appeal for Irish economic or political actors. By the time this case was put, key actors had not only developed a shared perspective, based on a high level of consensus and participation in Europe's path to EMU, but had seen it produce a dramatic transformation of the economy.

INTERPRETING THE ROLE OF EUROPE IN IRISH DEVELOPMENT

Europe's New Governance and Ireland's Transformation

Consider the number and variety of European influences identified in our survey of the first 25 years: inward investment, Structural Funds, developmental planning, monitoring and evaluation, competitive re-orientation of Irish industry, access to European markets in both products and services, a new regulatory framework in services and utilities, new standards and agencies for consumer rights, environmental protection and social regulation, financial discipline, low and predictable inflation, capital mobility without severe volatility, effective exchange-rate policy, a conception and language of social partnership and consensus, and support for policy innovation and experimentation, especially in the sphere of social exclusion and local development. There can be no doubt that the deepening of European integration, and the emergence of a new shared perspective on Ireland's place in Europe, was a profound influence on Ireland's economic and social experience, particularly in the past decade.

The reader might be tempted to ask whether this is to claim too much. Was Ireland unique in being so thoroughly influenced by the

Union's policies, institutions and laws? Why was Ireland so deeply affected? The answer to these questions can be found if we forget Ireland, and look at the same decade-and-a-half from a European perspective. Here I mention a few characteristics of the Union which show why it might have a profound effect on a country like Ireland.[16]

First, the completion of the European internal market is of historic significance. With it, the EU signalled that it did not intend to be by-passed by the dynamic change occurring in the world economy, did not intend to live off its past wealth, becoming a *rentier* continent. In the circumstances prevailing in the 1980s and 1990s, prioritising European integration (without a Fortress Europe) cut with the grain of fundamental changes in economic organisation, public administration, social life and technology. A significant part of that movement was the liberalisation and internationalisation of markets. The quantitative accumulation of market-opening measures produced a qualitative shift in the degree of integration, the pattern of market governance in Europe and, it seems, in the nature of the integration process.

Rather than amassing extensive and autonomous political authority, the Union gradually altered the exercise of national political authority by enmeshing the Member States in a web of collaboration and co-operation. The governance of the Union rests largely on embedding the national in the European and the European in the national. This is achieved through institutionalisation and constitutionalisation. The complexity of this enmeshing defies any neat division between Union and national competencies. The implications of integration were taken inside each national system, as a source of regime change and institutional adaptation. Scholars of European integration have been seeking a terminology to capture this aspect of the system. One emerging description is 'multi-level governance', which is contrasted with the 'state-centric' conception which dominated earlier analyses of European integration.

Second, openness to Europeanisation, and adaptation to internationalisation, varies from Member State to Member State, and across different social groups. In some states, and among some social forces, a nostalgia for the grand era of the West European state is still evident. Given Ireland's complete lack of nostalgia for the grand era of the European state, and a desire to escape from the not-so-grand era of the closed Irish state, it was very open to both Europeanisation and internationalisation.

Third, the EU is a strong example of what is becoming known as 'new governance'. Governing is no longer conducted exclusively by the state. It is undertaken by networks of public, private and voluntary groups. The function of governance is primarily regulation of activities, markets and risks, rather than state ownership or management. The new governance, when it works well, transforms 'bargaining' into 'problem-solving'. In research on the EU, there is much interest in identifying the degree to which problem-solving governance replaces lowest-common-denominator outcomes. While patterns of economic and social governance are moving in this direction in the Member States (and across the world), this is reflected more quickly and more visibly in the Union, since it is new, always part-formed, decentralised, and unburdened by the large-scale expenditure programmes of the post-war nation state.

Fourth, the Union should be seen as a new model of internationalisation. The European model of internationalisation involves voluntary freeing of trade and significant deregulation, combined with new rule-setting, the development of common policies, the creation of institutions for permanent negotiation and the development of redistributive mechanisms. This contrasts with the forms of internationalisation which have dominated world history for many thousands of years: imperial conquest, colonisation, freeing of trade under a hegemonic power and, in the post-war period, multilateral trade liberalisation.

These characteristics resolve much of the mystery about why European integration should have had such significant effects on Ireland since the mid-1980s. During this period it was profoundly altering the sovereignty, governance and government of all countries in the Union – transforming them from *nation* states to *member* states. But the effect on Ireland was likely to be greater. The EU was becoming a new model of internationalisation: one which goes far beyond free trade, constrains the naked use of economic and diplomatic power, is law-based and consensual. This could be particularly transformative for a country which had for centuries experienced the sharp end of internationalisation in several other guises: colonial conquest, undemocratic incorporation in an imperial state, de-industrialisation, catastrophic migratory flows, and, after independence, supplicant status in the international diplomatic order.

A similar view is expressed by Garvin in Chapter 4, who argues that 'in these islands Europe symbolises the end of empire and therefore the obsolescence of the ancient English-Irish quarrel'. This, he says, has been 'the true European achievement in Ireland', an achievement which far outweighs the undoubted economic benefits. 'The odd thing is, we have scarcely noticed that the 800-year war is over, dying quietly and unmourned sometime between 1972 and 1998.' Likewise, Fintan O'Toole has suggested that 'the strange paradox of the first 25 years of our participation in the EU is that in the act of pooling our sovereignty we have discovered why we wanted it in the first place'.[17] In Chapter 5, Martin Cullen argues that membership has 'developed and strengthened Ireland's capacity to engage the outside world' and suggests that our changed perception of and relationship with Britain would have 'been very much slower, and very much less self-assured, had we not had the European Community'.

If the emergence of a new model of internationalisation was critical, there was a further synergy in the Irish case. Different kinds of bankruptcy pushed the EU and Ireland in similar directions. The degeneration of the European integration process in the 1970s and early 1980s, and the sheer stasis of its larger continental Member States, pushed Jacques Delors to radical action; but, the constraints on Union action dictated a reliance on consensus-based, multi-level, associative, experimental approaches. The failure of Ireland's political, commercial, social and interest-mediation systems pushed Ireland to try something new; but, the limits of state-led development and policy, and the lack of support for neo-liberalism, dictated reliance on consensus-based, associative and experimental approaches. Both were in uncharted territory, and both had to achieve a move from bargaining to problem-solving – of exactly the sort described by Monnet in his 1962 essay 'A Ferment of Change', quoted at the head of this chapter. A summary interpretation of the role of deepening European integration in Irish development is presented at the end of this essay.

Differential Impact on Government, Interest Representation, Society and Party Politics

Membership has had a profound impact on Irish government, interest representation and society. By contrast, European integration would seem to have had less direct impact on Irish party politics. Here we summarise the impact in each of these spheres, and suggest an explanation for the differential influences.

Government

The impact of integration on government has been significant. As shown in Chapters 10 and 11, the high level of consensus on EC membership meant that civil servants and government ministers were free to deal with EC issues using existing procedures and norms. Irish ministers, civil servants, officials in the state-sponsored sector, and representatives of interest groups now participate in thousands of meetings at ministerial and official levels in the Council and the Commission. Committees and working parties are a core element of the Union's governance structures. Performance of the Presidency is highly valued, extremely demanding, but is a major focus for Irish civil servants and ministers. The impact of the EU varies across government Departments, depending on whether their engagement with the Union is over-arching, multi-sectoral or sectoral. After 1988, the Community had the effect of strengthening programming, monitoring and evaluation within the Irish system. The EU has added a new layer to the auditing of public expenditure. Membership has moved Ireland's approach to market and social regulation towards independent regulatory agencies. While EU policy has prompted Ireland towards new forms of regionalisation, this has not been at the expense of central government. The 25 years of membership have seen a significant strengthening of strategic policy approaches. There has been an emerging strand of experimentalism in Irish public policy, which has been supported, and sometimes prompted, by the Union. It is notable that almost every one of these changes in government has strengthened the executive relative to the Oireachtas (Parliament), but not relative to interest associations, market operators, the European Commission or the Court of Justice. In Ireland's case, this effect has been enhanced by the extent to which national policy is dominated by the CAP and the Structural Funds.

In regard to EU policy, the opposition is more like the snooker player who is not at the table than a traditional parliamentary opposition. They know that they would approach the issues in a very similar way. They know that vocal opposition, or undermining of the government's position, is likely to be futile, or damaging, or both. While perceived instances of gross clientelism, such as the Healy-Rae affair, create an opportunity to attack the government's approach, this is the exception rather than the rule. Reflecting the importance of national representation, O'Toole has argued that Ireland has taken extraordinarily well to the EU partly because it has spoken simultaneously to both our 'traditional' and 'modern' sides. 'While speeding up our often painful transition into a modern society, it has also, oddly, vindicated one of our stronger traditions: nationalism.'[18]

Interest Representation
Reflecting the experimentation with new policy approaches, there has been significant change in interest representation. From the outset, economic interests that were most affected by EU policies mobilised and established a presence in Brussels. As Laffan emphasises in

Chapter 10, mobilisation is not limited to economic interest groups. With the expansion of the remit of the Union, women's groups, environmentalists, local authorities, anti-poverty groups, consumer groups, citizens groups and welfare rights groups participate in the Brussels arena of politics. They are drawn into transnational politics by EU finance, the deliberate creation of networks by the Commission and the desire to influence the direction of EU regulation and policy. Revitalised community groups, a marked feature of Irish politics since the late-1980s, look to EU involvement for money, policy strategies and channels of influence over the Irish government. Validation by the Commission can be an important resource in dealing with the government at home. A voice on national policy can be found at both European and national level.

Society, Culture and Identity
The first 25 years of EU membership have also seen an astonishing set of social changes. Perhaps the most dramatic was that in the role of women in society, the economy and public life. The long process of reforming legislation and changing attitudes – which seemed an uphill battle in the 1960s and 1970s, and looked as though it might be reversed in the psychosis and reaction of the 1980s – suddenly bore fruit, as women emerged in every area of life. Mention has been made of urbanisation and the modernisation of rural society. A significant set of changes, as yet undocumented, is the emergence of an entrepreneurial culture and the adoption of radically new approaches to management and organisation. Without the unleashing of enterprise and improvement in management and organisation, the benign macroeconomic and market access conditions since the mid-1980s could not have produced the commercial breakthrough, so often referred to as the 'Celtic Tiger'. It seems likely that advance in enterprise, management and organisation is related to internationalisation and secularisation. Other social changes, particularly in the period since 1987, include: a continued increase in average levels of educational attainment; a new emphasis on the rights of children; a revival of local community and voluntary activity; a decline, and subsequent collapse, in the influence of the Catholic Church; a revival, or perhaps reinvention, of Irish culture, and a much increased confidence in Irishness; the emergence of a culture of revelation and investigation, which is a step on the road to a stronger culture of accountability; the spread of information technology through a large segment of the society; increased inequality in access to these new economic and social resources; and, finally, the discovery (or invention) of the Irish diaspora.

This staggering list of social and cultural change must be given its place in the story of Ireland's experience in Europe. It is clear that Europe should not be seen as the sole, or even primary, source of the social and cultural change which has occurred in Ireland in the past 25 years. But, as Garvin says in Chapter 4, the tendency to modernisation and urbanisation would probably have been far slower under the old British-Irish customs union that was evolving in the 1960s. In Chapter 9, FitzGerald argues that the success of Irish officials, politicians and business people in the demanding European environment 'has banished the inferiority complex which was such a debilitating feature of much of the post-independence period'. Hederman O'Brien also links EU membership with the growth of national self-confidence, noting the complex relationship between the two. Ryan argues that EC membership has given minority cultures and languages a new self-assurance. He also points out that the emerging dialogue between Member States and the EU institutions has yielded a more disciplined, programmatic and accountable approach to problems of social exclusion.

While the collapse in the influence of the Catholic Church is clearly not a direct result of EU membership, Ryan suggests that it reflects a fundamental reversal of roles between church and society, which has to do with internationalisation. From the 1930s to the 1950s, Irish society was introspective, while the Church was one of the few institutions which offered an outward-looking ideal. 'It is now the nation that is looking out at the world, taking its place among the nations in Europe, while the Church has become introspective and unsure.'

While the EU didn't create the conflict between tradition and modernity of the past 25 years, O'Toole says that membership meant 'that conflict could only be resolved in favour of modernity'. 'After 1973, it was simply impossible to imagine an alternative project for the Irish future which could even begin to compete with the European one.'[19]

The underlying idea, that Irish identity can only be understood and strengthened in open interaction with others, is well expressed by Ryan in Chapter 6. Membership has strengthened the very identity which we previously tried to protect by isolation. 'Today we realise that openness is more conducive to keeping us Irish, that Europe is the context in which we can be more comfortably ourselves.' This is not to suggest that in culture, any more than in business, membership of the EU has greatly diluted the American influence – something I discuss below.

A particular aspect of the change in culture and identity has been the discovery or invention of the Irish diaspora. For a long time, the prevailing view of Irish emigration was a tragic or catastrophic one, which meshed well with the classic concept of diaspora derived from the Jewish experience – although we did not use the word 'diaspora'. Because of changes in Ireland, changes in the nature of Irish emigration in the late 1980s and the advancement of Irish people abroad, the Irish diaspora has become something of an investment diaspora and certainly a predominantly cultural diaspora.

There was a shift (in both policy circles, the society and business) from the idea of emigration as a tragedy, to an idea of diaspora as an opportunity. During the late-1980s and 1990s, Ireland has partly *become* internationalised, and partly *rediscovered* that it has been internationalised for a very long time.

Party Politics
In contrast to these striking changes in government, interest representation and society, it is difficult to identify a clear impact of EU membership on Irish party politics. In a number of respects, the Irish political parties have sought to fend off the changes to domestic politics which might have been produced by European integration. Parties systematically attempted to continue domestic political competition. Indeed, O'Toole argues that the Structural Funds 'gave a whole new life to a clientelism that might otherwise have died'.[20]

Most importantly, the political parties did not let European integration divide them. Once the accession referendum was decided, the Labour Party accepted that Ireland's future was in the Community. This adaptation was, of course, aided by the fact that it was in government almost immediately afterwards. But this is more than an historical accident. It highlights something fundamental about the EU, at least as far as small states are concerned. EU membership, and the day-to-day policy issues which arise in Europe, are not political 'issues' in the conventional sense.

Within the cross-party consensus, there is a discernible, if slight, difference between the two largest parties in their approaches to European integration. The emergence of the cross-party consensus on Europe owes something to the fact that the larger parties have been hegemonised by the Labour Party on one important European issue, neutrality. At some point during the first 25 years, Ireland's pragmatic and nationalist position of neutrality in the Second World War was transformed into a wider notion of neutrality and elevated into a principle shared by all political parties. Conformity on this issue has the great advantage that the parties are rarely asked to explain what the principle or policy is. Nevertheless, Europe's increasing engagement with the external issues is slowly forcing Irish political parties to distinguish between foreign policy, security policy and defence.

It is, of course, an exaggeration to say that there is complete cross-party consensus on European integration. The Green Party has emerged as an opponent of integration and campaigned actively against the Single Act, the Maastricht Treaty and the Amsterdam Treaty. However, it is too early to assess the significance of Green Party electoral successes for the politics of European integration. The composition, and probably the policy, of that party would seem to owe something to the scattering of left-republicanism, as well as the emergence of an environmental consciousness in Ireland. In the long run, it seems unlikely that the increasing number of Irish citizens committed to environmentalism, and the enlightened internationalism which that entails, will want environmentalism conflated with ultra-nationalism and a thoroughly old-fashioned notion of state sovereignty.

The clientelist nature of Irish constituency politics and the weakness of a committee system in the both Dáil and Senate militated against their extensive involvement in EU affairs. As noted above, the executive has been largely unfettered in its management of Ireland's EU policy. The creation of the Foreign Affairs Committee and the Joint Committee on European Affairs represents an attempt to undo this occlusion.

Perhaps the most significant change in party politics is one which has accentuated its decreasing real significance: acceptance of coalition as the norm. Since accession, the party composition of Irish government has gone through rapid change, such that almost all parties have been in government. Ireland would seem to have moved to a system of permanent, but frequently renegotiated, coalition. This certainly brings Ireland nearer to a continental European form of government, which does not have the 'winner takes all' and 'oppositional' characteristics of the British system.

Explaining the Differential Impact
How should we understand the fact that EU membership has had a profound impact on government, interest representation and society, yet apparently little impact on Irish party politics? The main explanation, I suggest, lies in an historical shift in the nature of government, which is particularly pronounced in the European Union.

The complexity, volatility and diversity of economic and social problems, and of social groups, are undermining the capacity of traditional, post-war, legislative and administrative systems. Parliaments find it hard to pass laws which can accommodate the variety and unpredictability of situations which need to be addressed. Governments find it difficult to direct the operation of departments and agencies, and administer complex systems of delivery and scrutiny. These traditional roles are being replaced by new ones: policy entrepreneurship, obliging and assisting monitoring, facilitating communication and joint action between social interests, protection of the non-statutory organisations that now have responsibility in many policy spheres, and supporting interest-group formation. The relationship between policy-making, implementation and monitoring is changing, in ways which place monitoring, of a new sort, at the centre of policy development.[21]

These trends are particularly pronounced in the EU, because of its limited central budget and executive power, and its reliance on negotiated outcomes. Consequently, European integration is as much about change in the *nature* of government as change in the *level* of government.[22] These trends are creating a new kind of politics or public action, which is technocratic but also relies more heavily on firms, interest associations and citizens. Its main generic effect on party politics is to reduce the significance of traditional party competition, since this is based on an outdated view of the power, autonomy and effectiveness of central government. This effect is evident in most Member States.

The way in which this generic effect is felt, differs. It may result in the collapse of a dominant, corrupt, populist party, which behaved as if it owned the state (such as the Italian Christian Democrats). Or it may preserve the shell of inter-party competition, around a reality in which it is virtually irrelevant (such as in Ireland). Which of these outcomes occurs may be random, and of limited consequence.

There is, of course, a danger that the demise of substantive inter-party politics would leave party politics, and therefore government, to those interested only in the rents and patronage which remain available despite the new forms of governance. Yet the continuing role of national governments in the European Union, and the critical, if not yet defined, role of government in new forms of governance could make politics attractive to able people interested in the new society, economy and state.

FUTURE ORIENTATIONS

Ireland, Europe and America

Does Prosperity Alter Ireland's Interest in European Integration?
In its 1997 report, *European Union: Integration and Enlargement*, NESC asked 'Does Ireland's convergence towards average European income levels fundamentally alter its perspective on European integration and the direction the EU takes?' This question was prompted by the prospect of diminished Structural Funds, further reform of the CAP and EU enlargement to the east.

The Council's answer was that convergence does not justify a reversal of Ireland's approach to integration. First, while Ireland may no longer be a 'poor' state, it remains a small state. As a small state within the EU, Ireland retains an interest in an economic integration process which is shaped by European institutions, governed by law and accompanied by common policies. Second, although it is more deeply integrated than any other region, the EU leaves considerable scope for national policy in key areas which influence prosperity and social cohesion. Third, Ireland is well placed to understand and use the emerging, complex, multi-level, networked, decision-making system in the EU. Fourth, despite its convergence towards average European income levels, Ireland has a continuing interest in the EU having the authority, capacity and legitimacy to harmonise Member State actions and develop common policies. Fifth, the interest of a small peripheral Member State in progressive European integration is not inconsistent with an element of 'flexibility' or 'differentiated integration'. Similar arguments were advanced in the government's White Paper on foreign policy, *Challenges and Opportunities Abroad* (1998).

The acceptance of these arguments, suggests that, in Ireland, there is now an instinctive and widely shared appreciation of a key observation made by Abram and Antonia Chayes in their book, *The New Sovereignty*. They show that sovereignty no longer consists in the freedom of states to act independently, 'but in membership in reasonably good standing in the regimes that make up the substance of international life.'[23]

Does Ireland's Relationship with the US Qualify its Claim to be European?
In several chapters it has been pointed out that 25 years in the EU has not diminished Ireland's economic, political or cultural links with the United States. It is sometimes argued that this qualifies Ireland's involvement with Europe and contradicts its claim to be 'European'.

Is this view justified?

First, it is important to recall the critical role of the US in promoting and shaping European integration. Key characteristics of the new European Community, such as competition policy, were a direct reflection of American approaches to governance. Indeed, as Garvin notes in Chapter 4, Europe's shared popular culture is largely American. In recent years, the Italian political scientist Majone, has argued that the EU is emerging as a 'regulatory state', very much on the American model. Third, American (and Asian) companies are important in the European internal market. Finally, and most significantly, Ireland's close involvement with American enterprise is a key element in the economic breakthrough of the past decade.

For all these reasons, accounts which counter-pose Ireland's relationship with the US to our involvement in the EU – and see the former as some kind of contradiction, or qualification, of the latter – are misconceived, on numerous counts. They miss the very nature of the EU. They assume that an economic, monetary and political union requires as its basis a homogeneous cultural identity. Many Member States have complex external and internal relationships, many with America, and these are entirely consistent with European union. How can an economic connection which has promoted regional convergence in Europe be damaging to the EU? How can a political connection which has promoted peace in NI (in partnership with the EU) detract from Europe? At a more base level, would other Member States prefer that Irish migration in times of economic difficulty was exclusively to continental Europe? The view that Ireland's American and European attachments are in conflict is, ultimately, based on an old-fashioned idea of sovereignty and an inability to grasp the reality of multiple identities. As Cullen says in Chapter 5, 'We have avoided any suggestion of a "zero-sum" game in developing these relationships and this is one of the many successes of our participation in Europe.'

There is a further way in which Ireland's involvement with America can be a positive contribution to Europe. Ireland's position as a base for American companies might be seen as undermining Europe if certain conditions held: if international business transactions were a zero-sum game and if America was competing with a well-functioning European economic and social model. Neither of these conditions hold. As Cassells shows in Chapter 7, the European social model is urgently in need of reform, if not radical recasting. Europe needs to emulate the technological, organisational, financial and entrepreneurial drive shown by the American economy in the past decade. In a small way, the attraction of American companies to the European periphery – and the economic dynamism and political flexibility of countries such as Ireland, Finland, Portugal and the Netherlands – underline the relative stagnation of much of continental Europe, and demonstrate innovative approaches to balancing economic revitalisation with social solidarity.

Finding a Synthesis of Strategy and Pragmatism

Ireland's first 25 years in the EU have witnessed many policy successes and some policy disasters. Although the policy disasters were primarily at domestic level, it has been argued in this chapter that they can be interpreted as failures to handle internationalisation. The failures raise concern about the conduct of Ireland's European policy. As Laffan shows in Chapter 10, Ireland's approach to EU policy is reactive and agenda-driven. The co-ordination of policy is informal, not institutionalised, and achieved by ad hoc contact between senior civil servants. Given past policy failures, it is sometimes argued that Ireland needs a more 'strategic' approach to its European policy. Indeed, taking the first 25 years as a whole, lack of 'strategy' and 'preparation' have been the most common and trenchant criticisms of Irish government.

Are these criticisms justified, and do the ideas of 'strategy', 'co-ordination' and 'preparation' provide a basis for improvement of Ireland's policy approach? A number of points must be noted before these suggestions can be accepted.

First, criticisms of lack of strategy and co-ordination often cite agriculture, particularly successive governments' judgement that Ireland's national interest lay in maximising CAP prices and agricultural supports. There would seem to be some validity in the argument of Garret FitzGerald, NESC and others, cited in Section 3 above, that in the 1970s and 1980s this was sometimes short-sighted or deflected attention from other issues. NESC suggested that 'the criterion by which Ireland's membership of the Community be assessed should primarily be the kind of economy which evolved as a result of EC membership and only secondarily whether a particular strategy maximised receipts from the Commission'.[24] Ministers and officials might accept that, but argue that there was rarely a trade-off, let alone a conflict, between the CAP and other EC issues relevant to Ireland. They might argue that Ireland has never had to sacrifice gains on other fronts, such as Structural Funds, internal market or world trade, in order to retain CAP benefits. This could be so, in part, because of the fragmented nature of the Council system at EU level (see Chapter 10). Indeed, in discussing the idea of a government strategy balancing the CAP against the Structural Funds, Cromien observes, in Chapter 11, that 'the system does not seem to work that way'. Despite the role of package-deals in European integration, the sequential and sectoral element of EU negotiations seems to weaken the trade-off between the CAP and other policies.

Perhaps the issue is not whether Ireland might have adopted a radically different stance at European level, on the details of the CAP, the reform of the CAP or the balance between the CAP and other Community policies. One question is: could the enormous benefit which the CAP conferred on certain groups of farmers have been accompanied by national measures which rebalanced things in favour of other interests? Several such groups spring to mind: indigenous food companies, PAYE income-tax payers and, most of all, unskilled manual workers, the outright losers from economic internationalisation. Another question is: did the Department of Agriculture use the ongoing, if much postponed, movement towards liberalisation of world food markets as an instrument to push Irish agriculture and food industries towards genuine competitive advantage? These questions have more to do with domestic policy than 'strategy' or 'co-ordination' in Ireland's approach to the EU.

Second, the gross failure of Ireland's political and interest-mediation system in the 1970s and 1980s naturally gave rise to calls for more strategic policy and closer co-ordination. However, the huge benefits to be had from replacing opportunism with strategy can give rise to an exaggerated notion of strategy and planning.

Third, since the late 1970s, Ireland would seem to have had a strategic approach to European issues. Consider the clarity and success of Ireland's approach to the remarkable series of EU developments since the mid-1980s: the Single European Act, the Delors I package and increased Structural Funds, the internal market programme, the Delors Committee on monetary union, the MacSharry reforms of the CAP, the Uruguay Round, the negotiation of the Maastricht Treaty, the Delors II package and the Cohesion Fund, the negotiation of the Amsterdam Treaty, the transition to EMU and, most recently, Agenda 2000. In this context, calls for more strategy and co-ordination seem either unwarranted or imprecise.

Fourth, there are both advantages and disadvantages to having a small number of civil servants involved in major aspects of EU business, and an informal system of co-ordination. The possible disadvantages are obvious: overload, a focus only on key agendas and the risk of missing some significant item. Against these must be weighed the fact that Irish officials have a wider brief and can see more of the picture. In addition, small numbers mean that there is less need for formal, institutionalised, systems of co-ordination. Most observers agree with Cullen when he argues that Irish governments have 'punched above their weight' within the EU.

Fifth, the Irish experience clarifies what kind of strategy and co-ordination is most important to success in the EU. As shown earlier in this chapter, and in Chapter 9, Ireland adopted a highly conscious long-term strategy in the 1960s, and undertook meticulous forecasts of the effects of free trade on indigenous industry, yet displayed a distinct failure of adjustment. The contrast between the first period of membership, from 1973 to 1987, and the later period illustrates an important lesson. Successful adaptation of public policy and administration to EU membership can only be effective if there is a simultaneous adaptation of the party political and interest-mediation systems. Adoption of a coherent approach to social partnership and European integration since 1987 can be described as strategic, but involved abandoning the forecasting approach of earlier years. It seems that strategy and co-ordination are required at three different levels: within cabinet and the civil service, across the main political parties, and across the economic and social interests.

The need for a coherent approach across a range of actors, suggests that institutions which develop joint action and shared understanding are as important as high-level 'strategy'. Indeed, the Irish experience also clarifies the relationship between strategy and 'preparation'. The last months before EMU saw a frenzy of scepticism, cynicism and fretting, among journalists and some economists about Ireland's preparation for the euro, and calls for evidence of a 'policy' on sterling movements. This betrays a misconception about how complex organisations prepare for uncertain future events. It is the policy *system,* and *relations* between actors in the economy, which need to be prepared. Relations between actors are critical because the economic and social context is so unsettled and complex. An unsettled system is best dealt with by alertness and effectiveness, rather than a rigid strategy. Government and other actors are embroiled in the flow of events before they can develop a strategy, as traditionally defined. Actors who can co-ordinate their tactics and action are more likely to achieve a shared strategic overview.

This connection between action, institutions and strategy is sustained by the contributions to this volume. They show that Ireland's difficulties in the past 25 years reflected deep-set institutional and political weaknesses. For example, in Chapter 9, FitzGerald points out that the need for greater competition in electricity, gas, insurance, banking and building was recognised by the social partners as long ago as 1967. 'As in so many other cases our ability to identify problems and to point to how they might be resolved was not matched by an equivalent willingness to take possibly unpopular action to resolve them.' He identifies this as evidence of a more general truth: 'that democratic national governments tend to be subject to such strong pressure from vested interests within their own territories that many of their decisions operate against the interests of society as a whole'.

The Irish experience suggests that overcoming this problem requires four, inter-related, developments. One is the attraction to political office of able and principled people who will see that analysis is matched by action. A second is the sharing of sovereignty at European level, which 'has greatly improved the capacity of European politicians to govern in the public interest' (FitzGerald, Chapter 9). Third, is the building of institutional mechanisms, such as social partnership, which deepen and widen consensus on the need for change and strengthen the persuasive force of the reports and analyses which express that consensus. A fourth, more recent, response, used at both EU and Irish level, is to enlist relevant groups in the design and implementation of change.

Having critically examined the general argument for more 'strategy' and 'co-ordination', and suggested a synthesis of pragmatism and strategy, it is necessary to consider a more specific point raised by Laffan, in Chapter 10, and Cromien, in Chapter 11. Having outlined the strong performance of the Irish government system in the EU, Cromien suggests that 'there has been one obvious deficiency':

> It has proved very difficult to establish a way of appraising all the Community initiatives which are under consideration at any one time and deciding on an integrated national strategy for them, setting bargaining tactics and priorities, based on what is considered to be the best for the country.

If the wider aspects of strategy and co-ordination are taken care of, this may be read as an observation on the conduct of European business at the level of the civil service and cabinet. As such, it identifies a technical problem, which probably requires an expert solution. Given Ireland's apparent success in the series of epoch-making European advances since the mid-1980s, there would not seem to be a lack of co-ordination on major strategic European issues or portfolios. Perhaps the danger is that individual departments might adopt an approach to non-strategic issues – such as state aids or duty-free – which cut across Ireland's strategic orientation and damage relationships with the Commission, other Member States or the Parliament. Departments might not give EU issues the priority which they require, thereby leaving the Department of Foreign Affairs without sufficient guidance. A somewhat more formal system of co-ordination may be necessary to improve the performance of the system.

Will Irish Support for Europe Dissolve?

It was argued earlier in this Section, that Ireland has an ongoing interest in deep European integration, despite income convergence, the reduction (and eventual withdrawal) of Structural Funds and on-going reform of the CAP (leading towards free trade in agricultural products). But will this interest be recognised by the Irish population? There would seem to be a fear – even among officials with vast experience – that Irish support for integration could evaporate if the CAP and Structural Funds were significantly reduced and European security and foreign policy became more prominent.

If we unpack this view, we can see that it is implausible. Its first element is the belief that Irish support for integration has been based only on the CAP and the Structural Funds, and that these material motives are entirely separate from cultural or idealistic considerations. As such, it may derive from the bombastic focus of one or two office-holders on the size of the Structural Funds extracted from Brussels, and the ruthlessness of some sectoral interests in defending transfers. It is not clear that the society as a whole sees such a sharp distinction between the material, the cultural and the ideal, or sees them pulling in opposite directions. In any case, Ireland's future material interest will be based more on the market, and less on transfers or state aids; consequently, withdrawal of support for integration will make limited sense, even on material grounds. The second element is the idea that European foreign policy and security will be viewed negatively. As Hederman O'Brien notes in Chapter 2, Irish public opinion has, since the early 1960s, taken a positive view of involvement in peace-keeping and international affairs. There is no reason to believe that this positive attitude will change as Ireland's involvement deepens. Indeed, Irish people are likely to revel in the global role which the Presidency will periodically confer on Irish ministers.

This challenge to the pessimistic view is not based on a contrast between national self-interest and altruism towards a collective European ideal. Still less is it to argue that Irish support for integration was, will be, or should be, based on the ideal of European integration, rather than our interests. Rather than reverse the conventional wisdom, it rejects the terms in which it is cast: an excessive distinction between the cultural and the economic, the normative and the material, the actual and the ideal. Rather than reject national interest, it suggests a different view of how national interest is defined and pursued.

A significant future Irish contribution to Europe may concern the European social model. Taking the first 25 years as a whole, there is no doubt that Ireland has been a regime importer – on gender rights, environmental protection, health and safety, information and consultation, consumer protection, technical standards, service market regulation and public utilities. Indeed, at various times, there was an ambition to import a range of other European models: the German social market economy, with its co-determination, works councils and craft training; the Scandinavian model of social partnership, with low wage dispersion and high levels of social provision; the Danish national system of innovation, with a cluster of advanced sectors built around agriculture. While these models played a role in shaping policy, and facilitating social partnership, Ireland's economic breakthrough does not conform very closely to any of them.

At the same time, the larger Continental countries face severe difficulties, and their post-war systems of economic policy, sector regulation, industrial relations and social welfare are under strain. While most Member States pay homage to the 'European social model', there is a distinct lack of confidence about what its core elements should be. The sharp increase in European unemployment in the 1990s has drawn the Member States into an on-going dialogue on labour market policy through the so-called Essen process and the employment chapter of the Amsterdam Treaty. Cassells suggests, in Chapter 7, that rather than adopt a defensive approach, on issues such as corporation tax and state aids, Ireland should confidently promote those elements of its policy approach which have underpinned its economic dynamism, employment growth and social solidarity. While these were devised to address an acute Irish crisis, they are similar to the innovations in the more dynamic Continental economies, such as the Netherlands, Denmark, Finland, Portugal and Austria. He argues that the key general issue confronting the European social model is how to achieve greater flexibility and how to redefine the security which citizens require. Ireland can be both a learner and a teacher in Europe's search for a new combination of flexibility and security.

CONCLUSION: RE-INVENTING IRELAND

In summarising the effects and meaning of Ireland's first 25 years in the EU, I begin with a question raised over many years by Hederman O'Brien, and again in Chapter 2: what has Ireland contributed to European integration? The contributors to this volume have identified a range of Irish contributions. In Chapter 5, Cullen says that reform of the CAP, competition policy, the shape of regional and social policies and the development of structural and cohesion funding might all be said to owe something to Irish energies and ideas. As McAleese points out in Chapter 8, several of these inputs reflect Ireland's 'human contribution', rather than its 'policy contribution', since they arise from the impact of outstanding Irish individuals, such as Garret FitzGerald, Peter Sutherland, Ray MacSharry, Jim Dooge and Maurice Doyle. At a more general level, Ireland has held the Presidency five times, and is acknowledged to have handled it well. Indeed, there is some evidence that small Member States are more effective in the Presidency than larger ones. Smaller states can find it easier to lead the path to consensus, whereas larger countries have a wider range of interests of their own.

Perhaps Ireland's greatest contribution has been to have made a success of membership – economically, socially, culturally and politically. Recognition that this is the first, and greatest, contribution any country can make, is critical to an understanding of the European Union. It reflects the practical, pragmatic, and civic nature of the European project. Making a success of membership is by necessity a collective contribution, an achievement of the country, or society, not just of the state. Ireland's first 25 years shows that success in integration cannot be achieved by the state apparatus alone, however skilled, but requires a reorientation of systems throughout the economy and society.

To have made a success is a contribution in a more specific sense because of Ireland's background. Ireland's success proves that a small, peripheral, less-advanced, post-colonial country can catch up with the leading European post-imperial nations. It also proves that regional integration, of the sort developed in Europe, can facilitate such catch-up . This is all the more significant, now that the protectionist, authoritarian and non-democratic Asian models of catch-up and industrialisation are faltering, and new countries look to the EU. In a more specific sense, Ireland's use of the Structural Funds strengthens the case for the EU policy of 'economic and social cohesion'. While there are moral and analytical arguments for such a policy, and an undoubted element of solidarity in the EU's actions, effectiveness is the most compelling argument of all. The applicant countries are understandably interested in Ireland's experience.

Turning to the impact of European integration on Ireland, we face an obvious difficulty of interpretation. It is said that when James Joyce was asked in Paris when he had left Ireland, he replied that he never had. Those of us who grew up in Ireland between the 1920s and the 1960s, and live here now, have an exactly opposite experience. We live in the same place, but we might as well have emigrated. Without moving an inch, we live in a different country. Ireland at the end of the 20th century is unrecognisable from that of even the 1960s. What is the role of Europe in such pervasive change?

In seeking to identify the role of European integration in Irish development, I have distinguished between the early period of membership, from accession to the late-1980s, and the experience since then. At both domestic and European level, there was a significant difference between these two periods – in the content, temper and coherence of public policy. I have previously argued that the severe difficulties experienced in the first fifteen years of membership should be seen as, in large part, a failure to adjust to the demands of internationalisation and European integration. Ireland's political, administrative and interest-group system proved unable to identify and mediate increasing international competition and domestic needs. The turnaround achieved in the late 1980s involved both a more consistent domestic policy framework, achieved through social partnership, and a relaunch of the integration process at European level. I then identified the dramatic changes in public policy, institutions and behaviour since the late 1980s: four social partnership programmes, a shared Irish perspective on European integration and internationalisation, the European internal market programme, increased and reformed Structural Funds and the transition from EMS to EMU. These developments had an impact on almost all areas of public policy, business, society and interest mediation. The combination of social partnership and the European internal market provided an unusual, benign, combination of institutionalised co-ordination and pressure for market conformity. Consequently, I argue that the deepening of European integration, and the emergence of a new shared perspective on Ireland's place in Europe, was a profound influence on Ireland's economic and social experience. In particular, European integration and governance have been centrally important in the economic transformation that Ireland has experienced in the past decade.

To see why this was so, we need to understand the depth and

nature of change in the European Union since the mid-1980s. As noted above, the internal market programme was of historic significance. Its implementation produced a qualitative shift in the degree of integration, and the pattern of market governance in Europe. The Union altered the exercise of national political authority by enmeshing the Member States in a web of collaboration and co-operation. The EU is a strong example of the 'new governance', which in networks of public, private and voluntary groups transform 'bargaining' into 'problem-solving'. Since the mid-1980s, European integration was profoundly altering the sovereignty, governance and government of all countries in the Union, transforming them from *nation* states to *member* states. But the creation of this new model of internationalisation was particularly transformative for a country which had for centuries experienced the sharp end of internationalisation in several other guises.

In summary, the Irish economy and society have undergone a journey from closure, through a dependent and vulnerable openness, to a new combination of international involvement and self-confidence. Irish development since 1960 has been an evolution from deliberate strategy – through radical disruption, disorientation and loss of direction – to a new shared understanding of the constraints and possibilities of national and international governance.

Externally, we have experienced a movement from national sovereignty to a complex form of partnership in the European Union. Domestically, we have experienced a movement from state autonomy, and a reliance on the state as the driver of the economy and the agent of social change, to a partnership of the state with economic and social interests. This dual movement from sovereignty to partnership has transformed the relation of the external to the internal.

The complex interaction of domestic and international factors is clear. The common thread, the underlying transformation, is a switch from a long history in which external factors were constraining, to a new situation in which the external environment provides valuable inputs, and even its undoubted constraints can be used as opportunities. It seems that European integration has transformed Ireland's relation to its international environment, and social partnership has transformed its internal ability to mediate interests, adhere to coherent strategies and experiment.

It is remarkable, but clearly no coincidence, that the opponents of one (deeper economic and monetary union) are also opponents of the other (social partnership). Their opposition, negligible in policy terms but influential in academia and the media, is both to the substance of the prevailing consensus and to the idea and value of consensus itself – and, most of all, to the proposition that, in the circumstances of the past decade, these two interact. Yet those who achieved Ireland's transformation have little doubt that closing-off macroeconomic alternatives, and embracing deeper European integration, freed management, union and government energies for discussion of real issues that impact on competitiveness and social cohesion: viz., corporate strategy, technical change, training, working practices, the commercialisation of state-owned enterprises, taxation, public-sector reform, local re-generation, welfare reform and active labour-market policies. Closing off illusory alternatives forced all to engage in realistic discussion of change. Those involved in Ireland's transformation sense, even if they cannot say, that this approach was particularly liberating in a country whose political system tends to clientelism, whose enterprises had grown used to direct and indirect protection and whose trade union movement had developed in the British adversarial tradition.

To these two transformations – in Ireland's relation with its international environment and in its internal ability to mediate interests – we have to add a third. The social and cultural change of recent decades has transformed the individuals in Irish society in a way that has unleashed enterprise and demands new patterns of organisation. It is for this reason that the changes in the public sphere – European integration and social partnership – can be seen as the beginning of a reinvention of Ireland, much as the cultural movement of the late 19th and early 20th century were shown, by Kiberd, to have invented Ireland.[25]

The project of demonstrating and interpreting this third transformation – in the nature of individuality, enterprise and organisation – involves showing that the new culture does not exist despite the new economy, but that the two are related. That the internationalisation of the culture is not an entirely distinct process from the internationalisation of public policy, the economy and business. It requires an account of the managerial and entrepreneurial revolution which seems to have taken place in Ireland. It requires a characterisation of the forms of organisation and individuality which are emerging. It seems unlikely that 'individuality as personal freedom' is entirely distinct from the individuality in work and business. In other words, the project is to reunite our account of the cultural and the economic, the normative and the material, the actual and the ideal. Without, of course, overdoing it, and claiming a stable, organic unity, in a context which is pregnant with contradiction and change.

In Chapter 3, Halligan says that, at the time of accession, Ireland was in the midst of a reawakening, 'while half awake, it was still half asleep'. If it woke up in the 1970s and 1980s, then, to borrow from Mao Tse Tung, it 'stood up' in the 1990s. It is free to walk and run in the century that lies ahead. Ireland ends the 20th century in a position of unprecedented potential. It leaves the century free of the two masters that dominated and constrained it – London and Rome. It is now free to reinvent itself: an international people in a global world, a negotiated state in a negotiated Union. Europe is not so much the cause of these transformations, as their context. For they were only possible with the creation of an international regime which is voluntary, law-based and pluralist, which constrains the naked use of state power, protects small states in international negotiation and supports both individual and cultural freedom.

NOTES AND REFERENCES

1. NESC, *Ireland in the European Community: Performance, Prospects and Strategy*, Dublin, 1989, P. 214
2. Ibid, p. 206
3. Fintan O'Toole, 'The EU provides a clearer context to define our old problems', *The Irish Times*, 1 January, 1998
4. Damian Hannan and Patrick Cummins, 'The significance of small-scale landholders in Ireland's socio-economic transformation', in J.H. Goldthorpe and C.T. Whelan *The Development of Industrial Society in Ireland*, Oxford, 1992
5. See John Waters, J. *An Intelligent Person's Guide to Modern Ireland*, Duckworth, London, 1998
6. For a graphic account of the cultural crisis, see Fintan O'Toole, *A Mass for Jesse James: a Journey Through 1980s Ireland*, Raven Arts Press, 1990
7. The following argument draws heavily on NESC, *Strategy into the 21st Century* Dublin: National Economic and Social Council 1996 Chapter 1
8. Raymond Crotty, *Ireland in Crisis: A Study of Capitalist Colonial Underdevelopment*, Dingle: Brandon Book Publishers, 1986
9. Dennis O'Hearn, 'The Irish Case of Dependency: an Exception to the Exceptions?' *American Sociological Review*, 54, 1989, 578-96
10. See Rory O'Donnell and Colm O'Reardon, 'Ireland's experiment in social partnership, 1987-96', in Giuseppe, Fajertag and Phillipe Pochet (eds.) *Social Pacts in Europe*, Brussels: ETUC
11. See NESF, *A Framework for Partnership: Enriching Strategic Consensus through Participation*, Dublin: National Economic and Social Forum, 1997
12. O'Toole 'The EU provides a clearer context'
13. NESC, 1989 *Ireland in the European Community*, p. 218
14. Charles Sabel, *Ireland: Local Partnerships and Social Innovation*, Paris, Organisation for Economic Co-operation and Development, Paris: Organisation for Economic Co-operation and Development, 1996
15. Patrick Honohan, 'Fiscal Adjustment and Disinflation in Ireland', in Frank Barry (ed.) *Understanding Ireland's Economic Growth*, London: Macmillan, 1999, p. 94
16. These characteristics are identified in Brigid Laffan, Rory O'Donnell and Mike Smith, *Europe's Experimental Union: Rethinking Integration*, London: Routledge, 1999
17. O'Toole, 'The EU provides a clearer context.'
18. Ibid.

19. Fintan O'Toole, 'An ecu for old Ireland', *The Irish Times*, 6 May 1998
20. O'Toole, 'The EU provides a clearer context.'
21. These changes in government are discussed in more detail in NEFS, op. cit.
22. See Laffan et. al., *Europe's Experimental Union*, Chapter 9
23. Abram Chayes and Antonia Handler Chayes, *The New Sovereignty: Compliance with International Regulatory Agreements*, Harvard University Press, 1998, p. 27
24. NESC *Ireland in the European Community*, op. cit., p. 214
25. Declan Kiberd, *Inventing Ireland: the Literature of the Modern Nation*, Cambridge MA, Harvard University Press, 1995

IEA Foundation Members

The Institute is particularly indebted to its *Foundation Members* which
enable it to operate independently on a financially secure basis

Aer Lingus
Aer Rianta
AIB Bank plc
An Bord Tráchtála
An Post
Arthur Andersen
Avonmore Foods plc
Bank of Ireland
Bord Gáis
Bord na Móna
Bristol-Myers Squibb Co.
Cityjet
CRH plc
Deloitte & Touche
Electricity Supply Board
FBD Insurances plc/*Irish Farmers
Journal*/IFA
First National Building Society
FitzPatrick Hotel Group
Forbairt
FORFÁS
Glen Dimplex

Guinness Ireland Ltd
IBEC
IDA Ireland Ltd
Independent Newspapers plc
Irish Dairy Board
Irish Distillers
Irish Life
Irish Permanent plc
National Irish Bank
National Treasury Management
Agency
New Ireland Assurance
Company plc
RTÉ
Siemens Ltd
SIPTU
Smurfit (Ireland) Ltd
Eircom
The Irish Times
Ulster Bank
Waterford Crystal plc

IEA Corporate Members

Agriculture, Food and Forestry, Department of • All Party Oireachtas Committee on the Constitution • Arthur Cox • Arts, Heritage, Gaeltacht and the Islands, Department of • ASTI • Attorney General/Chief State Solicitor's Office, Office of the • Bizquip • British Embassy • Central Bank of Ireland • Centre for International Co-operation • Church of Ireland Working Group on Europe • Citibank • Committee on European Affairs of the Irish Episcopal Conference • Construction Industry Federation • County Tipperary (North Riding) VEC • Defence, Department of • Defence Forces Library • Department of History, UCC • Director of Public Prosecutions, Office of the • Dublin City University • Dublin Corporation • Education and Science, Department of • Embassy of Greece • Employment Equality Agency • Enterprise and Employment, Department of • Environment and Local Government, Department of the • European Commission Library Service • European Foundation for the Improvement of Living & Working Conditions • FÁS • Finance, Department of • Foreign Affairs, Department of • Fyffes • Government of Quebec, London Office • Gypsum Industries plc • Health and Children, Department of • Higher Education Authority • Howmedica International Inc • ICOS • ICTU • IMPACT • INTO • Irish Bankers Federation • Irish Ferries • Irish Intercontinental Bank • Irish Management Institute • Justice, Equality and Law Reform, Department of • Lansdowne Market Research Ltd • Léargas • Marine and Natural Resources, Department of the • McCann FitzGerald • Moore Europe Research Services • NCB Group • NESC • Northern Ireland Public Sector Enterprises • Ombudsman, Office of the • Public Enterprise, Department of • Revenue Commissioners, Office of the • Royal Danish Embassy • Royal Norwegian Embassy • Ryan Hotels plc • Social, Community and Family Affairs, Department of • Taoiseach, Department of the • TSB Bank • UCC • UCD • Údarás na Gaeltachta • University of Dublin, Trinity College Dublin • Wavin Ireland Ltd • Zeneca Ireland Ltd

Index

United States of America (USA), 13, 19, 30, 36, 37, 40, 74, 100, 112, 196
  cultural influence, 39, 61
  cultural influence of, 39, 61
  investment from, 85, 104, 119, 182, 201–2
  relations with Ireland, 44, 48–9, 200–2
Uruguay Round, 203

V
Vatican II, 60

W
Waters, John, 173
Werner Report, 102
Western European Union (WEU), 47
Whitaker, T.K., 21–2, 29
White Paper, 1972, 27–8, 29, 166, 167
White Paper on Growth, Competitiveness and Employment, 1994, 71, 73
Wolfe Tone, Theobald, 37
women, role of, 25, 66, 75, 172, 195
World Bank, 93, 148, 186

Y
Yeats, Jack B., 58
Yeats, Michael, 8
Yeats, W.B., 58
Yugoslavia, 47